Social exclusion

Second Edition

DAVID BYRNE

OPEN UNIVERSITY PRESS

Open University Press
McGraw-Hill Education
McGraw-Hill House
Shoppenhangers Road
Maidenhead
Berkshire
England
SL6 2QL

email: enquiries@openup.co.uk
world wide web: www.openup.co.uk

and Two Penn Plaza, New York, NY 10121-2289, USA

First published 2005

A catalogue record of this book is available from the British Library

ISBN 0 335 21594 7 (pb)   0 335 21595 5 (hb)

Library of Congress Cataloging-in-Publication Data
CIP data applied for

Dewey no.	Subject headings
305 BYR	Social policy Social theory Equality
Location H & H	Abstract Social exclusion Sure Start
3 Week ✓ 1 Week LUO Reference	Inequality JK Order details Po 22932E 20.05

Typeset by RefineCatch Limited, Bungay, Suffolk
Printed in Poland by OzGraf S.A.
www.polskabook.pl

Contents

Part Two

Part Three

Acknowledgements

I would like to acknowledge the domestic support and attention of Alissa, Sally, and Clare Ruane, to whom this book is dedicated. Those who helped me with ideas and discussion include Sally Ruane, Tim Blackman, John Ditch, Gill Callaghan, Liz Wilkie and Tim Rogers. In the preparation of this second edition I benefited considerably from discussions with Dale Parent. I remain endebted to Kazimiera Wodz for her guidance on Polish matters. I would like to acknowledge the encouragement and support of Tim May, the editor of this series.

Series editor's preface

The social sciences contribute to a greater understanding of the workings of societies and dynamics of social life. They are often, however, not given due credit for this role and much writing has been devoted to why this should be the case. At the same time we are living in an age in which the role of science in society is being re-evaluated. This has led to both a defence of science as the disinterested pursuit of knowledge and an attack on science as nothing more than an institutionalized assertion of faith with no greater claim to validity than mythology and folklore. These debates tend to generate more heat than light.

In the meantime the social sciences, in order to remain vibrant and relevant, will reflect the changing nature of these public debates. In so doing they provide mirrors upon which we gaze in order to understand not only what we have been and what we are now, but to inform ideas about what we might become. This is not simply about understanding the reasons people give for their actions in terms of the contexts in which they act, as well as analyzing the relations of cause and effect in the social, political and economic spheres, but about the hopes, wishes and aspirations that people, in their different cultural ways, hold.

In any society that claims to have democratic aspirations, these hopes and wishes are not for the social scientist to prescribe. For this to happen it would mean that the social sciences were able to predict human behaviour with certainty. This would require one theory and one method applicable to all times and places. The physical sciences do not live up to such stringent criteria, whilst the conditions in societies which provided for this outcome would be intolerable. Why? Because a necessary condition of human freedom is the ability to have acted otherwise and to imagine and practice different ways of organizing societies and living together.

It does not follow from the above that social scientists do not have a valued role to play, as is often assumed in ideological attacks upon their place and role within society. After all, in focusing upon what we have been and what we are now, what we might become is inevitably illuminated. Therefore, whilst it may not the province of the social scientist to predict our futures, they are, given not only their understandings, but equal positions as citizens, entitled to engage in public debates concerning future prospects.

This international series was devised with this general ethos in mind. It seeks to offer students of the social sciences, at all levels, a forum in which ideas are interrogated in terms of their importance for understanding key social issues. This is achieved through a connection between style, structure and content that is found to be both illuminating and challenging in terms of its evaluation of topical social issues, as well as representing an original contribution to the subject under discussion.

Given this underlying philosophy, the series contains books on topics which are driven by substantive interests. This is not simply a reactive endeavour in terms of reflecting dominant social and political pre-occupations, it is also pro-active in terms of an examination of issues which relate to and inform the dynamics of social life and the structures of society that are often not part of public discourse. What is distinctive about the series is an interrogation of the assumed characteristics of our current epoch in relation to its consequences for the organization of society and social life, as well as its appropriate mode of study.

Each contribution contains, for the purposes of general orientation, as opposed to rigid structure, three parts. First, an interrogation of the topic which is conducted in a manner that renders explicit core assumptions surrounding the issues and/or an examination of the consequences of historical trends for contemporary social practices. Second, a section which aims to 'bring alive' ideas and practices by considering the ways in which they directly inform the dynamics of social relations. A third section then moves on to make an original contribution to the topic. These encompass possible future forms and content, likely directions for the study of the phenomena in question, or an original analysis of the topic itself. Of course, it might be a combination of all three.

The first edition of Dave Byrne's book was written with this ethos in mind and the new edition take this further. Here we see not only an up-dating from the original, but also the inclusion of new material. This new material focuses upon New Labour and its record in office. However, as he notes, this is not parochial in the sense of being restricted to the U.K., but actually concerns the democratic left and its potential across different continents to offer a viable alternative to a capitulation to the altar of the free-market. This is seen from the point of view of a strong version of social exclusion which does not individualize the problem according to the characteristics of those who are marginalized, but also focuses upon those who are doing the marginalizing. After all, when it is asserted that we are living through a political epoch defined by a 'third way', this encapsulates not only an assertion of difference from past programmes of social reform, but is also seen to represent a vision of an alternative mode of organizing society and social relations that does not replicate mistakes of the past. To this extent it might be reasonable to assert that a balance is needed that does not appear to take the thesis of an 'end of history' for granted: that is, capitalism is vindicated and the administration of 'inclusion' is the topic for consideration, as opposed to an explanation of the dynamics of exclusion based upon the system under and through which people operate in their daily lives.

To offer a critique of the consequences of a system which is so much taken-for-granted is bound to be controversial. At the same time, within academic discussion it is modernity and postmodernity that seems to preoccupy authors, whilst mention of the dynamics and effects of capitalism as an economic system is not so prevalent. As critiques so often end at the point of possible forms of organization, it is possible to gain the distinct impression that there are no alternatives and those analytically inclined are marginalized, or regard intervention into policy and practice with suspicion. Therefore, by default, it is as if we must live with an economic system that the process of historical evolution has vindicated as being its final resting place. To even imagine alternatives via a critique of present conditions thereby becomes a daunting task in the face of such overwhelming complacency and indifference to the plight of the excluded.

By drawing upon complexivity theory and by being robust and spirited in its style and methodical and comparative in its content, no reader will emerge from this book believing that the author prevaricates when it comes to the dynamics and consequences of social exclusion. Arguing that post-industrial capitalism and its related social politics is converging around a norm of structural social exclusion and labour market flexibility, Dave Byrne argues that this is driven by ideology and the subordination of social policies to an anticipation of business interests, *as if* such interests were simply separate from the process of social reproduction.

This 'phase shift' in the social order through which we a living in the West, encapsulated by the term post-industrial capitalism, is not an inevitable process, but the outcome of interactions between decisions that inform the construction of social policies and the economic order. He argues that whilst social exclusion is an inherent feature of contemporary capitalism and that chaotic processes are deterministic, agency can nevertheless make a difference. To that extent, actions, either at the level of the single household or the collective, can make a difference; the question is with what overall effects?

Seeking comparative explanations for social exclusion according to the tenets of complexity theory raises serious issues for the construction of social policies. In particular, it does not relieve individual nation-states of the burden of responsibility for ameliorating and responding to the consequences of an unbridled capitalism in the age of globalization. It also directly challenges the idea that the solution to the problem of social exclusion comes with changing individual skills in order to make people more marketable according to the demands of market capitalism. From that point of view, this book is controversial in directly challenging contemporary trends. Yet in an age where the complacency of some is bought at the cost of the misery of others with its effects on the fabric of social order for all, the arguments in this new edition deserve serious consideration and debate. Quite simply, they inform the possibility for a form of politics whose time has not past, merely the understanding and commitment of those who claim to speak in its name.

Tim May

Introduction

Exclusion [original emphasis] is an idea which poses the right
kind of questions.

(Donnison 1998: 5)

The expression 'social exclusion' is everywhere in contemporary UK social
policy, not only in the processes of policy development but also at the sharp
end of policy implementation. Since the first edition of this book was
written, a 'Social Exclusion Unit' has been established, first in the Cabinet
Office and then transferred to the Deputy Prime Minister's Department,
with the remit of making 'inclusion' central to the whole of governance in
this country. The UK has become the world leader in the development
of policies that have a 'third way' character – which seek to reconcile the
supposed imperatives of a globalized economy with the political aspirations
of the masses of people in postindustrial countries for some sort of security,
social provision, and even equality in their lives. Resolving 'social exclusion'
is central to this programme. However, the term itself and the processes it
describes are deeply contradictory and contestable. I will argue that the
character of UK 'anti-exclusion' policies and the form of understanding of
the meaning of social exclusion that informs them actually contributes to
the development of an excluding postindustrial capitalism based on poor
work for many and insecurity for most. 'New Labour' has pioneered the
abandonment of the objective of increasing equality through the political
management of market capitalism, which informed post-Second World War
social and Christian democratic politics in industrial societies. To sustain
that argument we must examine all aspects of 'social exclusion'. These
include the historical development of the idea, the linguistic content of the
term, the processes of social restructuring from an industrial to postindustrial society within which social exclusion is embedded, and the policies
which are asserted to be in the interests of inclusion. That is the purpose of
the second edition of this book.

By the mid-1990s, the expression 'social exclusion' had to a considerable,
and welcome, extent replaced that pejorative US import, 'the underclass', in

discussions about the poor in 'postindustrial' society in the UK in particular. There were advantages in this development. The two words 'social' and 'exclusion' when put together conjoin society as a whole, as opposed to the discrete individuals within society, with ongoing process, as opposed to timeless state. When we talk and write about 'social exclusion' we are talking about changes in the whole of society that have consequences for some of the people in that society. We are dealing as C. Wright Mills (1959) suggested we always ought to in sociology, with the intersection of history and biography – with the way the social world changes and with the consequences of those changes for the lives people lead.

Note that the term is inherently dynamic – exclusion happens in time, in a time of history, and 'determines' the lives of the individuals and collectivities who are excluded *and* of those individuals and collectivities who are not. Note also that although the term is clearly systemic, that is to say it is about the character of the social system and about the dynamic development of social structures, at the same time it has implications for agency. 'Exclusion' is something that is done by some people to other people. The central tenet of popular versions of 'the underclass' argument is that miserable conditions are self-induced – the poor do it to themselves. Political theorists of 'social exclusion' allow that it can be a consequence of economic transformation – it is the fault of 'society' as a whole. Only dangerous radicals, like the Catholic Bishops of England and Wales, admit that the people who stand to gain might have something to do with it – that they might be shaping the character of economic and social arrangements, the very stuff of social politics, to their own advantage and to the disadvantage of others.

It is important to distinguish the idea of 'social exclusion' from the somewhat simpler notion of 'poverty'. Walker and Walker do this:

> . . . we have retained the distinction regarding *poverty* [original emphasis] as a lack of the material resources, especially income, necessary to participate in British society and *social exclusion* [original emphasis] as a more comprehensive formulation which refers to the dynamic process of being shut out, fully or partially, from any of the social, economic, political or cultural systems which determine the social integration of a person in society. Social exclusion may, therefore, be seen as the denial (or non-realisation) of the civil, political and social rights of citizenship.
>
> (1997: 8)

Another definition is offered by Madanipour et al.:

> Social exclusion is defined as a multi-dimensional process, in which various forms of exclusion are combined: participation in decision making and political processes, access to employment and material resources, and integration into common cultural processes. When combined, they create acute forms of exclusion that find a spatial manifestation in particular neighbourhoods.
>
> (1998: 22)

This book will work with an approach that is closer to that of Madanipour et al. than to that of Walker and Walker. I want emphasize both the multi-dimensionality of exclusion understood in terms of the complex dynamics of life trajectories, and the significance of spatial separation within the urban areas of advanced industrial societies.

For Walker and Walker, the opposite of exclusion is integration, with integration understood in relation to the idea of citizenship as it was formulated by Marshall (1950, 1963). This view represents a considerable development beyond the passive conception of poverty as a state. However, it takes up only one of the two competing projects of modernity, that centring on the notion of individual rights founded on the doctrine of 'possessive individualism' (MacPherson 1963). This is part of the liberal project of individual emancipation, with the individual understood as unique subject and agent. There is another project, the democratic socialist project of collective transformation, in which the collective actor is the universal working class. Theorists of postmodernity, with that term and that category understood in the most general sense, argue that there is no universal collective social actor, even in terms of inherent potential. Instead, we must recognize the existence of a multiplicity of differentiated and potentially competing social collectivities founded around identities which may be as much matters of voluntary choice as of structural determination.

The argument presented here will be unashamedly old-fashioned: social politics in 'postindustrial' capitalism are necessarily organized around the disputes which, at an ideological level, take the form of confrontations among the three positions of classical liberalism with its foundation in possessive individualism, democratic socialism with its foundation in solidarity, and conservatism with its foundation in the pre-modern conception of an appropriate status-based social order. These categories in practice intermingle and cross-fertilize, but they are what matter, precisely because they can be associated with absolutely real and very general material interests.

Another important weakness of contemporary versions of the Marshallian citizenship approach is a relative neglect of issues of power. Marshall himself did not ignore power, but he did not get beyond a consideration of the extension of the franchise in representative democracy. The new school of 'citizenship', even when it does engage with anything more than a very passive conception of rights, seldom gets beyond the notion of the active citizen as the fulfiller of reciprocal obligations of general do-gooding and busybodying. In contrast, those, like Madanipour et al., who discuss social exclusion with an urban frame of reference are inevitably confronted by power, as it is exercised by competing interests in the processes of urban governance.

'Social exclusion' is not simply a term in social politics. It is also a central concern of social science. However, there is a problem. The academic debate on social exclusion provides an excellent illustration of the problems posed by the reification of disciplinary boundaries within the contemporary academy which prompted the recent Gulbenkian Commission's injunction to *Open the Social Sciences* (1996). The processes that engender social exclusion and the issues which derive from it are the subject matter of investigation both by a range of academic disciplines including sociology, geography, economics, history and political science, and by inter- and multi-disciplinary fields that have become established as distinctive academic areas: urban studies, health studies, labour studies and education. In the UK in particular, but increasingly on a European scale, they are the subject matter of that strange academic entity 'social policy', perhaps the oldest of the distinctive inter- or multi-disciplinary fields with its origins in late nineteenth- and early twentieth-century liberal collectivism's concern with poverty, and now making claims to stand as a discipline in its own right. There is a cross-discipline/-field debate and discussion about this topic, but it remains at best only partially coherent, primarily because there are fundamental dissonances in the way in which the processes of social change, which can be subsumed under the heading of 'social exclusion', are conceptualized and, above all else, measured.

This book was originally written in part as an attempt at a synthesis to tackle the problem of the focus on the individual as the object of measurement and conceptualization, characteristic of economics, social policy, and much of quantitative sociology's examination of change through time. In the social sciences there is now a clear recognition of the dynamic character of social process, but there is also a failure to integrate the individual with the social entities through which individuals lead their lives: households, the complex and multi-layered components of social space, and the social order as a whole. The synthesis we need must be able both to bring together concepts and to provide an account of complex and interacting levels in society.

This synthesizing objective remains central to the second edition. We will attempt to clear the ground, establish just what we are dealing with, consider what the origins of this are, and review proposals for doing something about it. The book will draw on a range of disciplines and fields, and it will employ the understanding of social dynamics offered by the application of the conceptual tools of 'chaos/complexity' to the complex nested systems of the social world. I am far from neutral on the politics of these matters, but will endeavour to be honest in my presentation of ideas or 'facts' and clear about my own views, so that readers can decide to what extent they influence the presentation of argument and account. I reserve the right, following on from an honourable tradition that will be represented here by citation of Hazlitt, to name things for what they are and to be polemical in so doing, although the text will remain primarily in academic mode with polemic confined to some asides and to the conclusion. However, I really do feel that the democratic left has been far too shy in showing that it can bite if vexed. Bite I will.

And now a note of caution. John Veit-Wilson makes a very important distinction between 'weak' and 'strong' versions of the idea of social exclusion. He puts it like this:

In the 'weak' version of this discourse, the solutions lie in altering these excluded peoples' handicapping characteristics and enhancing their integration into dominant society. 'Stronger' forms of this discourse also emphasise the role of those who are doing the excluding and therefore aim for solutions which reduce the powers of exclusion.

(1998: 45)

He goes on to note that many consider the development of the discourse of 'social exclusion' in France in the 1980s as being: 'a discourse deliberately chosen for closure, to exclude other potential discourses in European political debate and to depoliticize poverty *as far as income redistribution was concerned*' (1998: 97, original emphasis). I think that is right, so long as we talk about the weak version of the idea. Certainly, the use of 'social exclusion' in the UK in the late 1990s by New Labour seems to be exactly as a method of closure in relation to challenges to inequality as a general social issue. In this book, unless explicitly qualified, the idea of social exclusion will always be used in its strong sense. Social science has been, rightly, accused of adopting a posture of palms up to the rich for the receipt of funding and eyes down to the poor as part of the surveillance necessary for their control. Here, the eyes are definitely looking up more than down.

Let me now state a central tenet underpinning this whole book: there has been a recent categorical change in the character of advanced industrial societies. The word categorical is used to indicate that this is a change of kind, of quality, rather than some matter of incremental continuous development. To use the vocabulary of chaos/complexity, there has been a phase shift. This book will use the ideas of chaos and complexity to explore the dynamic character of our changing social order. The objective here is to extend our understanding of the significance of the dynamic so that we can use it to describe how our sort of society changes. Indeed, we can go beyond description. A proper understanding of the complex character of social dynamics offers the possibility of an informed and engaged social science which plays a role in the shaping of the character of the future. Leisering and Walker are absolutely right when they identify the dynamic perspective as:

. . . the beginning of an intellectual revolution, one that blends insight from across the social sciences, merges quantitative and qualitative methodologies, combines micro and macro views of society and exploits the power of international comparison.

(1998: xiv)

My point is that once we go dynamic, we must go non-linear. We are dealing with emergence, bifurcation, complexity, and the possibility of willed alternatives. We are in the realms of a science that deals with the possibility of different forms for the future. That matters a great deal.

Before proceeding to outline the organization of the book, I want to say something about the background to the production of this second edition. The original version was written during 1997, before and in the first months of the Labour government elected in the United Kingdom in that year. The Conservative administration under Thatcher, and to a rather more muted extent under Major, had endorsed a very harsh neo-liberal view of the consequences of social change. Indeed, their social policies were informed by a conception of the nature of social politics which closely resembled the *laissez-faire* doctrines of the early Victorian era. 'New Labour' was elected because it seemed to be something rather different. However, 'New Labour' was not 'Old Labour'. It did not represent itself as such, even though many party activists and voters did not grasp the qualitative change in objectives. I have to say that I, personally, did. I resigned from the party, of which I had been a member for most of my adult life, which I had represented as a local councillor for twelve years, and with which my family had been engaged across three generations. However, I did so in relation to the industrial politics of the party – that is, in response to the complete and sustained failure of 'New Labour' to commit to a restoration of the organizational capacity of trade unions. The irony is that the Labour Party had originally been created with the defence of that capacity as its central objective.

In terms of social politics outwith the workplace, 'New Labour' looked as if it had more to offer. In opposition it had resisted the privatization of welfare and criticized the massive transfer of resources to the very affluent which derived both from the opening up of the differentials in original incomes between most people and the top 1 per cent of income earners *and* from the radical reduction in higher rates of tax. It is true that 'New Labour' believing that the 1992 election had been lost because of 'Old Labour's' tax and spend image, had explicitly rejected a reversal of the tax cuts, but it still – on the social if not industrial front – looked like a social democratic party. This second edition has been written in the light of 'New Labour's' record in office. This has significance far beyond the parochial politics of Britain. 'New Labour' stands as the prototype for political parties that are transmuting social and Christian democratic forms to fit with the 'inevitable' market-dominated logic of postindustrial and post-democratic capitalism. In this context 'social exclusion' – always understood in the weak sense of that term as identified by Veit-Wilson (1998) – is a concept with great political force. 'Inclusionary' policies serve two vital purposes for such parties in government. They maintain order by dissipating sources of anomic disorder through the integration of the anomic into regulating institutions and processes, and particularly into work. At the same time, they lend a 'reformist' colour to political agendas which serve the interests of capitalism as an abstract system and of capitalists as real people. It is ironic that there are individuals in the 'New Labour' system of governance (which term is employed because policy advisors and other unelected actors may have just as much or even more power as ministers, although this category includes ministers as well) who as 'Marxist' critics of social democratic welfare earlier in their careers argued that 'the welfare state' – including both services and the general system of redistribution – was a giant confidence trick worked on the proletariat in order to maintain the capitalist system. Those of us with a more historicist understanding of the creation of the welfare states of post-war Europe saw things somewhat differently. Apparently on the principle of 'if you can't beat 'em, join 'em', they are now engaged in the dismantling of welfare and redistribution on a wholesale basis.

This book is divided into three parts dealing respectively with 'social exclusion – understanding and argument'; 'the processes and experience of social exclusion'; and 'tacking social exclusion'. Part One seeks to establish the content of the academic and political debate which deals with these issues. This section comprises four chapters. The first will examine the classical liberal tradition of political economy with its historic identification of the surplus population/residuum recast in contemporary terms as 'the underclass'. It will deal with perspectives that are essentially founded around the doctrines of possessive individualism as these were influenced by the social pessimism of Malthus and by classical political economy's assertion of the market as the epitome of rationality. It should be noted that in this chapter I will deal with much of the debate on citizenship, precisely because the late twentieth-century version of that idea is constructed around an individualistic conception of rights, and with Etzioni's version of communitarianism, which for me remains essentially founded on individual interests expressed in a utilitarian form, rather than on any notion of emergent solidarity. The general discussion of the residuum/'underclass' will also be considered here, not because those concerned with that debate necessarily identify with the politics of the 'New' or old Right, but because the debate seems to me to revolve around two themes which are part of the Right's repertoire. These are the notion of surplus population after Malthus and the notion of the non-elect which comes from Calvinistic Protestantism. The introduction of the term 'New Right' illustrates the difficulties of actual classification. That expression describes not only those who assert the economic logic of classical liberalism, an inherently anti-conservative doctrine, but those who do this in association with a reassertion of traditional social, and especially sexual and familial, values, as part of a programme of neo-conservatism. Protestantism's concern with individual salvation through faith without works and Calvinism's justification of the expulsion of the non-elect seem to me to be the linking features here.

The next chapter will examine approaches which to a greater or lesser degree reject the doctrine of the possessive individual and assert that it is the business of politics to regulate or even abolish markets in the pursuit of collective human goals. We will begin by looking at the combination of Rousseau-influenced 'republicanism' and catholic social thought that underpins the idea of social exclusion, with its Durkheimian overtones of organic solidarity, and the 'collectivist' version of liberalism which is found in the ideas and programmes of Keynes, Marshall himself and Beveridge. What these positions have in common at the most fundamental level is that they are prepared to put politics in control of markets, although they all seek to retain the market as the fundamental form of economic organization. It has to be recognized that there are some real contradictions here. The French Revolution asserted 'fraternity' which has an exact non-sexist synonym in socialism's subsequent conception of 'solidarity'. For all the influence of Locke on republican and democratic thought, the popular masses were able to force their discourse of solidarity into the political lexicon. From the point of view of liberal political economy, the discourse of solidarity is deeply reactionary. It is a version of romanticism, often informed by a looking back to some imaginary ideal past. In this respect it has a common element with the Catholic hierarchy's inherent conservatism and defence of the old order, with its ranked statuses in which people were included by insertion in their proper place.

However, Christian doctrine, as expressed in that dangerous and revolutionary set of texts known as the New Testament, does not advocate hierarchy. On the contrary, it is profoundly egalitarian in its expression of solidarity. Catholicism had to contain within itself by accommodation the radical challenge represented in the Middle Ages by the Franciscan tradition. It failed to contain, but succeeded in suppressing, the later Hussite opposition. Within the social doctrines of Catholicism there is a contradiction, which the Church sought to resolve in practice in the nineteenth century through its condemnation of the consequences of Godless political economy and endorsement of workers' rights and state welfare. Nonetheless, this contradiction remains immanent in Catholicism: witness the difficulties with the worker priests' tradition in Europe and with the general programme of liberation theology on a global scale.

The common element in the approaches discussed in the first part of Chapter 2 is that while they are solidaristic in objective, they do not assert the necessity for a transformation of capitalism into something else. They are efforts to accommodate an element of solidarity, and its inevitable tendency towards equality, with the continued existence of a market economy and its inevitable tendency towards inequality. For this reason, I will include in the discussions in this chapter a consideration of the set of approaches most usually known by the name of the archmage of the tendency, Keynes. Keynesianism is the most important coherent system derived from the collectivist shift taken by much of the UK's liberal intelligentsia in the later nineteenth and early twentieth centuries in response to the intellectual stimulus of the English Hegelians and to the political reality of the emergent power of an organized working class. The ideas reviewed in this chapter come from the domain of the 'social market economy', of the non-totalitarian third way, in its different forms in the post-World War II period. What we will examine here is the convergence of Keynesian/collectivist liberal, Christian democratic and non-transformational social democratic approaches in a broad rejection of unfettered markets. The contemporary 'third way', as proposed by Giddens (1997, 2000) and endorsed by Blair, is really an attempt to impose a neo-liberal agenda on politics while retaining some sort of emotional overtone of solidarity. It will be reviewed in Chapter 3 in relation to its rhetoric and in Chapter 8 in relation to the policies of social inclusion that embody it.

The remainder of Chapter 2 will deal with the Marxist account as founded around the notion of exploitation and with its contemporary expression in terms of the underdevelopment of 'the social proletariat'. The separation of classical liberal and social market approaches is a commonplace of discussion of these issues. The introduction of the Marxist critique is an unfashionable reassertion of the traditional alternative to those accounts that accept the inevitability of the continuation of capitalism as a system. This reflects the intellectual power of the Marxist critique, as is has been developed particularly by C.L.R. James and Raya Dunayevska and those who have been influenced by their ideas, and the considerable role of socialist ideas in the formation of the programmes of European social democracy and even of the UK (Old) Labour Party. The examination here will be of approaches that are founded in principle on the notion of an inherent contradiction of interests between a universal proletariat composed of those who own nothing but their labour, and the capitalists who own the means of production, although some versions have left behind the practical implications which flow from this. Of course, this formulation is simplistic and in real historical process things are much more complicated, but the core idea is that if the objectives of solidarity are to be achieved, then capitalism will have to become something else, not founded around the exploitative wage/labour relationship.

These two chapters will be concerned with ideas as expressed in social politics and policy. They will be histories of ideas in reflexive interaction with politics, rather than histories of ideas taken alone. For illustrative purposes, I will make reference to the contemporary social politics of four nation states, the United States, the United Kingdom, France and Poland, although the United Kingdom will dominate this second edition to a far greater degree than was the case previously. The United Kingdom has undergone a transformation from classic liberalism to initially liberal and then socialist collectivism and back again, with the explicit endorsement by almost all its political elites of the necessity for a 'flexible' labour market in a competitive globalized world. Moreover, since the election of the Blair government in 1997 it has embarked on an unparalleled and prototypical raft of policies informed by 'third way rhetoric' and directed towards 'social inclusion' which offers a model for neo-liberal governance in societies with strong collectivist cultural and political traditions. In consequence, more of the book is taken up with UK initiatives precisely because these demonstrate what might well be a general model for the future.

Part One will continue with Chapter 3, new in this second edition, which reviews two related and interwoven ways in which social exclusion is conceptualized. It will begin with a deconstruction of the rhetorical use of the expression in what are now generally referred to as political discourses. There has to be some qualification of this Foucauldian language, and, frankly, I would prefer to talk about 'ideology' rather than discourse because there are very real material interests and informed political actions in play here that have a substance far beyond the merely linguistic. However, for once, the linguistic turn is useful to us because in postindustrial politics what is said and how it is said is of crucial significance and the language games surrounding social exclusion require careful consideration. Here we will draw on the work of a range of social scientists and social critics who have done this job for us.

Chapter 3 will continue with a critical consideration of the social science of exclusion and in particular of the ways in which this complex idea has been operationalized in order to facilitate measurement of the extent of social exclusion and, with reference forward to Chapter 4, the dynamics of exclusion through time. This is not an esoteric methodological issue. Social statistics matter enormously, since social measurement is essential to governance in any complex social order. This general significance is even greater when the actual processes of governance are guided by target setting in a fashion which is wholly inappropriate for any sort of radical politics in a complex social system. Getting into the guts of measurement is really important for critique and the development of alternative practice.

Chapter 4 will deal specifically with social dynamics. This is the most theoretical chapter of the book and will seek to integrate three strands in contemporary social science. One is the concern with grand transformations in the character of the social order as a whole. This has already been identified here as involving a phase shift, a transformation of kind. The most coherent account of this transition is that provided by regulation theory in its various forms, a school which will also be discussed in Chapter 3 as part of the Marxist tradition. Here, the focus will be on the implications of a shift from a Fordist to post-Fordist social order, considered explicitly in terms of the language of complex dynamics. The second strand has already been introduced by citation of Leisering and Walker (1998). This is an emerging school in social science made possible by the availability of new data sets which describe the trajectories of individuals and households through time. These longitudinal data sets, measures of the experience of people through time rather than of their condition at a point in time, are the product of the macroscopic range of vision of the social order that becomes possible as a result of the data management capacities of contemporary computing resources. They are inherently micro in form. They deal with biographies, although it must be noted that those working with them are well aware that biographies occur within a social order that has its own dynamic of change. However, there has not as yet been a systematic integration of the micro level described by, to use complexity theory's term, these ensembles of biographical trajectories and the macro level of social transformation which is described by ideas such as that of a shift from a Fordist to a post-Fordist world. My argument is that such an integration is possible if we draw on the concepts of complexity/chaos theory, and in particular on Reed and Harvey's very fruitful notion of nested systems (1994). The last strand in this chapter will provide a summary introduction to these concepts (see Byrne 1998 for a fully developed account) as applied to a consideration of social exclusion. I am convinced that future discussions of social issues will always be dynamic and optimistic, in that I believe that the tools of complexity/chaos theory do provide us, not with an elite technology of social engineering, but with a social science that can be applied as part of a programme of dialogical learning and social transformation.

Part Two of the book comprises a set of chapters that draws extensively on empirical materials and does so with an absolute emphasis on the dynamics of social change, again using illustrations from the USA, the UK, France and Poland. It comprises three chapters dealing respectively with: the dynamics of income and exclusion; the dynamics of space and exclusion; and the dynamics of exclusion in everyday life in relation to education, culture and health. In all three chapters considerable emphasis is placed on the constitutive role of social policies in the creation of the contemporary forms of social division. In other words, changes in the whole social order should not be understood as comprising two separate domains of 'economic change' (the organization of production and private consumption) on the one hand, and 'policy change' (the organization of collective social reproduction) on the other, with the former being autonomous and proactive and the social domain representing reactive policy responses to the changes which are generated by economic transformation. On the contrary, it will be argued that the general contemporary character of economic and market relations, which will be described using Nelson's conception of 'postindustrial capitalism' (1995), would not be possible without crucial changes in the character of social policies from the form such policies took during most of the post–World War II period.

The areas of dynamic change to be considered in these chapters include changes in the social distribution of income taken together with the form of individual/household life-term income trajectories, and changes in the socio-spatial organization of urban life, here with an emphasis on the dynamics of neighbourhoods within urban systems and of individuals/ households around urban space over life terms. These two areas have been selected for closer examination because income differentials and spatial segregation are the core foci of two somewhat separate literatures examining social exclusion and two somewhat separate sets of programmes directed towards its redress. Moreover, information about them is available across the range of societies being considered.

An examination of income distributions is central to any consideration of processes of change towards or away from equality. Although income is only a proxy for exclusion as a whole, by examining the character of its distribution and changes in the form of its source, which for most people is wage labour or wage substitution benefits, we can get a grip on processes that are central to exclusion considered in relation to exploitation. If we look at potential life-course trajectories in terms of both income and its sources, we can start to develop a chaos/complexity-founded understanding of the emergent forms of social classes 'in themselves'. Work and wages (and wage substitution and supplementation benefits) do matter a very great deal. We can get a sense of the consequences of social change by looking at these things in some detail.

The examination of exclusion through space is vital for two reasons. First, much of the actual expression of exclusion in urban industrial societies is through spatial segregation. This both defines immediate everday living conditions and determines, at least in part, subsequent life-course trajectories. Such determination is a consequence of differential access to spatially defined collective services and in particular to schools. Second, the restructuring of urban life as a process illustrates very clearly the forms of exclusion from the exercise of power. In postindustrial capitalism the organized working class and its immediate political agents have had the capacity to determine the form of social space taken away from them. In these two chapters, four 'thematics of differentiation' will be considered in relation to the processes of exclusion through income and through space: class, gender, ethnicity and age. Much of the argument and illustration in the empirical chapters will show that, with two crucial exceptions, the development of the doctrines of possessive individualism in the form of programmes of 'equal *individual* rights' has tended to reduce the significance of income and spatial exclusion around principles of ethnicity and gender. The two exceptions are the position, albeit highly differentiated, of black Americans in the USA, and the position of female single parents and their children, albeit subject to non-linear change, in postindustrial societies in general.

The examination of 'exclusion in everyday life' in Chapter 7, which is a new chapter in this second edition, is very much UK-focused. It first explores the constitutive role of education in social exclusion, with particular reference to the role of educational systems for social mobility in postindustrial societies. The Giddens/Blair neo-liberal version of the third way has explicitly abandoned the social objective of equality of outcome, but equality of opportunity is vital to its legitimating rhetoric. Education is crucial here, and we will see how limited opportunities for access to elite status actually are in the contemporary UK. Indeed, secondary education perhaps more than any other area of social policy illustrates the degree of social closure which can be achieved under the guise of a rhetoric of choice and encouragement of individual aspiration. The subsequent discussion of 'cultural policy' is important for three reasons. First, it addresses the dimension of cultural exclusion which informs all conceptualization of exclusion as a process. Second, it connects with the cultural aspect of urban regeneration programmes which are central to the actual generation of exclusion in postindustrial urban systems. Finally, a central argument of this book is that anti-exclusionary political struggle must begin in the arena of popular culture, understood with all the meanings that can be attached to the word 'culture'. The discussion of cultural exclusion here will connect with the discussion of radical alternatives in the last chapter of the book. To conclude the chapter, there will be a brief discussion of exclusion and health, which will refer to the voluminous literature on the social determination of health inequalities, but will focus particularly on the development of non-democratic governance in health in order to facilitate the privatization of social health systems.

This seems an appropriate point to make it clear that the exclusion being examined in this book is internal exclusion within postindustrial societies. It is to do with the consequences of what Madanipour et al. describe in these terms:

> The processes which link the unification of the western European space and the fragmentation of its urban life are complex. At their root, however, is the changing nature of work in contemporary society. Increased global competition leads employers to transfer risks onto the workforce wherever possible. As the balance of employment throughout Europe has shifted from manufacturing to the new service industries the transfer of risk breeds new forms of insecurity among large segments of the workforce, through increasing part-time and temporary working and self-employment, and creates new pressures on household and kinship structures in providing support for their members. As global competitiveness has become the rallying cry of neo-liberal governments throughout Europe and as a commitment to the convergence criteria for monetary union has come to be seen as a key element in achieving it, welfare state systems of support for households and individuals are being reconstructed in order to reduce public expenditure.
>
> (1998: 7–8)

Exclusion can be external. It can be to do with keeping other people out of a particular nation or bloc (Fortress Europe). Lister (1998) deals with the term almost exclusively in that sense in her recent book discussing feminist perspectives on citizenship. The ethnic diversity which is in considerable part produced by immigration and which may be a basis for exclusion will be considered in this book, but the focus is on change within industrial societies, rather than on their relationship with the non-industrial world. Here, I want to identity a very important but necessary omission in this text: a neglect of the links between the postindustrial world of the relatively affluent and the rest of humanity. When I wrote the first edition, it was impossible to imagine that Chinese nationals working illegally in the UK would not only be picking cockles in Morecambe Bay and drown in consequence, but that another illegal Chinese worker would be literally worked to death in a manufacturing plant in Hartlepool. The US and Continental Europe have a long history of 'illegals' working below and outside the system of citizens' rights in relation to work regulation that runs across most of the labour market. The scale of illegal work is of its very nature difficult to assess, but the UK, which is probably the most difficult large postindustrial country to enter illegally, is estimated to have at least half a million such workers. These people are essentially a reserve army of labour and are absolutely excluded. They are not dealt with in this book because there is limited information about them, and because our focus here is on the dispossession of the citizens of what were supposed to be industrial democracies. They do, however, matter, and matter a great deal.

The countries chosen as illustrative examples for this text are all 'developed'. They are all part of the 'first' or former 'second' worlds of industrial capitalism. If not exactly Western–centred (although Poles are of course very firm about their historical Western status), this choice is none-theless of countries of 'the North'. I agree that this is a serious issue, but I want to justify the choice in terms of more than convenience. It seems to me that Nigel Harris (1987) was right when he argued that development (combined and uneven of course) is now general as a world process. My view is that these advanced industrial societies, in a world now dominated by systems of economic organization, if not always of political form, which they developed in the first place, stand as prefigurative of likely developments on a world scale.

The third part of the book will examine action against exclusion. In Chapter 8 there will be a highly critical review of the actual nature of third-way policies as implemented in practice. Again, the emphasis will be on the UK, although particular attention will be paid to the way in which the Clinton administration in the US pioneered the revival of the Speenhamland system for the subsidizing of low wages in order to make work a rational choice for the citizen poor. The rest of the chapter will review UK developments with reference to 'New Deals' and related inclu-sionary policies. We will look again at education, both in relation to pro-vision for pre-school children through Sure Start – which is intended to promote equality of opportunity *and* to facilitate the entry of mothers into the labour market – and at policies directed at NEETs, that is adolescents and young adults who are Not in Education, Emploment or Training, and therefore represent a potential source of crime and disorder. There will be a particular focus on processes of participation through New Deal for Com-munities and Local Strategic Partnerships, because these represent an attempt at the development of new forms of governance, which address the problems for democracy and social legitimacy posed by the neo-liberal dominance of the political systems of postindustrial capitalism.

Participation is of particular significance, and a central argument of Chap-ter 9 – which proposes a radical alternative against exclusion – is that a key strategy is the subversion of participation through informed and engaged social confrontation. In this chapter, the themes already identified will be drawn together with special reference to the potential that exists for the development of both a social politics and a set of social policies that might eliminate social exclusion. The combination of the expressions 'social politics' and 'social policy' is quite deliberate. The argument will be that there are no simple technical fixes to these issues. What is required is a new form of social politics founded in a recognition that at the least there are competing social interests at stake here, and that those interests may very well be irreconcilable. This is not just a matter of objectives; it is also a matter of process. In the conclusion, I will draw on the ideas of Freire as a starting point for thinking about how such a set of processes might be developed in a way that allows for a real partnership between an engaged social science and those who are negatively affected by the process of exclusion in consequence of the transition to postindustrialism. A development from the first edition of this book will be the emphasis placed on the politics of culture as central to any realistic transformational politics.

All the chapters in this book have been updated with reference to both new data – particularly data about income distribution – and the academic argument as it has developed since the publication of the first edition. Here, I will say only that the general tenor of both sources of information is that things were bad and have become worse. There is still time to 'make it different' but that time is running out.

PART ONE

Conceptualizing social exclusion: the political foundations – classical and neo-liberal

Concepts do not arrive from nowhere, descending from some blue sky of abstract thought and translated through empirical investigation into the development of policy. They always have a history both in specific form and in relation to their precursors, and for concepts with political salience that history is always contested. This is particularly true for 'social exclusion'. In this chapter we will begin to explore the way in which social exclusion has emerged from an intermingled process of ideological formation, political argument and social analysis which is as old as that modernity that began in the political discourses of the late seventeenth and eighteenth centuries. From the nineteenth century onwards, three distinctive approaches to the issues this concept seeks to address have coexisted, merged at the boundaries, and simultaneously stood in radical opposition to each other. We can describe these as the classical liberal position of 'possessive individualism', with its emphasis on the negative liberties of the self, the optimizing function of the market, and that at best residual role of the collective sphere; the 'traditional conservatism' typified in many respects by nineteenth- and early twentieth-century Catholic social teaching, with a Durkheimian emphasis on integration of individuals into a traditionally legitimized and coherent social order; and the radical and potentially transformational socialist position, most clearly expressed in the work of Marx, which sought to eliminate inequality and exploitation through the transformation of capitalism to socialism.

The purpose of this chapter is to delineate this history in terms of the first of these three strands as the basis for the empirical and methodological presentation and argument which will constitute the core of this book. In Chapter 2 we will examine the different versions of the collectivist alternative – both those that accept capitalism but seek to modify the character of its operations, and those that challenge capitalism and seek to transform it into something else.

The possessive individualists – blaming the poor redundant populations

. . . when we see the lower classes of English people uniformly singled out as marks for the malice or servility of a certain description of writers – when we see them studiously separated like a degraded *caste*, [original emphasis] from the rest of the community, with scarcely the attributes and faculties of the species allowed them, – nay, when they are thrust lower in the scale of humanity than the same classes of any other nation in Europe . . . when we see the *redundant population* [original emphasis] (as it is fashionably called) selected as the butt for every effusion of paltry spite, and as the last resource of vindictive penal statutes, – when we see every existing evil derived from this unfortunate race, and every possible vice ascribed to them – when we are accustomed to hear the poor, the uninformed, the friendless, put, by tacit consent, out of the pale of society – when their faults and wretchedness are exaggerated with eager impatience, and still greater impatience is shown at every expression of a wish to amend them – when they are familiarly spoken of as a sort of vermin only fit to be hunted down, and exterminated at the discretion of their betters: – we know pretty well what to think, both of the disinterestedness of the motives which give currency to this jargon, and of the wisdom of the policy which should either sanction, or suffer itself to be influenced by its suggestions.

(William Hazlitt 1821, 1982: 466)

Hazlitt was writing against capital punishment, against a method for the elimination of the 'useless' poor – which took the form in principle of suspending them from the neck until dead for stealing goods worth more than a shilling, although in practice most were disposed of by geographical separation through transportation to penal colonies, first in the Americas and then in Australia. In Hazlitt's era, the poor were punished not only for crime derived from poverty, and especially for criminalized collective action directed at resisting poverty, but, after the establishment of the New Poor Law of 1834, for the very fact of being poor itself.

Inglis (1972) noted that the workhouse regime of less eligibility – relief was to be 'less eligible' than the condition of the 'meanest employed labourer' – was opposed, not only by popular movements, which were to develop into the Chartists, but also intellectually by proto-Keynesians, including the authors of the interventionist report of the Irish Poor Law Commissioners of 1837. However, the combination of Malthus's warning of the implications of a reproducing poor with the utilitarian and market logic not so much of Adam Smith as of Bentham and Ricardo led to public policies that denied the poor any social rights (beyond minimal and punitive maintenance), separated from the obligation to work if able for whatever wages the labour market would provide. These approaches derive from the political doctrine of possessive individualism (Macpherson 1962). This principle, originating from Locke, provides a coherent rationale for the rights of individuals both to control their own persons and to possess their own distinctive and private property. It is the foundation of liberalism as a component of modernity and was of the greatest significance for both the American and French revolutions in politics and for the development of the ideological content of political economy as a set of economic doctrines. Note that it is inherently anti-collectivist. It is a principle directly set against both the estate-based conception of hierarchical natural orders which it was instrumental in destroying, and the collectivist conceptions of universal human solidarity that inform the socialist and social Christian doctrines which oppose it.

The late eighteenth and early nineteenth centuries in the UK were crucial for the development of social ideas that have a new, contemporary salience. As well as the doctrine of possessive individualism, there was the social demography of Malthus with its prediction that population would grow geometrically while resources would increase only arithmetically. We must never forget that the United Kingdom then included Ireland. In 1841 a third of the UK's population was Irish. The Irish experience seemed to be a practical illustration of the problems of too many people and no use for them. Even the socially conscious and proto-Keynesian Irish Commissioners on the Poor Law had no solution to the problems posed by this surplus population and its resistance to dispossession of land tenure, than to propose subsidized emigration to the 'empty' colonies. The idea of a useless surplus is one of the most dangerous of all social propositions, particularly when associated with the assignation of moral turpitude and worthlessness to the apparently surplus poor.

English commentators forget that early nineteenth-century Ireland was a colonized society on which English institutions could be imposed; Scotland was a free partner with a different legal code and civil society. The distinctive Scottish Poor Law was profoundly influenced by the Calvinisitic doctrine of predestination, in which the elect of God are separated from those who on the Day of Judgement will be cast into the outer darkness, a doctrine without sympathy for the poor – they deserve everything they get because it reflects their sinful and depraved state. Classical political economy in its pure forms is a non-judgemental, if harsh, doctrine. When it has added to it the moral judgements of individualistic forms of Protestantism, then insult is added to injury. This combination underpins what might otherwise be seen as the fundamentally contradictory neo-conservative position where possessive individualism does not lead to a libertarian absence of judgement, as with the utilitarian conception that the poor have to 'stand by their accidents and suffer for the greater general good', but that their poverty is an accident, not something derived from their inherent worthlessness. For the neo-conservatives the poor deserve everything they get.

In postindustrial capitalism, possessive individualism has experienced a remarkable resurgence. For example, 'counter-revolutionary economics' (that is, anti-Keynesian developments after the 1970s) regards unemployment as a choice:

> Unemployment as choice places the emphasis on the individual. The unemployed can find a way into work by demonstrating a willingness to accept lower wages, less attractive working conditions, longer journeys to work or by transferring to other occupations, industries and locations. Insufficient flexibility results in unemployment 'by choice'. The counter-revolution represents the relationship between employer and employee as remarkably shallow. The loss of job security for an individual, the loss of a way of life for a community are depoliticised and described in a way that minimises their consequences. Unemployment is seen as a voluntary choice or as the result of government policies that provide incentives to workers to remain unemployed.
>
> (McKay 1998: 50–1)

There is an essential continuity between such positions and 'godless economics', the 'dismal science' of political economy developed in Britain in the late eighteenth and early nineteenth centuries. Silver regards such understanding as characterized by explanations of poverty/social exclusion in terms of specialization.

> In Anglo-American liberalism, exclusion is considered a consequence of *specialisation* [original emphasis]: of social differentiation, the economic division of labour and the separation of spheres. It assumes that individuals differ, giving rise to specialisation in the market and in social groups. It is thus individualist in method, although causation is situated not simply in individual preferences but also in the structures created by co-operating and competing individuals – markets, association and the like. Liberalism, thus conceives of the social order, like the economy and politics, as networks of voluntary exchanges between autonomous individuals with their own interests and situations.
>
> (1994: 542)

These ideas exist not just as technical propositions in welfare economics. They constitute the basis of a liberal political philosophy founded around the concept of negative freedom (Berlin 1969), defined in terms of freedom of the individual *from* coercion and constraint. In contrast, positive liberty, which is freedom *to*, based on the collective provision of resource systems, extends the role of social action of individuals who would otherwise be constrained. The main exponent of the necessity for negative freedom in the post-World War II years was Hayek (1944), who regarded collective interventions, originating in the social programmes of the Christian and social democratic and collectivist liberal (Keynesian) positions, as representing 'the road to serfdom'.

It is important to distinguish those who argue for unfettered markets and absence of individual constraints on the basis of optimizing efficiency from those who assert the absolute primacy of negative liberty. The first category are utilitarians. They accept the illfares of some in order that the total of human welfare may, as they assert, be maximized – the greatest good – although not necessarily calculated to be of the greatest number; this is a programme of overall maximization without regard to any distributive effects. The second are individualists in an essentialist way. Their ethical commitment is anti-collectivist because they assert anything else diminishes the value of the individual self.

The three elements of this position are essentially inseperable. We cannot separate the absolute emphasis on individual freedoms from economic restrictions imposed by the collectivity, from the notion that developments that result from the operation of markets may engender a surplus and unnecessary population. Equally inherent is the moralist condemnation of the poor which derives from Calvinism. Paulin (1998) has reminded us that Hazlitt's political radicalism was founded in a theological unitarianism which rejected absolutely the notion of singular and selfish salvation – the covenant of faith. The US is the great bastion of the covenant of faith, but Mrs Thatcher's atheistical protestantism reflected it rather well.

In Anglo-American social thought, notions of blame and exclusion have crystallized around the related conceptions of the 'underclass' and 'benefit dependency', and constitute the core of the 'neo-conservative' position. These are not merely intellectual abstractions. They inform public policies, in particular policies directed at encouraging those dependent on state benefits 'from welfare into work'. The next section of this chapter will be devoted to an elaboration of these crude perspectives, which must be contrasted with Lewis's subtle original conception of the idea of a culture of poverty which we will consider in Chapter 5. We will then turn to a consideration of the way in which contemporary Anglo-American conceptions of citizenship and the related proposals of 'communitarianism' are inherently individualistic in form and remain part of the possessive individualist programme.

Residuums, underclasses and redundant populations

There is nothing new about the idea of an 'underclass': 'versions of the general concept of an inter-generational "underclass" have figured prominently in social debates during the past one hundred years' (MacNicol 1987: 293). Different terms have been used at different times. The commonest nineteenth-century expression was 'residuum', and the idea of a group that has been somehow left behind is an important component of all versions of the idea. The notion of a cycle of deprivation in which disadvantage is transmitted from generation to generation has been expressed in both genetic and cultural terms, although it is important to realize that the idea of an underclass can be expressed without reference to either. The term's recent reappearance comes from debates in the United States which are largely a continuation of the debate about 'cultures of poverty' that began with the Moynihan Report (1965). The main referent for the notion of a culture of poverty was Lewis (1966), although most of those who picked up the idea failed to pay any attention to the role Lewis assigned to culture as a resource of the poor. The concept has become a central part of the intellectual armoury of the dominant neo-conservative tradition in the New Right, notably in the work of Murray (1984, 1990).

Murray reiterated Ricardo's account of the genesis of the 'underclass'. For him, welfare benefits promoted a culture of dependency. Young women 'settled down' on benefits available to lone mothers and raised successive generations acculturated to behave in the same way. The account was originally racialized largely by implication – a disproportionate number of lone welfare mothers were black. Murray was brought to the UK in 1989 by *The Sunday Times*, and in 1990 the right-wing think tank, the Institute of Economic Affairs, published his account together with a number of criticisms of it. Dennis (Dennis and Erdos 1995; Dennis 1997) wrote in the same vein from an 'ethical socialist' position, seeking to provide a UK-based evidential basis for the view that inadequate parenting, and in particular the absence of respectable fathers, is the causal element for a life course of deprivation and deviance.

The United States debate about the underclass has largely been concerned with the position of Afro-Americans in cities. The arguments of the New Right have not gone unchallenged. In particular, Wilson (1987, 1989, 1992) and his co-workers have reiterated the criticism Valentine (1967) made of simplistic versions of the notion of the 'culture of poverty', pointing out that different behaviour can be explained by constraints without any need for recourse to cultural accounts:

> . . . if the concept of underclass is used, it must be a structural concept: it must denote a new socio-spatial patterning of class and racial domination, recognisable by the unprecedented concentration of the most socially excluded and economically marginal members of the dominated racial and economic group. It should not be used to designate a new breed of individuals moulded freely by a mythical and all powerful culture of poverty.
>
> (Wacquant and Wilson 1989: 25)

We must note here the emergent rather than nominalist character of Wacquant and Wilson's account. They are not dealing with individual status but with a social collectivity which is more than the sum of the individuals who make it up.

The significance of the notion of surplus population is enormous. The classical liberal position does not judge that uselessness. The neo-conservatives equate uselessness with worthlessness. Indeed, they have a theory of causation for such worthlessness. It is self-inflicted through the inter-generational transmission of the 'culture of poverty' and consequent habits of welfare dependency.

Subsequently, we will consider the notion of a culture of poverty as an emergent form, which originates with Oscar Lewis (1966). In his formulation the idea is subtle and important. However, here I want to deal with the use made of the notion of a 'culture of poverty' when the poors' own attitudes and values are identified as the source of their poverty in a process of blaming them for their own condition – the contemporary version of Protestantism's excluded and morally deficient non-elect. Lawrence Mead (1988), perhaps the most important US neo-conservative, has argued, in terms that are foundational to the counter-revolution in economic theory, that the condition of the poor derives in large part from their obdurate refusal of 'poor work'. Poor citizens, as opposed to immigrants, argue that they want to work, but they refuse to take low-paid and unpleasant work, demanding instead 'decent' or 'proper' jobs. In consequence, they fail to obtain any sort of work record and cannot gain access to reasonable work on the basis of proven work commitment. Their failures become internalized and lead to apathy and defeatism. That this approach assumes no discontinuity, no barriers of kind, between 'poor work' and 'decent work' should be obvious. We shall see in subsequent chapters that such an assumption is wholly wrong.

Mead asserts that his own approach is that of non-moralist utilitarianism and that the policy proposals that flow from it are essentially behaviourist rather than judgemental. For him, the task of public policy is to create incentive systems with both positive carrots and negative sticks, which make work preferable to benefit dependency. However, a moment's reflection on the moral element, which seems inseparable from any programme that sees the problem in terms solely of individual behaviour, suggests that this economistic rationalizing is disingenuous. Only mainstream economists and policy wonks ever confine themselves to a rationalist account of individual poverty, and not even all of them. In the hands of politicians we always get the moral argument, the judgement of the poor as unworthy, if perhaps redeemable, sinners.

Citizenship?

> . . . citizenship is a strategically important concept *intellectually* [original emphasis], not least in Sociology and Social Theory. It is important in principle because it provides a common field (1) for the sociological study of society to meet the study of social policy and politics and (2) for social theory to meet explicitly normative analysis in political theory and moral philosophy.
>
> (Roche 1992: 2)

For many years T.H. Marshall's discussion of citizenship was not an important theme in sociology or political theory. It surfaced only in social administration as the philosophical contribution to the study of the field of social policy. Marshall's account is one of an evolutionary development of the defined rights of individuals expressed in terms of individual persons acquiring progressively judicial, political and social rights. It is an account founded in a Whig history interpretation of the development of the social politics of modernity.

From the point of view of proponents of possessive individualism, Marshall's account is inherently contradictory. They have no problem with judicial rights. Indeed, the existence of such rights and of mechanisms for their enforcement, including the enforcement of rights derived from processes of contract, are central to any programme based on negative conceptions of liberty. Democratic rights are more tendentious, although few now publicly argue that they should be available only to those who possess a property-based stake in the social order. It is the social rights, the components of 'positive liberty', that are dismissed by those arguing from a classical liberal position, because they inevitably involve claims made through political mechanisms which challenge the property rights of others.

Given this, it may seem surprising that I have chosen to discuss citizenship in a chapter that deals essentially with the individualistic tradition. After all, Marshall's framework was shaped absolutely by the character of universalist social service provision through a tax-based welfare state in the UK after 1945. However, I want to argue, first, that the approach is not actually founded in a universalist programme but rather represents a rather traditional gloss placed on events which were not a product of actions of the elite who had the privilege of describing them; and, second, that late twentieth-century discussions of citizenship have forgotten the collectivist context in which Marshall developed the idea. Citizenship, and its derivative communitarianism, derive from the doctrines of possessive individualism and negative liberty. They are an intellectual accommodation with the necessity for social arrangements, but they remain inherently anti-social (in both the sociological and popular sense of that word) at the core. This is true even of sophisticated conceptions of exclusion in terms of incomplete citizenship as proposed by Bhalla and Lapeyre (1999), so long as citizenship is conceived of in terms of rights possessed by individuals rather than as something that is collective.

To understand the significance of the historical context of Marshall's ideas, we have to consider the anomalous character of the UK welfare state. Esping-Andersen (1992) had considerable difficulty locating the UK in his typology of welfare regimes, based as it was on contemporary institutional forms. In some respects the levels of welfare provision were not high, but there was a universalist free at the point of need National Health Service – a massively important representation of what Westergaard (1995) has described as the expression of a 'welfare aim beyond the market'. This is not a residual welfare state, neither is it the welfare state to be found under conditions of accommodation between Catholic social teaching and civic republicanism. Rather, it is a welfare state created by working-class social democracy but profoundly influenced in its development by collectivist liberalism. If subsequent debate about its character and future has been largely conducted between collectivist and classical (free market) liberals, with a period of structuralist Marxist ranting to add spice, the relative silence of a social democratic voice does not mean that the topic being discussed is not inherently social democratic in character. Indeed, Esping-Andersen explicitly endorses the view that the system immediately after its implementation represented a high point of democratic socialist achievement in terms of decommodification (1992: 53–4).

In effect, the historical product of a process of mass collective action, culture and disaffection, of what Williams called *The Long Revolution* (1962), has been appropriated as an intellectual practice by a liberal intelligentsia schooled in deductive philosophizing rather than in empirical investigation and account. These approaches ignore the social consciousness as developed by wartime experiences which was the origin of Labour's 1945 victory and of the universalist welfare state. There is ample evidence in the reports of mass observation of the character of social views in this period. Even that elitist (if radical) Liberal Beveridge ended his *Full Employment in a Free Society* with the exhortation:

> The British people can win full employment while remaining free. . . . But they have to win it, not wait for it. Full employment, like social security, must be won by a democracy; it cannot be forced on a democracy or given to a democracy. It is not a thing to be promised or not promised by a Government, to be given or withheld from Olympian height. It is something that the British democracy should direct its Government to secure, at all costs save the surrender of the essential liberties. Who can doubt that full employment is worth winning, at any cost less than surrender of those liberties? If full employment is not won and kept, no liberties are secure, for to many they will not seem worth while.
>
> (1944: 258)

Citizenship has been considered almost entirely in terms of abstract philosophical discussion rather than by reference to the real historical social politics, the long revolution, that created its modern form. It is this stripping out of the history which has made possible the appropriation of what can be a transformational and collectivist conception by proponents of possessive individualism.

This critique does not apply to Marshall himself. On the contrary, he belongs within the intellectual and political tradition that can be dated in the UK from the Newcastle programme of the Liberal Party in the 1890s, when the original ideological foundations of that party in free-market individualism were replaced by an accommodating collectivism drawing on Collingwood and the English Hegelians for its intellectual provenance. This was the mindset of Beveridge and Keynes, as well as of Marshall, and we will consider it in the next chapter. Turner describes the original conception thus:

In the work of Marshall, the concept was developed to answer a problem in liberalism. In capitalism, liberal values were successful in emphasizing freedoms and individualism, but there was no easy answer to critics who pointed out that the classic freedoms . . . were ineffective tokens for the majority of the population who lived in poverty. In part, the institutions of citizenship, especially in the British case, functioned to ameliorate the condition of the working class without transforming the entire property system. While 'citizenship' functions as a description of certain institutions, it covertly carries the implication that they *ought* [original emphasis] to exist in the interests of social harmony.

(1993: 176–7)

It is the dominant contemporary 1990s usage of citizenship that is individualistic to the core. Jordan expresses this well when he dismisses 'the analysis of poverty and social exclusion in terms of citizenship, especially within the liberal tradition' because of:

. . . the narrow focus of this concept on individual rights and responsibilities, at the expense of interdependency and collective action. Indeed the whole debate about 'social citizenship' has been largely directed into this cul-de-sac – the search for a 'balance' between rights and responsibilities conceived as formal reciprocities between individual members of market oriented systems.

(1996: 85)

It has to be said that citizenship expressed in these sorts of terms is a profoundly unsociological idea. It is a micro-theory that ignores the macro-structures, the social order, within which citizenship as a practice must be embedded. There is one sociological proposition of the New Right which must be exempted from that criticism. This is the absolute standard argument. If minimum standards are high enough in absolute terms, then whatever the inequalities that may exist in relative terms, there is no longer any need for collectivist intervention which impinges on negative liberty. This kind of argument implicitly incorporates a crude version of the view, much more coherently expressed by Eder (1993), that the rise in overall real living standards (for Eder among other factors) has not only eliminated any social justice case for major redistributive intervention in the name of citizenship, but has also eliminated the causal processes that created an emergent and self-conscious class-based collective politics demanding such redistribution. However, at least we have sociology here.

Absolutist liberals have the virtue of logical consistency in their views on these matters. Neo-conservatives are inherently inconsistent. Roche summed up the neo-conservative dilemma in these terms:

Neo-conservatism is to a considerable extent ambiguous and incoherent in its conception of the poor and underclass citizen as simultaneously capable of moral reform by authoritarian reminders about duty *and* [original emphasis] socially incompetent and psychologically incapable of rational self-control and thus of consistent moral action . . . Overall probably the major underlying weakness in the neo-conservative challenge to the dominant paradigm has been its inability to connect systematically its two main values. On the one hand it supports 'morality' and 'traditional' patriarchal, familistic and 'work ethic' morality in particular. On the other, it supports capitalism as an economic system, which is arguable inherently anti-traditional.

(1992: 49)

There is an important additional contradiction here. Neo-conservatism asserts a work ethic but cannot assert a right, as opposed to a duty, to work, precisely because full employment recasts the basis of the relationship between labour and capital around the wage relationship. Capitalism must always have its reserve army in position and available on demand.

'Communitarianism' has been proposed as a way of resolving the crucial problem for neo-conservatives of reconciling the idea of rights for individuals with obligations which those individuals may owe to the wider collectivity (Etzioni 1995). It is important to distinguish this from the organic approaches which will be the subject of the next chapter. US communitarianism is firmly grounded in the tradition of possessive individualism, even if the core of the approach is based around an assertion of the need to move back from a social order characterized by excessive individualism founded on an overgenerous interpretation of personal rights.

There is a deal of confusion in the account, but it hinges around a kind of reverse principle of subsidiarity, of the Catholic doctrine that functions should be handed down below the level of the state to that level of social organization that is best fitted to their execution. Catholic organicism works down from the universal. Communitarianism works up from the individual. It does, of course, challenge the notion of the ultimate sovereignty of the individual through its imposition of community-ordered moral and civic obligations, but it does so in relation to an undifferentiated conception of the character of citizens. For example, Etzioni calls for a moratorium on the 'manufacturing of new rights' and is scathing about the 81 per cent of Americans (US citizens I assume he means) who regard health care as a right and the 66 per cent who likewise see decent housing as a right, asking 'who will pay for unlimited health care and adequate housing for all?' (1995: 5). The answer could well be all the rich who have benefited so massively out of the existing systems, including among them the US medical profession, by reducing their incomes to approximately those of physicians in other advanced industrial countries; the owners of capital in unnecessary private health insurance companies, by introducing an efficient single purchaser model on Canadian lines; and the exploitative rich in general by (a) paying their taxes at all and (b) paying more in taxes. In other words, the possessive individualistic origins of communitarianism presumptively, if not absolutely, leave intact the very tightly possessed property rights of those who have them, regardless of the consequences for the fabric of the social order. They readily impose obligations of behaviour on the poor, but there is no equivalent discussion of the obligations of the rich.

In the UK, typical contemporary proponents of this sort of theory are Dennis (1997) and Green (1996, 1998). Green states his position thus:

> . . . if too many people look to the government for the means of life, then this dependency has harmful effects which accumulate over time. The initial harm results from people organising their affairs so that they qualify for benefit. Having crossed the boundary between independent self-support and reliance on the work of others, individuals are inclined to neglect friendships or relationships with people who could provide a helping hand in a spirit of mutual respect. Because their self-respect diminishes, they often become more shameless in their determination to live at the expense of others. They also fail to join organisations like churches or voluntary associations, where they would meet people who would gladly provide temporary restorative help. As a further consequence, they acquire fewer skills of co-operating with others, and face fewer challenges. In turn, they have fewer opportunities to strengthen their characters by overcoming adversity. As a result, they are more prone to manipulation by politicians, some of whom are only too willing to 'buy' their votes with promises of 'more'. Politicians whose model of society is one of leaders and led are very happy to preserve in being a section of the population that will trade its votes for cash rewards.
>
> (1998: vii)

The reality is that far from the poor being a constituency of politicians in the UK and even more in the US, they are now so alienated from a political process which seems to disregard them as a significant social group, that they increasingly don't vote in the former state and don't really vote at all in the latter. However, it is the 'moral' fault argument that is central to Green's position.

These kind of accounts are the 'moralistic' and 'astructural' version of communitarianism. Küng has understood them exactly:

> . . . moralism and moralizing overvalue morality and ask too much of it. Why? Moralists make morality the sole criterion for human action and ignore the relative independence of various spheres of life like economics, law and politics. As a result they tend to absolutize intrinsically justified norms and values (peace, justice, environment, life, love) and also to exploit them for the particular interests of an institution (state, party, church, interest group). Moralism manifests itself in a one-sided and penetrating insistence on particular moral positives (for example, in questions of sexual behaviour) which make a rational dialogue with those of other convictions impossible.
>
> (1997: xiv–xv)

There is one further topic we must consider before we leave the doctrines founded in individualism. It is the inherent tension between an economic system founded on possessive individualism and ordered through free markets on the one hand, and democratic majority government, especially when informed by the principle of subsidiarity, on the other. Crouch and Marquand put this rather well:

> One of the central assumptions of the new right is that choice is maximised through the market, not through politics: that the frictionless, undisturbed market is a realm of freedom and the polity a realm of domination and manipulation. Grant that and it follows logically that the sphere of the political should be curtailed; one obvious way to do this is to limit the scope of subordinate political authorities. On new right assumptions, provided people have the chance to vote in national elections and to participate in open political discussion and lobbying, they should find variety, choice and delegation through market activity alone, and not through further political forms.
>
> (1989: viii–xi)

The New Right will only accept lower-level political entities when these are considered to act as a bastion against the collectivism of a higher level, for example in the way the doctrine of 'states' rights' can be used against what has, since the New Deal, been seen as the collectivist tendency of the federal level in the US, or the basis of 'Eurosceptic' defence of the UK nation state against the European Union. It is thus adamantly opposed to the principle of subsidiarity – that is, the principle of the necessity for and necessary autonomy of lower spatial levels for the management of political life. Indeed, there is a tendency in practice, if not much these days in formal principled expression, for New Right politics to revert to the conception that citizenship rights of political determination are only available to those with property.

The clearest indication of the consequences of this is the withdrawal of the mass of people from political engagement in those societies, particularly the US and the UK, where neo-liberalism dominates the political system. The membership of the British (since it does not organize in Northern Ireland) Labour Party is now generally understood to be less than 250,000. In the 1950s it exceeded a million, and at Labour's election victory in 1997 it was over 400,000. Conservative Party membership is down to less than 350,000 from its figure of a million in the Thatcher years. In 2001, turnout in the UK general election fell below 60 per cent, the lowest ever in the country's history of democratic adult suffrage. In the US 2000 presidential election, only half of the voting-age population voted, and the figure for registered voters was 68 per cent. As we shall see in 'post-democratic' societies, corporate interests dominate the political system. The relevance of this here is that throughout the modern history of politics, market-orientated political ideologues and practitioners have sought to limit the political engagement of the mass of people and to restrict the capacity of political systems in relation to economic life. In mass democracies, achieving popular political disengagement is an important means to this end.

The argument against what is now called neo-liberalism was stated at the beginning of industrial capitalism by Hazlitt. The political and social doctrines which flow from possessive individualism, and the division of people into the worthy and the depraved, serve particular and restricted material interests. They are ideological in essence. All political and social doctrines serve interests. The issue is whether those interests are particular or universal – or at the very least of the relative size of the interests served. All social accounts are ideologically coloured. However, the realist position that informs this book does not accept that all accounts are merely expressions of interests – this is not a relativist text. We can establish how things are – there is a truth to be got at. Subsequently we will try to do that. Let us now examine two other sets of doctrines, recognizing always that the distinction between social doctrine and account of the social is simply heuristic, that are certainly different from each other, but which do share an essential commitment to the social and collective as the foundation of any social politics.

2

Order, solidarity and transformation: collectivist political traditions

In this chapter we will examine the intellectual origins and contemporary form of an internally varied set of social ideas/programmes which can nonetheless be distinguished from those reviewed in Chapter 1 by the emphasis placed on the importance of the social order as a whole and on the obligations which all members of the collectivity owe to that social order. We will begin by examining two positions which share the collectivist objectives of the Marxist position but can be distinguished from even the most reformist versions of Marxism by their belief that the capitalist social order can deliver in terms of collective social goals. For the exponents of these positions, market capitalism must be corrected by political action but it is a corrigible system. We will then turn to variants of the Marxist understanding of the nature of capitalism both in terms of development and contemporary condition. Of course, we are dealing here with fuzzy sets. Communitarianism represents a set of approaches which provide a bridge between the classical liberal conceptions discussed in Chapter 1 and the positions reviewed here. The boundary must be drawn between 'moral communitarianism', in which the responsibility is assigned to individuals, and 'socio-economic communitarianism', which displays some awareness of the significance of social structures and of the faults of capitalism as a mode of production (see Driver and Martell 1997). Likewise, the social democratic tradition links perspectives which deny that fundamental class conflict is inherent in the capitalist order, to Marxist accounts which assert the reality of such fundamental conflict and its role as the active contradiction of capitalism itself.

Capitalism can be tamed – the social market and related approaches

The approaches reviewed in this section all agree that market capitalism is an unstable system which requires collective regulation. They accept that:

> If the great scenarios teach us anything, it is that the problems that threaten capitalism arise from the private sector, not the public. The saturation of demand and the degradation of the labour force that are the great difficulties of Smith's conception; the crises and contradictions of Marx's model; the inability to reach full employment that Keynes selected as the great flaw; the cultural erosion of Schumpeter's scenario – these are all failures that arise from the workings of the capitalist economy, not from any interference with those workings by the polity. What solutions, what counter-measures can there be to problems caused by the private realm except those that originate in the public realm?
>
> (Heilbroner 1993: 112)

In summary, we might say that the approaches outlined in Chapter 1 argue that market capitalism will work well and that the only role of the political systems of the collectivity is to ensure that the recalcitrance of the idle is overcome by appropriate discipline. In contrast, the perspectives being reviewed in this section accept the need for the collective regulation and management of capitalism in order to ameliorate excesses of inequality and maintain stability in an inherently unstable system. Marxist socialist perspectives, which we will consider in the next section, argue that capitalism is not a long-term option and that the future sustainability of human societies depends on its transformation into something else, by a process of what may well be a long revolution based on the accretion of the effects of social reform.

The sources of non-transformational collectivism are various. They include Catholic 'solidarism', its mirror image in the solidarism of Jacobin republicanism, non-transformational socialism, and Keynesianism, which came together in the post-war years in Western Europe as the basis of a social politics which is best described by the now neglected expression 'social market economy'. The theologian Küng locates this approach in a post-World War II desire to realize a 'new third form' between the totalitarian controlled economy and the purely liberal market economy:

> Beyond doubt the social market economy had more realist presuppositions than ultraliberalism, which professed itself to be so realist. After all the fearful experiences of twentieth-century Europe it was no longer possible to maintain the ultraliberal idea that a natural harmony of interests had to be the model for economic and social life. Conflicts, not harmony, are the realistic starting point for the social market economy;

to this degree there was an agreement with Marxism. But at the same time there was a concern not to rake up the old 'class struggle' between labour and capital all over again: . . . A positive effect of this was that here ideas of Protestant social ethics were combined with those of Catholic social teaching, the foundations for which were laid in the papal encyclicals *Rerum Novarum* (1891) and *Quadrigesimo Anno*. These had been thought through above all by advocates of the concept of solidarity . . .

(Küng 1997: 201–2)

Küng notes that these positions developed an understanding of solidarity and subsidiarity: 'Long before any communitarianism' (1997: 202). This is something more than the stockholding conception of social practice ascribed by Jordan to the European mercantilist tradition in which the poor are seen as: 'more like sheep and cattle to be farmed (regulated and provided for as part of the creation and conservation of national wealth), than wild animals to be tamed' (as in the Anglo Saxon liberal tradition) (1996: 3). It is also qualitatively different from the kind of organicism which asserts a social order formed of natural ranks and places to which people are properly allocated, and sees departure from the allocated places as threatening to the integrity of the whole system. Non-transformational collectivism is not conservative in that sense. It allows for change and indeed regards some change as not only desirable but probably essential.

It certainly has to be distinguished from the version of the term 'third way' presented by Prime Minister Blair in his speech to the United Nations of September 1998. For Blair, as for the Borrie-chaired Commission on Social Justice (1996) before him, the power of global markets is so great that no political system can stand against them. The best it can achieve is tendential modification. The original idea of the third way does not subordinate politics to economics in this way. On the contrary, it is precisely founded on the use of state power to regulate economic systems so that they do not challenge social goals.

Silver argues that: 'At the heart of the question "exclusion from what?" lies a more basic one, the problem of social order during times of profound social change in society' (1994: 541). We must remember that this is by no means the first period in which this question has been asked. Küng makes it very clear the social market economy programme as developed by Erhard in the first 20 years of the Federal Republic, originated in the regulated liberalism of the Freiburg school: 'which called for a strong state capable of establishing an ordered framework for free competition whilst at the same time pursuing a policy of order to maintain competition' (1997: 199). The 'order liberals' who pursued these objectives were very different in their approach from the classical liberals exemplified by Hayek. They argued for: 'the interdependence of society, the state and the economy' (Küng 1997: 200), in marked contrast to classical liberalism's absolute privileging of the market economy. At the same time they did not endorse the organic totalitarianisms both of the old regimes and of fascism. They were trying to make a non-totalitarian capitalism work, and of course they succeeded for many years.

European Christian Democrats combined ideas from an analytical and atheological programme, order liberalism, with the theologically informed account of solidarity which underpinned Catholic social teaching after *Rerum Novarum*. French Republicanism, to the considerable degree that it is inspired by Rousseau's ideas, emphasizes solidarity in terms of integration into the social order to an even greater degree than its old Catholic antagonist, hence the ease with which Gaullism in post-war France could reconcile Catholic perspectives with a godless republic.

The social democratic case is more complicated with two different reconciliations going on. The first is in French and Belgian socialism of social democratic and Catholic perspectives. The second is in Swedish, German and British socialism of formal socialist objectives with a Keynesian programme of macro-economic management. These combinations had broadly similar objectives, but very different mechanisms were to be employed to achieve them. All 'organicist' programmes depend on the development of institutions which represent both means for the formal attachment between individuals and the collectivity, and processes through which individuals are integrated culturally into the social order. The German combination of education and social insurance shows this very well.

The two aspects to this institutional integration need to be spelled out. First, in Germany high general levels of education meant that most citizens have the qualifications necessary in principle for well-paid jobs. When there is insufficient demand for the available volume of qualified labour, then integration was formerly achieved through the institutional mechanism of generous income substitution benefits, the Bismarkian model. This, of course, suggests that 'Welfare to Work' schemes will not work unless low wages are accepted by workers qualified to levels which would normally command higher wages. It is the failure of the supply side mechanism to achieve solutions – the delivery of highly qualified labour by educational systems does not create employment unless there is demand for the products of that employment – which is the origin of the contemporary crisis in Western European welfare systems. However, a major tension in German politics in the early years of the twenty-first century has centred exactly on the preservation of the rights of German workers to rely on high-level income substitution benefits as an alternative to work below their levels of qualification and expectation. At the same time, German workers are being forced to work longer hours for the same pay under the threat of the movement of their jobs to new accession members of the EU. The neo-liberal agendas have penetrated deep into order liberalism's heartland.

This is where the Keynesian perspectives become particularly interesting. They were much discussed in the early 1980s but have almost disappeared from the formal content of contemporary debate. Held pointed out that:

The crisis of the Keynesian social democratic state is in essence, the loss of faith in its continuing efficacy as a political accommodation of both universal suffrage and organised labour with a market oriented economy.

(1983: 258)

Why should this mechanism, which was so successful for so long, have ceased to work? One important explanation is that the Keynesian programme was implemented in a period when the general level of capital in the economies of the advanced industrial world was low. There were deficits in productive capital which reflected the impact of wartime destruction. There were deficits in social capital, particularly in housing and transport infrastructure, which reflected both wartime destruction and the poor quality of social capital developed in the nineteenth century. There was a massive military industrial complex engaged in both a Cold War involving competitive technology development and a series of hot post-colonial wars. All this served to maintain global aggregate demand.

The system suffered a severe shock from the 1970s' rapid rise in oil prices which drained from the expenditure-based demand of the Western economies. This, coupled with the filling up of productive and social capital deficits and massive productivity gains in manufacturing industries in general, created a situation in which the intrinsic demand for labour weakened in advanced industrial economies. There was a crucial collapse in demand for skilled manual labour. Productivity gains depended on the replacement of skilled labour by a combination of machinery and less skilled labour. At the same time, the 'product mix' of the global capitalist economy has moved away from the heavy engineering products which were the main locus of skilled manual employment towards both light electronic goods and a range of services. These changes in the nature of the real economy are part of the story of the weakness of classic Keynesian policies over the last two decades. Another important factor has been the globalization of finance capital based on new communications technology. For nationally based Keynesian policies to be effective, the political forces vested in nation states had to be able to control capital flows. After the early 1980s, they no longer had the capacity to do this.

It is conventional to discuss the account of social exclusion offered by the perspectives being reviewed here in terms of the failure of integration, particularly into work but also with general social systems including family, friends and local community. Levitas (1996) identifies this aspect as a strongly Durkheimian element in the 'middle way'. However, her entirely correct emphasis on the significance attached to integration through work actually misses the point that the demand for work in previous eras has been radical. The idea of a 'right to work' was the project of two political responses to the socialist objective of the transformation of society. It has been part of both Keynesian 'bourgeois liberalism' – the new order liberalism of the twentieth century, and of Catholic-influenced Christian democracy. I agree with Levitas that the main institution created by these positions, the European Union, has abandoned these perspectives. In its policy documents we find that:

> The cause of exclusion is not the fundamental nature of capitalism (which never gets discussed) but the 'contemporary economic and social conditions' which tend to exclude some groups from the cycle of opportunities.
>
> (1996: 8)

However, the Christian democracy, non-transformational social democracy, and new liberalism all recognize that there are problems with the fundamental nature of capitalism, and with the balance of power within it of labour as against capital. These perspectives come together in an interesting way in the recent publication of the Council of Churches of Britain and Ireland dealing with *Unemployment and the Future of Work* (1997) and an exegesis of that text is a good way of illustrating their implications:

> The most fundamental question we have had to address is this: should we still, as church leaders have in the past, argue the case that enough paid work should be created for everyone, or should we adopt a new set of values in the belief that full employment is essentially a thing of the past? . . . We have concluded that the value of work is central to the Christian understanding of the human condition, not an optional extra. Society should not give up on paid work . . . 'Enough good work for everyone', has to become an explicit national aim in its own right . . . The aim of enough good work cannot be allowed to remain a hoped for, but ultimately optional, by-product to economic growth.
>
> (1997: 7–8)

The interesting thing here is the emphasis on 'good work':

> Work is rightly seen as a form of service to one another, to the community and to the well-being of the world. All those who are called to such service should accept it. But willing service should never become a kind of servitude. The wish to do useful work, indeed the need to earn a living, should never be exploited by employers offering pay and conditions which are unfair and offensive to human dignity.
>
> (1997: 102)

The common conflation of the views informed by a radical theology with those of conservatism as a single paradigm describing positions on social exclusion is mistaken. Catholic-influenced politics will always contain a deeply conservative strand of reactionary organicism. However, this is not informed by the principle of 'solidarity/fraternity'. Rather, it revolves around an intrinsically hierarchical conception of proper place. In contrast the principle of 'solidarity/fraternity' is essentially anti-hierarchical and inherently radical. It is probably a key element in the formation of potential coalitions for social change. We can see this by attempting to consider what these perspectives make of the idea of 'citizenship'.

Citizenship considered from a solidaristic perspective is very different from that idea as understood by 'possessive individualism'. Citizenship is a new idea of modernity, despite important reference back by those who developed it to the political ideas of classical Greece, and in particular to conceptions of the proper relationship between citizen and *polis*. It must also be recognized that solidaristic discussions of citizenship did borrow from liberalism and allow a separation of the appropriate spheres of private existence and the public domain – for a *limited* sphere of individual possession.

In so far as 'liberal' discussions of citizenship confine themselves to issues of 'rights' and 'duties', they neglect the notion of 'powers'. This is the case even when the term 'active citizen' is brought into play. The active citizen is either implicitly confined to the sphere of civil society, or explicitly directed there by those such as Green (1997) who argue from an extreme liberal (possessive individualist) position for a 'community without politics'. Marshall cannot be accused of this fault. His three levels of citizenship involved equality under the law, the necessary precondition of the negative liberties which constitute a minimalist possessive individualist basis for citizenship's access to social rights, the basis of positive liberties; and the franchise which involved access to processes of political determination. There were definite obligations imposed along with this extension of political liberty and hence political power, particularly in relation to military service. At the high point of citizen power in the UK, in the period which led to the writing of Marshall's book, this obligation of military service was extended to women. The doctrine of military participation ratio is rather important in understanding citizenship in all its aspects.

We have already noted the inherent tension between the assertion of negative liberty and the existence of democracy. There is also a tension between organicism and democracy. Organic polities are traditionally corporatist. This conception of the role of 'estates' in the political sphere was the intellectual core of Italian and Spanish fascism and played an important role in the development of Catholic political thinking in the twentieth century. The European Union's emphasis on 'social partners' is a corporatist idea involving collaboration between the elites of labour and capital – the classic social partners – in a system mediated by the state. With the development of 'partnership' as an active device directed against social exclusion we see the invention of a third partner, 'the community', in which local representatives from the voluntary sector, active citizens in Green's 'community without politics' are drawn into the corporatist process. In the UK, trade unions were excluded from the corporatist bun fight by the Tories and remain excluded by a Labour Party originally founded expressly to represent their organizational interests. It is important to distinguish corporatism from democracy. Under corporatism the leaders of interest groups act without any clear mechanism through which they are

accountable to the constituencies they represent and crucial decisions
are likely to be secret.

There is no direct role for the political citizen in the corporatist framework. They are included only through membership of the group or estate to
which they belong. The identification of the 'community' as an estate of the
poor is at best a dangerous and self-deluding myth, and at worst a cynical
device for facilitating their continued exclusion in terms both of their condition and from any active participation in real politics. There is an alternative which represents the most radical end of radical Catholicism. Indeed, in
its liberation theology form this is closely related to Marxist approaches, but
it should be introduced here. Again we are dealing with fuzzy sets. The key
word is Freire's – 'empowerment'.

> . . . *Empowerment* – For poor and dispossessed people, strength is in
> numbers and social change is accomplished in unity. Power is shared,
> not the power of a few who improve themselves at the expense of
> others, but the power of the many who find strength and purpose in
> a common vision. Liberation achieved by individuals at the expense
> of others is an act of oppression. Personal freedom and the development
> of individuals can only occur in mutuality with others.
>
> (Heaney 1998: 2)

Teague and Wilson say something important here:

> The civil republican model of citizenship stands in sharp contrast to the
> liberal individualist version. In particular, it places much more emphasis
> on the idea of collective good and social duties and responsibilities of
> individuals. Thus civil republicans are strong advocates of political
> communities and active participation. The idea that citizenship is
> simply some type of legal status that confers on individuals certain
> rights against the state is rejected as impoverished. Individuals are
> regarded as only being fully enriched through social co-operation and
> in circumstances where they play an active role in public life and abide
> by community norms and rules.
>
> (1995: 93)

They remark that in Northern Ireland there has been a hypertrophy of what
Arendt (1959) called 'communities of meaning', but that with the weakness
of civil society, there is no foundation for 'communities of action', 'through
which decentralised collectivist solutions are to be found to the question
of order and authority' (1995: 94). Freire's notion of empowerment is a
specification both of a means of social pedagogy through which poor
people transform themselves in interaction with others, and of an end, an
outcome in which civil republican citizenship is expressed through communities of action. It is about outcome, but also about process. People have
to be able to do it for themselves.

Plainly, organicist corporatism is not a means to this end but is rather a
way of excluding most people from decision making. Freire developed his

approach in a Brazil dominated by economic and political elites with the mass of the population excluded from any role in determining the course of the social order, and in which the degree of emmiseration and social deprivation was (and remains) extreme. This system was highly corporatist, but with both organized labour and the rural poor kept out. In practice, the introduction of a formal ideology of classical liberalism and of institutions facilitating liberal market reforms has virtually no effect on these kinds of arrangements. For now, we can see, I hope, that there are two versions of organicism. One, whilst concerned with inclusion in the sense that people are to have a place, is not concerned with emancipation. The other is absolutely about emancipation. The one is typified by the theological attitudes of John Paul II. The other is characteristic of liberation theology. For the first, inclusion is about condition. For the second, it must be about process. For Freire, struggle against what we now call 'exclusion' is a cultural process founded around ideas or it is nothing.

The politics of transformation – Marxist and related perspectives

The key Marxist concept in understanding the phenomena with which this book is concerned is that of the 'reserve army of labour', sometimes also referred to as 'the industrial reserve army'. Bauman's analysis (1987, 1997, 1998, 2004) hinges exactly on the notion that the 'socially excluded' do not constitute a reserve army of labour under the present conditions of accumulation in late capitalism.

> . . . the poor are less and less important to the reproduction of capital in their traditional role as the 'reserve army of labour'. They are no longer the object of concern for the twofold political task of recommodification of labour and limitation of working-class militancy. The previously taken-for-granted principle of social responsibility for the survival – and, indeed, the well being – of that part of society not directly engaged by capital as producers has suddenly come under attack.
>
> (1987: 21)

This is a deeply Marxist analysis in form – Bauman has gone right to the heart of the matter. This is the crucial issue. The burden of this chapter will be an argument that he is wrong – that those discussed under the contemporary heading of 'social exclusion' are indeed a reserve army of labour and that we have to understand the contemporary character of capitalist restructuring as one which depends absolutely on a simultaneous development and underdevelopment of the forces of production and of the class elements which contribute to those forces of production.

Let us begin with consideration of the classical Marxist account of the 'reserve army', followed by a review of the way in which 'regulation theory', the currently fashionable (and indeed even intelligible and often sensible) version of Marxist academic theory deals with these issues. However, regulation theory remains a system-centred account in which all the autonomy is yielded to capitalism and capitalists. Nelson's discussion of postindustrial capitalism, which will also be considered here, is one that recognizes the significance of political action, but again see this as monopolized by capitalist interests. The discussion of 'autonomist Marxist' perspectives which will conclude this chapter takes a very different view of things, at least in terms of potential.

The industrial reserve army

Marx was an assiduous reader of the Blue Books, of the investigations conducted by Royal Commissions and House of Commons Committees which described the profoundly changing society administered by the British state during the Industrial Revolution. I would be very surprised indeed if he had not read the reports of the Royal Commission on the Irish Poor Law, and especially Lewis's *Report on the State of the Irish Poor in Great Britain* (1836). Let me quote A. Carlile in his evidence to Lewis:

> The boundless coal fields beneath us and the boundless mines of labour so to speak, existing for us in Ireland, form together one of the great secrets of this part of Scotland. We are in the rare predicament of being able to obtain any required increase in our working population, without being obliged to pay the usual high penalties for creating such increased supplies viz. increased wages, loss of time and valuable commercial opportunities.
>
> (A. Carlile 1836: 463)

Marx went to school with these students of capitalism and he learned his lesson well. The immediate function of a reserve army of labour is twofold. It exists in order to enable expansion of production without increase in unit labour costs. It exists in order to discipline employed workers through the threat of substitution. Note that Marx goes beyond this account. His reserve army is differentiated. A crucial element in order to facilitate special branches of accumulation. We will come back to that idea in a moment.

Contemporary literature dealing with social exclusion pays justified attention to 'income dynamics', that is movements around position in the distribution of household incomes (see Webb 1995; Goodman et al. 1997; Leisering and Walker 1998). It is important to understand the duration of 'the state of being excluded', and this matters for public understanding and public policy. Short term with the probability of recovery matters much less than permanent differentiation. What really matters is movement between the reserve army and poor work. It is this dynamism that is the basis of the functionality of the poor as a reserve army.

Dynamism is an aspect of the capitalist social order as a system as well as of the household units nested within it. The significance of the industrial reserve army lies not just in its role in disciplining labour within a given condition state of capitalism as a system, that is within a period when capitalism operates with a relatively stable form in terms of the social relations of production. The industrial reserve army is crucial to processes of restructuring when capitalism is in crisis. O'Connor (1981) identified the term 'crisis' as originating in classical Greek medicine to describe a 'turning point', a situation in which continuation in present state was not possible but in which things had to change to one or another of two possible outcomes. This is exactly analogous to the idea in chaos/complexity theory of a bifurcation point. O'Connor describes capitalism as a 'crisis-dependent system'. This is by no means specifically a Marxist viewpoint. Schumpeter understood capitalism as driven by waves of creative destruction, another theory of capitalism as crisis driven, but, whereas Marxist accounts see crises as stages in the transition from capitalism to socialism, for Schumpeter capitalist crises are the means by which the system develops to ever higher levels of production and general welfare achievement. We shall return to a Schumpeterian account when we consider Nelson's (1995) discussion of the development of the service sector in postindustrial capitalism.

O'Connor dismissed both the traditional 'scientific' Marxist theory of crisis as being an interruption in the accumulation of capital – accounts in which 'the subject is capital itself' (1981: 302) - and neo-Marxist accounts in the radical Durkheimian tradition of critical theory, in which crisis is an interruption of the normative structure of social action. In autonomist mode, he asserted that crisis involves social conflict and class struggle. His account of the role of the reserve army in relation to crisis runs thus:

> . . . crisis induced recreation of the reserve army of labour is a lever of accumulation to the degree that it is a level of 'capital restructuring'. This means that layoffs during the early stages of economic crises permit capital to re-establish its domination over the working class which in turn is a pre-condition for restructuring the means of production and relocating industry. . . . It is not the original layoffs . . . but the 'second round unemployment' which theoretically makes the next boom possible without excessive upward pressure on wage rates. In this sense, the reserve army is the key to restructuring the means of production and also the system's capacity to enter into a new phase of expansion.
>
> (1981: 315–16)

O'Connor is saying exactly the same thing as Paisley businessman Carlile said in 1836, although Carlile's reserve army was the latent reserve army of a dispossessed peasantry from Ireland rather than the unemployed within the capitalist industrial order itself. As we shall see, the dispossessed peasantry can come from very far away in postindustrial capitalism. The significance of the latent reserve external to metropolitan capitalism but importable into it is immense.

I want to push O'Connor's position further than he takes it. His discussion deals with the slump/boom cycle of capitalist production. We need to consider that dynamic as a dynamic within phases of capitalism. I would argue that the recreation of a reserve army is even more important as a means towards the dynamic phase shift from one form of capitalism to another. Essentially, my argument is that the reserve army is a crucial means to the restructuring of the capitalist social order as a whole – it is the means within a Schumpeterian account whereby the countervailing power of labour is overcome and the forces which drive change, including new technologies and new forms of managerial control, are given the sway they need.

Recently, Auyero has reintroduced a development of the classical Marxist conception of the reserve army which derives from Latin American development sociology of the 1970s. He has reminded/informed us that:

> The structural historicist perspective on marginality . . . understood that the functioning of what they called 'the dependent labour market' was generating an excessive amount of unemployment. This 'surplus population' transcends the logic of the Marxian concept of the 'industrial reserve army' and led the authors to coin the term 'marginal mass'. The 'marginal mass' was neither superfluous nor useless; it was marginal because it had been rejected by the society that created it.
>
> (1997: 508–9)

This term and the conception it embodies is extremely valuable because Auyero is picking up the spatial segregation element and linking it to the role of the 'excluded' in the general logic of the development of capitalist production through underdevelopment. The 'bringing back home of underdevelopment' is a crucial aspect of the autonomist account, although we will find subsequently that marginalization is not the strategy by which postindustrial capitalism is seeking to achieve underdevelopment in its metropolitan core. Rather, we will find a programme of control rather than abandonment, of formal work and incarceration as a way of integrating the dispossessed into an exploitative social order. Let us turn from O'Connor's account of the means of restructuring to the most general account of the nature of the outcome of that restructuring: regulation theory.

Regulation theory: transition codified – postindustrial capitalism: the means specified

'Regulation theory' has been described by Amin as the product of an intellectual current which wanted to develop:

. . . a theoretical framework which could encapsulate and explain the paradox within capitalism between its inherent tendency towards instability, crisis and change, and its ability to coalesce and stabilise around a set of institutions, rules and norms which serve to secure a relatively long period of economic stability.

(1994: 7)

However, it is not stability but change which preoccupies contemporary regulation theorists. They posit, as Esser and Hirsch put it: 'a nonlinear theory of capitalist development' (1994 73). The regulation theory school at its most general distinguishes between 'the regime of accumulation', that is the general pattern of organization of the processes of capitalist production towards the end of accumulation, and 'the mode of regulation' which describes the complex of institutions and normative structures which surround and govern the processes of capitalist reproduction. It is changes in these which constitute the kind of transition shifts in the forms of capitalism.

Amin describes regulation theory's concept of 'mode of societalization' as referring to: 'a series of political compromises, social alliances and hegemonic processes of domination which feed into a pattern of mass integration and social cohesion, thus serving to underwrite and stabilise a given development push' (1994: 8). The Keynes/Beveridge welfare state, coupled with the rights of trade unions to effective organization, can be considered to have 'represented a crucial compromise between organised labour and capital'. In particular, it channelled accumulation away from absolute surplus value expropriation which depended on the exploitative emmiseration of workers and towards relative surplus value expropriation which involves the use of technology and labour process organization to increase the volume productivity of workers. This latter was the essence of Fordism. It was the basis of a general raising of all metropolitan sector incomes during the Fordist era. The owners got more absolutely but wages still rose. This applied both to direct wages and to components of the social wage in the form of welfare services in kind.

Jessop considers that the shift from Fordism has led to the development of a Schumpeterian workfare state: 'governed by the aim "to promote product, process and market innovation in open economies" (hence Schumpeterian) and "to subordinate social policy to the needs of labour market flexibility and/or the constraints of international competition" (hence workfare)' (Amin 1994: 27–8). Jessop himself remarks that:

post-Fordist growth need not generalise core workers' rising incomes to other workers and/or the economically inactive [as Fordism had]. Indeed, as post-Fordist accumulation will be more oriented to world-wide demand, global competition could further limit the scope for general prosperity and encourage market-led polarization of incomes.

(1994: 254)

Regulation theory in the hands of Jessop and many others is a distinctly sad song with little potential for stirring up social action for change. Even Lipietz, who makes a genuine effort (1994) at constructing a politics, is left with little more than palliation. In the language of autonomist Marxism, this is Marxist analysis as 'mere political economy' and 'for capitalism'. Certainly regulation theory underpins the continuing wailing of 'globalization is inevitable and capitalism has won' which is the fundamental political economy of the 'new centre politics of flexibility'.

The problem with regulation theory is that it has no prescriptions to make other than moral ones. Lee's interesting article ends by arguing for the 'exogeneity of the social reproduction of labour' (1995: 1577), that is the relative independence of the forms of the social reproduction of labour from determination by the specific forms of capitalist production and reproduction of commodities in general. This means that under capitalist social relations we can develop 'circuits of power independently of the circuit of capital' (1995: 1593), and on the basis of these establish a different moral economy in the social sphere. This is really a kind of political economy version of the line expressed by Bauman. It seems to me that Lee has slipped from exploitation to domination as the central relation of capitalism itself. This is a very general shift in social analysis, but it is perhaps surprising to find it coming from a writer with such a political economy style. Regulation theory is full of interesting ideas but at the end is a deeply gloomy and disempowering account of potential for change because of the systemic power it gives to the organizational forms of capital.

Nelson's account of the development of 'postindustrial' capitalism seems to have been written in isolation from the literature on post-Fordism. They have much in common, although Nelson's is the better because he identifies the role of managerial agency expressed in production, marketing and politics, in the reformation of the social context. His approach is explicitly Schumpeterian, in that he produces a description of a social order of which he thoroughly disapproves, but which he does not see as being in any sort of crisis at all. The implications are summarized thus:

> . . . postindustrial capitalism does not involve any shift in the funda-
> mental processes of capitalism, as reflected in the competitive search for
> economic advantage or political dominance . . . What his new and
> blended form of capitalism does, however, is produce a transformation,
> a qualitative and discontinuous shift in class structure. That is, the con-
> trast of past and present is indicated not merely by the blended form
> capitalism assumes but also by its influences on inequality. In a previous
> time, economic development fed social development by diminishing
> inequality; today economic development escalates inequality.
>
> (1995: 14)

Nelson attacks the 'Latin American' analogy exemplified by Therborn's thesis of the 'Brazilianization of advanced capitalism' (1985) which argues that advanced capitalism is likely to develop a tripartheid system of division among an excluded poor, an insecure middle mass, and an exploitative rich, but he is not attacking the account of polarized inequality it represents. Rather, he sees not a disjointed economy with a marginalized poor, but rather: 'a functionally integrated economy with a top and a bottom both part of the same fabric, the same overall master trend toward escalating rationalisation in business' (1995: 39). In this respect the evidence supports his account for the United States, and it is clear that the development of workfare as an integrative mechanism is intended to have the same effect in the UK.

This account is a complete refutation of Bauman's (1997) notion that the new poor are an economically irrelevant surplus population who are not even required as a source of consumption. Far from it – in the new sectors through which consumption is delivered by large-scale private capital – and here we must pause to note the almost complete neglect in 'consumptionist' sociology of any consideration of the actual production of that consumption, are crucial in contemporary capitalism: 'What is new (and news) about the working poor is their connection to corporate growth – to industries in the core sector rather than in the margins of a peripheral undermodernised economy' (Nelson 1995: 54).

Nelson's account of the organization of the new low-waged service sector in the US with a division between highly skilled and credentialized management and a low-wage insecure workforce, is convincing and significant. It represents a real political economy of 'poor work' and places the generation of profits from the exploitation of those who are forced to do 'poor work' (Welfare to Work after Gordon Brown) as central to the development of advanced capitalism as a whole. However, Nelson, as a Schumpeterian, is profoundly pessimistic about the development of any kind of counter to these changes. This concerns and worries him, but he concludes that what we are experiencing is 'inequality without class conflict'.

Let us turn to an account that understands the potential of class action as the determinant of which sort of future we shall actually have.

Social proletarians – underdevelopment as exclusion

A central proposition of the autonomist position is the notion of 'the social factory', the arena of the reproduction of labour power in a capitalist system as well as of the production of commodities in that system. Cleaver explained this thus:

> (Mario Tronti) focuses on how the analysis of circulation and reproduction in Volume II of *Capital* also involved the reproduction of classes. This insight meant that the equation of capital with the 'factory', characteristic of Marxist political economy, was clearly inadequate. The reproduction of the working class involves not only work in the factory

but also work in the home and in the community of homes. This realization brought into sharp focus the importance of Marx's long discussion of the reserve army in Volume I's chapters on accumulation. Accumulation means accumulation of the reserve army as well as the active army, of those who work at reproducing the class as well as those who produced other commodities (besides labour power). The 'factory' where the working class worked was the society as a whole, a social factory.

(1979: 57)

From the autonomist perspective the contradictions in a capitalist system do not stem from abstract aspects of the logic of the system as such, the classical mechanist Marxist position, but instead are represented by the working class as the active contradiction which in denying exploitation, denies the validity of capitalism as a system in general. Thus crises and transformations are points at which, to use the Gramscian terminology, the war of position characteristic of 'stable' periods within capitalism is replaced by a war of movement in which the terms of engagement between capitalism, on the one hand, and the working class, on the other, are redefined.

This account actually corresponds perfectly well with capitalism's Marxism as expressed by those who endorse globalization – capitalism has liberated itself in space through the use of global repositioning of both money and plant, and at the point of production trade union power has been so reduced that managers have had restored to them 'the right to manage', that is the right to direct the trajectory of production against any competing vision of how it should be. The new 'hybrid' forms of service – delivering capitalism (Nelson 1995) represent an innovative development based on reflexive expertise of managers, in the domination of workers, which actually seems to have led to the renewed significance of absolute emmiserating surplus value expropriation.

The significance of the idea of the 'social factory' is that conflicts between capital and labour occur not only at the point of production, but around all aspects of reproduction as well. Capitalism and capitalists seek to control not only the making of commodities in general, but the terms and conditions under which labour power is reproduced in particular. This cannot be left 'exogenous' from the relations of production in general. The political implication of this analysis is that no privilege attaches to class action at the point of production, to, in the Italian autonomist's expression, 'the politics of Fiat'. All struggles over both production and reproduction matter.

The central autonomist idea which relates specifically to social exclusion is that of underdevelopment. Let me quote again from Cleaver:

(D)evelopment and underdevelopment are understood here neither as the outcome of historical processes (as bourgeois economists recount) nor as the processes themselves (as many Marxists use the term). They are rather two different *strategies* [original emphasis] by which capital seeks to control the working class ... they are always co-existent because hierarchy is the key to capital's control and development is always accompanied by relative or absolute underdevelopment for others in order to maintain that hierarchy ... By development I mean a strategy in which working class income is raised in exchange for more work ... The alternative strategy, in which income is reduced in order to impose the availability for work, I call a strategy for underdevelopment.

(1977: 94)

Underdevelopment in this sense is a synonym for the processes that constitute social exclusion. The socially excluded are those who have been actively underdeveloped. In globalized capitalism all of us are potentially subject to the regime of a social factory in which capital is pretty much in charge.

Therborn's thesis of the 'Brazilianization of advanced capitalism' is a thesis of underdevelopment. The idea of a 'fourth world' as employed by Harrison (1982) to describe places within the localities of advanced metropolitan capitalism is likewise an underdevelopment account. Harrison uses this term to describe neighbourhoods within which social conditions are so relatively disadvantaged that despite being only three or four miles from Hampstead, one of London's most affluent areas, they have more in common in terms of conditions of life with third–world slums.

The crucial point about the thesis of underdevelopment is that it is a thesis of exploitation and a thesis of emmiseration. Sweezy, in his preface to Braverman's *Labor and Monopoly Capital*, remarked that:

Marx's General Law of Capital Accumulation, according to which the advance of capitalism is characterised by the amassing of wealth at one pole and of deprivation and misery at the other ... far from being the egregious fallacy which bourgeois social science has long held it to be, has in fact turned out to be one of the best founded of all Marx's insights into the capitalist system.

(1974: xii)

The 'social proletariat', the 'stagnant reserve army of labour', are not irrelevant to the accumulation logic of contemporary capitalism. On the contrary, their existence is absolutely crucial to it. They matter because they are necessary as a means to bringing the new social order into existence. They matter because the exploitation of them is crucial to the continued accumulation process in the new form of capitalism which is being created. No capitalism of a post-Fordist/postindustrial general form can do without them. The account of underdevelopment suggests that social exclusion is not an accidental by-product of capitalist development but absolutely intrinsic to it. Thus when Silver correctly considers that:

... there are differences of opinion within the (regulation) school as to the likely course of global capitalism since the crisis. It is not clear whether the emerging regime will pursue high quality employment in a post-Fordist regime of flexible regulation or revert to a competitive strategy of externalizing market uncertainties through low-quality, low-wage jobs subject to numerical flexibility.

(1994: 551)

the crucial point is that it will do both at the same time and in the same places.

I regard the autonomist account as profoundly optimistic and hopeful. This may seem somewhat strange since it identifies 'social exclusion', if that term is interpreted as I argue it should be as a synonym for 'under-development', as an essential characteristic of the dynamic transformation of contemporary capitalism *and* as a necessary characteristic of the form of capitalism that capitalists want. I have deliberately used the class rather than system label here. The point is that the system has potentials, attractor states to use the vocabulary of complexity, but which of them actually comes into being is a matter for class action. Capitalists are functioning as class warriors. They are certainly on the advance, but they won't necessarily win. It can be done differently. The social proletariat, the excluded, are not passive observers in all of this. They are certainly not, as Cleaver puts it: 'spectators at the global waltz of capitalism' (1977: 86). On the contrary, their own activity, their autonomous self-organization, is crucial to the struggle about which kind of social order can be brought into being.

The account being presented here is one that emphasizes people's role as producers. Those like Bauman (1998) who are putting a postmodernist gloss on Marxism have followed critical theory's obsession with people not as producers but as consumers, and have thereby interpreted the 'excluded' as largely irrelevant to processes of consumption under capitalism. The thesis being expressed here is that production remains central and that it is as producers that we can best understand the poor.

Conclusion

MOST is a UNESCO programme engaged with the Management Of Social Transformations. The second policy paper produced by MOST deals with social exclusion on a world scale. At first the participants in the symposium on which it reports seem to be agreeing with Bauman et al.:

The concept of exclusion has come into ever greater use with the deepening of the social crisis. Contrary to what occurred in the Industrial Revolution of the last century, the rich now have less and less need for the labour power of the poor. Exclusion seems to have replaced exploitation as the primary cause of poverty.

(Bessis 1995: 13)

However, they immediately qualify this position:

The two phenomena of exploitation and exclusion are not, however, totally independent of one another. Can one say, as does Philippe Van Parijs that the successes obtained by European welfare states and trade unions in the struggle against exploitation rendered exclusion the predominant form of social injustice? . . . These questions regarding the respective importance of the two phenomena are not a matter of simple quarrel among specialists. The response one gives to them generates policies that assign priority either to the struggle against exploitation or the battle against exclusion.

(Bessis 1995: 13)

My argument is that exclusion is a crucial contemporary form of exploitation, and that indeed there is nothing new about it. It has a great deal in common with the form of exploitation that characterized the beginning of the Industrial Revolution itself. Hence the renewed utility for elites of the ideology of that period, expressed with a deal less honesty and clarity than it was by Ricardo and Nassau Senior, but expressed in essentially the same terms. The battle against exclusion must be a battle against exploitation.

Of course, this argument requires not only analytical assertion but also empirical demonstration. That will be the purpose of much of the rest of this book. It is important that the statement that exclusion is exploitation is also a statement about what exclusion is not. Exclusion is not domination. It is not to do with identity considered as something either intrinsic or self-chosen. It is to do with specific economic relations. This is a highly contentious point. Let me say straight away that I actually do think that a neo-Durkheimian treatment of exclusion in relation to identity is worthwhile and that exclusion can really be thought to have a lot to do with excluded identities, but that is not what the current debate on social exclusion is essentially concerned with. In other words, 'identity exclusion', although always subject to modification by the economic relations of phases of capitalism, has an intrinsic content of its own and may exist under all forms of economic relation.

However, I can't understand domination without an economic dimension. There is a tendency in contemporary social theory to write class relations out all together, to such an extent that some postmodernists are having to rather shamefacedly say that it too is a domain of identity. In the contemporary academy the notion of any sort of struggle for socialism tends to be replaced by much more generalized notion of emancipation from domination. The contrary equation of exclusion with exploitation will inform the rest of the analysis in this book. Following those who developed the ideas of autonomist Marxism, the autonomy of struggle for what postmodernists call identity groups will always be recognized and asserted. There are no lead elements in the social proletariat in the social factory which is society as a whole. However, it is class relation that counts, however distinctive identity makes that relation, and with the distinctiveness of that relation always recognized. We have a universal project here.

3

Conceptualizing social exclusion: the language and social science of social exclusion

'Social exclusion' is a phrase with enormous power. That power derives both from the way in which it is used in the language of the linked set of political discourse, policy formation, and policy implementation, and from the salience of the term in the conceptual debates and empirical investigations of the social sciences as academic practice. The ordering in the last sentence is deliberate and indicative. 'Social exclusion' came into the social sciences from the world of politics and governance. Its origins lie in originally rather abstract and theoretical responses by Continental European social, political and religious thinkers to the social consequences of industrialization and the dominance of market forces and relationships within capitalist societies. This is in marked contrast to the essentially empirical concern with poverty as a phenomenon which marked the 'social problems' social science of late nineteenth- and early twentieth-century Britain, exemplified by the work of Booth and Rowntree. The British tradition can be understood as one in which empirical demonstration was an important factor, if never of course the only factor, in the political debates and processes that led to social reform and the creation of a welfare state. In contrast, in much of Europe political debate was primarily informed by a more abstract consideration of general principles of social organization, culminating in the sophisticated synthesis of social Christianity and reformist social democracy developed by order liberal thinkers and implemented by Christian democratic, Gaullist and social democratic/socialist governments in the European core in the post-war years. When the European Union was founded in that European core, the value system that informed its general understanding of social organization was precisely that of order liberalism. The key concept was that of the social market economy – of a society in which market capitalism remained the dominant mode of economic organization, but in which social intervention was understood as essential in order to maintain an acceptable and legitimate inclusive social order. Of course, the idea of a 'social market' is inherently contradictory. The principles of the free market will always clash with the political objectives of inclusion. The point is that the order liberals understood the role of governance as always involving the mediation of this conflict with neither of the contesting principles having priority over the other.

In the fortunate third quarter of the twentieth century when Keynesian regimes of accumulation in societies with overall deficits of capital operated to ensure social growth, full employment, and expanding welfare, this process of mediation was generally highly effective and, being effective, was not generally much observed or even understood by the population at large. The increasingly globalized last quarter of that century and the early years of this one have seen a massive reduction in the capacity of national states, and even of the European Union as a bloc, for mediating between the competing demands of capital and capitalists for the maximization of returns, and of populations for security within an inclusive social order. We are faced with the paradox that the term 'social exclusion' was not much employed in political discourse and scarcely at all in academic social science during the period when the general character of macro-economic policies and the political formation of social institutions operated to achieve a very high degree of social inclusion, especially across Europe but also in North America and Australasia. In contrast, in an era when globalized flexible capitalism is generating social exclusion on the same scale as the original unrestrained capitalism of the early phase of industrialization, 'social exclusion' and its redress has become the mantra of politics and a central principle of all public administration and related aspects of governance in postindustrial capitalist societies with the single, but enormously important, exception of the USA.

The time ordering of the usage of the phrase matters a great deal. Contemporary debates and discussions about 'social exclusion' began in the domain of political discourse and only then entered the discourses of academic social science. That time ordering provides a rationale for the structure of this chapter. We will begin by reviewing the political usage of 'social exclusion', particularly by 'New Labour' in the UK, but also with reference to its employment in other national political discourses including the very interesting Canadian case. The Canadian instance provides a marked and informative contrast to the absence of the term in US political discourse. We will also consider the 'European' usage of the term, with reference both to the politics of the European Union as a whole and to the particular politics of the European core – France and Germany. Finally, in this first half of the chapter we will examine the 'global' use of the expression in the political discourses of international organizations, and particularly the United Nations and its agencies, and in the processes of development, aid and global migration. The second half of the chapter will review how academic social science has responded to the emergence of 'social exclusion' as a key issue for contemporary governance. The focus will be on issues of definition and measurement and relate both of these to the dynamic understanding of social change which will be the central theme of Chapter 4. This review of academic discussion of social exclusion and the general character of social scientific research in this field will be generally and assertively critical. The criticisms will focus on the rather unsophisticated and simplistic definitions and measurements employed in empirical research into the topic, which will be contrasted with the possibilities offered by even the most minimal attention to the actual character of wider debate about classification and the mapping of social trajectories as this is developing in general discussion of social research methodologies as a whole. This is by no means an abstruse methodological issue. The focus on specific and isolated dimensions of exclusion translates in an audit culture of public governance at the meso level into a wholly inappropriate specification of targets which is both a misrepresentation of the real processes of social change and an important method through which effective popular politics are disabled at the local level.

Social exclusion as discourse – the language of caring neo-liberalism

The eruption of the phrase 'social exclusion' into the language – discourses – of politics and policy has prompted several commentators and critics to focus on the actual employment of the expression as a component of language itself. The most interesting such approach has been the explicitly linguistic investigation conducted by Fairclough (2000), but before reviewing that innovative contribution it is appropriate to consider Levitas's (1998) careful review of the 'discourses' of social exclusion which provides a useful bridge between traditional social policy/political studies approaches and Fairclough's employment of the traditional tools of socio-linguistics. Levitas takes up themes originally proposed by Silver (1994) but develops them in an interesting way with specific reference to the language, politics and policies of New Labour in the UK from the beginning of the 1990s.

Levitas rightly considers the use of the expression 'discourse' to be itself an issue. She notes that traditionally social science, with a nod to the ghost of Marx, has tended to employ the word 'ideology' or one of its grammatical derivatives in describing bodies of understanding and principle articulated in relation both to specific social issues and the general character of the social order. The term 'discourse' seems to have replaced ideology for two reasons. The first is that it is a better expression for describing a body of argument, debate, and multi-faceted collective contribution than the rather unitary expression 'ideology' with its implications of an agreed specific account. In other words, discourse implies continuing conversational process rather than finished product. The second is that discourse is neutral in a way in which many but not all usages of ideology are not. All usages of ideology do imply that a body of ideas represents and corresponds to a specific set of social interests. Many usages take the adjectival qualification 'false' as given – ideology is understood as systematic misrepresentation of social structure and process in the interests of a dominant and exploitative elite. Levitas does recognize that we lose something when we lose that sense of power relations by turning from ideology to discourse. Nonetheless, discourse is now the usual word.

In terms of her specific discussion, Levitas's position makes a deal of sense, provided we always retain a sense of unease about discourse's relative lack of specificity in relation to power and exploitation. Levitas identifies three discourses of social exclusion which she characterizes as:

- RED – the traditional redistributionist discourse of left-leaning social policy discussion in the UK. Essentially this approach would be typified by the relationship between academics associated with the Child Poverty Action Group (CPAG) and Labour social policy in the 1960s and 1970s when CPAG and related academics had considerable influence on Labour's social policies as a whole. Levitas equates this with traditional social democratic approaches to social policy, but it was rather the approach of the centre right of social democracy. Left social democrats always adhered to a transformational conception of the role of politics.
- MUD – the moral underclass/dependency discourse. Levitas correctly associates the contemporary form of this discourse with the influence of right-wing US commentators – and in particular Murray – on the UK debate. However, as we have seen in Chapter 1 it is simply an old song sung again – the principles which informed the New Poor Law resurrected in a less coherent and much less honest form. This was very much the position of the dominant strand of government in the Thatcher years. Note that this is not simply classical liberalism. Classical liberals would let the excluded poor suffer for the greater good but did not extend that injury to the insult of labelling the poor as morally inferior.
- SID – the social integrationist discourse. The objective here is integration into the overall social order. Levitas places particular emphasis on the role of work – of being employed – as the key mode of integration for contemporary proponents of this position. In relation to the UK and USA, this is absolutely correct but European versions of social integration have traditionally placed considerable emphasis on non-employment social contributions – and in particular the rearing of children in societies threatened by demographic competition. Levitas describes SID as part of a new Durkheimian hegemony. In terms of the general character of the position that is a good label to employ, although SID's intellectual pedigree descends far more from German order liberalism than from any direct citation of Durkheim's social politics.

For Levitas, the social politics of the UK Labour Party have moved from RED to a combination of MUD and SID. The rich have become invisible. If they are considered at all, they are simply the most affluent of the normal non-excluded middle mass. Her account of the development of the political discourses and consequent policies of New Labour is informative and interesting, particularly in relation to the role of 'think tanks' in what she appropriately describes as the privatization of policy formation. However, there is a singular absence in her account – the role of the Social Democratic Party (SDP) as a split from Labour in the early 1980s. Although a failure as a political project in and of itself, the creation of the SDP (with the improbable but real support of elements in the Communist Party of Great Britain on a direct trajectory from Stalinism to neo-liberalism with no intervening stops on the way) was probably the major factor in Labour's disastrous electoral performances of the 1980s, and individuals associated with it have been influential both in think tanks and as New Labour policy advisers across a range of policies and programmes. The role of political organizations is extremely important, and we will return to this issue in our discussion of 'ways forward'.

In brutal summary, Levitas sees the combination of MUD and SID characteristic of New Labour employment of the expression 'social exclusion' as representing a way in which New Labour can differentiate itself from uncaring and unsocial Thatcherism whilst remaining committed to the neo-liberal, anti-collectivist and globalizing agendas which Thatcherism made central to UK governance. This seems accurate, with the necessary qualification that Thatcher retained some sense of national as opposed to global interest, and New Labour has been far more enthusiastic about the neo-liberal agenda with particular reference to the privatization of core public services than Thatcher either dared or even wanted to be.

Fairclough (2000) brings the skills of a professor of language in social life to an analysis and interpretation of New Labour's New Language. He begins from the proposition that New Labour is an enthusiastic institutional proponent of neo-liberalism and globalization, and addresses the interests of the winners in the globalization process: 'despite its claim to "tackle" the social exclusion of the losers' (2000: viii). His method is to analyse the actual linguistic form of New Labour's usage of words and phrases, and he devotes particular attention to social exclusion. His central conclusion is that:

> In the language of New Labour social exclusion is an outcome rather than a process – it is a condition people are in rather than something that is done to them.
>
> (2000: 54)

This conclusion is supported by a careful review of the way in which the term is used in New Labour-speak. In contrast with earlier European Union documents in which the word exclusion was used in its verb form almost as often as adjectivally, for New Labour the adjectival form is almost entirely predominant. People and places are excluded, but there is no sense of there being any agent – other than by implication themselves, Levitas's MUD discourse – which might be responsible for that condition. As Fairclough notes, a significant absence in New Labour's world view is invisibility of multi-national corporations, and indeed of capital in any form, as economic agents. He concludes that:

> The long-standing Labour Party objective of greater equality has been displaced in 'New Labour' by the objective of greater social inclusion. The objective of equality in left politics has been based on the claim that capitalist societies by their nature create inequalities and conflicting interests. The objective of social inclusion by contrast makes no such claim – by focusing on those who are excluded from society and ways of including them, it shifts away from inequalities and conflicts of interest amongst those who are included and presupposes that there is nothing inherently wrong with contemporary society as long as it is made more inclusive through government policies.
>
> (2000: 65)

Plainly, New Labour's inability to conceive of social exclusion as a process engendered by any agents other than the excluded, commits the party to the weakest possible weak version of the concept as a basis for social politics. Mulderrig, in her interesting linguistic review of the rhetoric of UK educational policy, sums up the situation very well:

> The power of the rhetoric of globalization lies precisely in its self-representation as an abstract challenge to be met, rather than the agent-driven process of capitalist development. Policies are thus represented as simply meeting the challenges of a contemporary world rather than as contributing to capitalism's ongoing globalized construction.
>
> (2003: 127)

There is much in common between Fairclough's linguistically founded account and Steinert's (2003) sharp identification of the way in which the term 'social exclusion' in its weak form is founded on a horizontal rather than vertical model of social inequality. Steinart contrasts this with traditional vertical conceptions in which there is an ordered hierarchy in which the top level is dominant, exploitative, affluent and possessing, in contrast to the bottom which is subordinated, exploited, poor and without means. In vertical conceptions of inequality, the affluence and comfort of the elite is dependent in large part on the poverty and misery of the poor. In contrast, in a horizontal model the majority are included within a circle of acceptable conditions whereas the excluded are marginalized – marginalization being a synonym for exclusion in this formulation – and outside that circle. Again the rich and powerful are invisible through their simple subsuming into the normal and ordinary. The social politics that took inequality to be hierarchical sought to eliminate inequality. Steinart does not really recognize any social politics that depends on a horizontal conception of inequality. Instead, we have individual aspiration to stay inside the circle. Steinart, in common with Levitas and Fairclough, regards what is essentially the weak usage of 'social exclusion' as part of an ideological project of: 'making the reality of globalized neo-liberalism appear inevitable' (2003: 46). However, Steinart actually seems to reinforce the significance of individualization in social practice and the impossibility of social politics by endorsing individual autonomy against both the neo-liberal emphasis on market primacy and collectivist projects based on collective social actors. This is somewhat odd given that Steinart proposes participation as the proper antonym of exclusion, rather than inclusion. This is a radical idea since it rejects the SIP model in favour of something which begins to look like politics. Steinart's participation is individual – not collective.

Williamson (2003) addresses the issue of the language of social politics from the opposite direction in a fascinating piece of historical sociology dealing with 'The Language of Mutuality'. The editor of the collection in which this appears makes the vitally important point that: 'By shaping the way in which people conceive of their inter-dependence with others, the government has effected profound cultural changes that have far greater consequences than the actual measures it has taken' (Tönnies 2003: 7). This is important because, as she notes, we are dealing with what Du Gay and Hall have identified as a 'circuit of culture' – the continuous reflexive relationships in which: 'the actual conditions of production and consumption are shown to influence and be influenced by state regulation at the same time interacting with the realm of representation and with the identities constructed by people and/or projected into fictional worlds' (Tönnies 2003: 9). Williamson, as he has done before, fruitfully uses his own family history over five generations as a frame in considering how people articulate their ideas about their place in the social world and their capacities and objectives as actors. He takes the idea of discourse into the popular domain:

> The way people talk about welfare and the ways in which they construe their rights and their obligations to one another have altered. These changes are facets of cultural change. They involve subtle alterations over time in the ways people interact with, represent and encounter one another. Such changes lie at the base of public attitudes to the welfare state. They shape the willingness of people to pay taxes for the care of others, to act as 'good neighbours' or to vote for political parties committed to high standards of public welfare provision. Such sensibilities define social boundaries of sympathy and mutuality in our society. They are not often visible in public policy debates about the welfare state, but they are a vital backdrop to all of them.
>
> (2003: 148)

For Williamson, what has changed is the language with which people engage with mutuality in their lifeworlds (*lebenswelten*) and he does so by reflecting on the specific role of welfare reform in relation to the political actions of his parents' generation with profound implications for his generation (and mine), and contrasting it with the Blair project including the usage of 'social exclusion' as description and policy tool. His is not a romanticized reflection. He is fully aware of the contradictions of the welfare state, and not least the very different meanings of it for the respectable working class and those below them. However, things have changed.

Williamson's method works by considering changes at the three levels of macro – the level of changes in national policies and social values; the meso – the level of administrative practice – of policy formation and implementation; and the micro – the level of relationships among people in everyday life. He documents how the language of 'the project' includes the:

> . . . moral language of social inclusion. Social exclusion in this particular linguistic register is a state 'East of Eden' to be deplored for its wastefulness, inefficiency and moral unjustifiability. New Labour's strategy of modernisation is embedded in a social vision of empowered citizens acting responsibly and caringly in their own communities, working to secure the welfare of themselves and their families. . . . It is more than a moral language. It is a managerial language too.
>
> (2003: 157)

This language is not confined to the level of high politics or public rhetoric. It is, as we shall see in Chapter 7, absolutely central to what Williamson calls the 'Initiative Culture' of public governance at the meso level. However, it is in his discussion of the micro level of everyday lived experience, and in particular of the language of that level, that Williamson has the most interesting things to say. He identifies the tensions among consumerism, residual collectivism, a desire for good services to benefit oneself and significant others (a term that can have a wide range but is not general), a reluctance to allow for too much downward distribution – based in large part, I will argue, on the extraordinary simultaneous celebrity presence and political invisibility of the rich, and a prevailing insecurity, particularly among the young.

As Williamson says, we simply don't know about the: 'private conversations that take place in families working to secure their futures and trying to accommodate to the needs of their neighbours and friends' (2003: 163). But what we do know is that such conversations are the start of political projects and that in postindustrial capitalism, the collectivism that derived from industrial experience is at best what Raymond Williams described as a residual cultural force. Of course, as we shall see, the project of New Labour, which must be recognized at the prototypical project of post-democratic politics in postindustrial societies with a social democratic past, is driven in considerable part by devices for assessing public opinion and attitudes which originate in the marketing strategies of those engaged in selling products to mass and/or differentiated consumers. The point Bill Williamson is making, which resonates absolutely with Steinart's conception of the relationship between social exclusion as a concept and horizontal inequality as a model of social order, is that individualization and identity as consumers/recipients is part of the everyday language of contemporary Britain.

The UK position is an extreme one, but it can be regarded as a prototype for neo-liberal language and politics in societies with a history of collectivist politics. Rieger and Liebfried (2003) have commented on the general European politics of welfare. Again in brutal summary, they argue that the historical legacy of welfare in Europe means that electorates as consumers will defend high levels of welfare provision for relatively privileged 'insured' groups, and that this means that the problem is not the weakness of welfare but rather its strength and consequent inflexibility. There is considerable truth in this in the sense that in Continental Europe – at least in the core states – there is no major political party that has endorsed the neo-liberal position in unequivocal and forthright terms. Instead, social democratic parties alternate with republican/Christian democratic parties in power, both seeking to introduce neo-liberal policies, and both punished by defensive electorates for so doing. The significance of institutional histories is enormous, but it must be said that the general tenor of politics in societies with a history of social/Christian democracy/one nation conservatism is still towards a neo-liberal consensus among elites on the inevitability of globalization and the triumph of capital. Indeed, so pervasive is this view that even the former Italian Communist Party's largest successor, Olive Tree, endorses it. What is significant is that in Continental Europe, civil society does not.

Here the language of social exclusion – in the weak, conditional sense – is extremely important. It seems as if babble – no other word is strong enough – by political elites about exclusion can serve as a kind of linguistic trick in order to assert a continued commitment to the values of order liberalism/reformist social democracy, whilst the actual tenor of policy supports globalization and neo-liberalism. In the US, where collectivist politics have always been weak, there is no need for this elision in language and the politics of greed and benefit to the most affluent can be pursued merrily, something which derives in large part from the significant impact of political contributions from the wealthy and corporate capital on the whole US political process. In this context the Canadian instance is illuminating.

Although Canada in the post-war years often figures in typologies of welfare regimes alongside the US, the continued existence of a real social democratic party with strong trade union connections – the New Democrats (NDP) – coupled with an immediate post-war political and cultural interest in UK welfare developments, has had profound implications for social politics. The introduction of something like a UK range of welfare provision was very gradual, but with the development of federally funded, although provincially delivered, health insurance in the form of Medicaid in 1970, Canada had a developed welfare system. Likewise, there was a considerable commitment to full employment. Essentially, Canadian social politics approximated to a Keynes/Beveridge mode of social regulation.

Baker (1997) charts both the development of the Canadian welfare system and the beginning of its dismantling in the 1980s and 1990s. Although, as Baker indicates, a powerful factor in dismantling was the nature of the funding relationships between federal and provincial governments, and the change in the Canadian political landscape consequent on the collapse of the Conservative Party and the federal Liberals' dependence on Quebec as a stronghold, this was embedded in a context of economic and political change. The weakening of the NDP, and of the trade union base which underpinned it, was in large part a consequence of shift in economic relationships that began with the establishment of the Canada/US Free Trade area and has continued with NAFTA. McBride (2001) points out that this was by no means simply an externally imposed process. The activities of the Canadian Business Council on National Issues in the 1980s created a lobbying power which resonates exactly with Nelson's account of the role of corporate power in post-democratic political systems. The consequences for Canadians have been considerable. Not only have real incomes stalled for 80 per cent of the population, with any benefits of economic growth going only to the best-off 20 per cent, Canada has adopted the governance and economic forms which the non-elected institutional agents of globalization assert with extensive privatization of and reduction in social programmes.

The social democratic elements in Canadian political culture have been massively reduced. And yet there is an anomaly. The term 'social exclusion' is widely employed in Canadian policy-related debates in much the same way as in the UK. This is in marked contrast to the US, where there is virtually no policy discourse of social exclusion. The agencies asserting the significance of 'social exclusion' in Canada are remarkably similar to their European counterparts. At both the federal and provincial level, there are a number of policy documents in which the term is explicitly employed. The rhetoric of social exclusion in Canada is essentially European in tone.

In summary, we can say that the weak usage of social exclusion, Fairclough's adjectival as opposed to verb form use of the expression, the usage that sees exclusion as a condition rather than an oppressive and exploitative process, is exceptionally important in constructing the range of possible social politics in postindustrial societies in which there is a history of political parties and programmes which have in the past challenged the notion that market capitalism is the only possible form of future social arrangement. This usage is everywhere at the macro and meso levels. What will matter most is how it relates to the privatization of the micro discourses of everyday life – the domain towards which Williamson points us as the source of real popular politics.

From definition to measurement: 'social exclusion in applied social research'

There has emerged a broad consensus that, in addition to basic income and consumption measures, poverty must take into account social indicators such as education, health, access to services and infrastructure. Similarly, there is broad agreement that less tangible aspects need to be added – risk, vulnerability, livelihood insecurity, social exclusion, loss of dignity/humiliation, deprivation, lack of choice, powerlessness. And above all, there is emphasis on consulting the experts – the poor themselves – in defining their own poverty and their needs. Thus poverty is seen as a complex, multi-dimensional problem arising from a matrix of assets, markets and institutions. Thus poverty is not amenable to simplistic solutions but needs a holistic multi-dimensional approach and strategy.[18] *Definitions of poverty and their link to Health, AIDS and Population objectives.*

(European Union 1999)

In conceptual discussion at the intersection of policy discussion and the formation of the research agendas of social science, social exclusion is generally asserted to be multi-dimensional, in contrast to poverty, which is considered to be uni-dimensional and concerned with material resources taken alone. Sen's approaches (Sen 1992, 2000) have been of considerable influence, in particular his extension of poverty to include the absence of 'capabilities'. We find conceptual definitions such as that proposed by Barry:

An individual is socially excluded if (a) he or she is geographically resident in a society but (b) for reasons beyond his or her control, he or she cannot participate in the normal activities of citizens in that society, and (c) he or she would like to participate.

(2002: 14–15)

being operationalized in terms of the measurements based on multiples of attributes for individuals and households at the level of micro-data. In contrast, when examining areas, aggregate data is typically combined into a single index using derivatives of regression analysis.

The micro-level approach for households is typified by the approach of Burchardt et al. (2002) in which four indicators derived from the British Household Panel Survey are employed to separate the excluded and non-excluded:

Equivalized household income is under half mean income

The economic activity category was none of employed, self-employed, student or 'looking after family'.

The person did not vote in the general election and was not a member of any campaigning organization.

The person lacked someone who 'will offer support (listen, comfort, help in crisis, relax with, really appreciates you).'

(Burchardt et al. 2002: 34)

A polythetic classification of this kind can be represented by a cell in a four-dimensional contingency table. With a longitudinal study based on a panel, the snapshot classification can have the added dimension of time with each wave representing another variate dimension. Here we can think of a series of four-dimensional tables arranged by time points – slices through five-dimensional space – as constituting a description of the trajectory of the case through time. The cell in which the case is at any given time point indicates the particular contingent condition of the case at that time point. Note that here the classification is essentially imposed on the data by those who propose it. It does not emerge from the data and is not – an absolutely crucial failing – based on comparisons made among cases in a systematic fashion. Reality is fitted into a procrustean, and essentially arbitrary, cell structure in a contingency table. Is there another approach?

The point of this discussion is to explore the implications of thinking about social exclusion in terms of 'dimensions' and to extend that consideration from the static – that is, specification of position at one point in time – to the dynamic in which we examine the trajectories of cases over time. The language of dimensionality necessarily implies that we think about cases as having positions at points in time, in which positions are described by the values of the 'dimensions' which specify the coordinates of the cases in a multi-dimensional state space, with the trajectory of the case being the track through this state space at different time points. We can quite readily visualize this in three dimensions, but it is important to realize that we can extend to as many dimensions as we wish.

A crucial problem in the use of statistical indicators in arguments about the nature and extent of 'social exclusion' is that almost all indicators are regarded as 'variables' which have a reality separate from the cases – whether individuals or at any other level – within which they are embodied. Consequently, the designation of any case as 'socially excluded' becomes a property of scores on variables – usually taking the form of an Aristotelian polythetic classification in which the case must satisfy all of a number of conditions to be regarded as falling into the category.

The alternative begins conceptually from a radically different notion of the nature of classification. Instead of a case having to fulfil all of a set of predetermined conditions to be a member of a given category, it is compared with some 'ideal' form – some prototype. Here classification starts with a broad picture and works by comparing that which is to be classified with the sets of prototypes available. However, this account of prototypical classification (after Bowker and Starr 1999: 62) assumes that we have a set of prototypes available in advance. Now we might consider that in the social world we are all of us experts because we have to act within that world on a continuing basis. However, the social world and the sets of social prototypes it contains do not remain constant. At the social constructionist extreme, the very specification of a category in official or related processes can create a real entity in the world of social actors. That said, 'official categories', whilst always social constructs, can be made out of something which reflects the character of changing social reality itself. In other words, most of social science's operationalizations of concepts as measures correspond to something which matters for most people in their daily lives and guides the way they act in those lives. Here, the evident example is that of 'socially excluded neighbourhood'. Most people have a very good grasp of the social geography of the locality within which they live and can generate descriptions of sub-locales which are essentially isomorphic with the kinds of categorizations which can be generated from social indicator sets. This offers us a hint as to how we might proceed.

There is another very important point to be made here about the idea of a range of prototypical classifications. Sen (2000) has noted that one of the key advantages of the concept of social exclusion is that it is inherently relational. In other words, being socially excluded is a matter of relational context in time and place. Any classification must be based on comparison with others. Numerical taxonomy techniques, and in particular the range of clustering procedures (see Everitt 1991; Byrne 2003) produce classifications which are based on comparison across cases. Typologies generate category memberships which are essentially attributes when considered at the level of cases. Comparative methods generate prototypical classifications. The classifications emerge from consideration of the relative positions of cases as a whole. The excluded are not somehow separate but are to be understood in relation to the social order as a whole. This way of thinking, of course, has much in common with traditional assertions of the relative nature of poverty, but it takes the idea into a multi-dimensional domain. It is rather important to note than recent clustering procedures allow for 'fuzzy clusters' and for membership of a set to be a matter of degree rather than absolute. This has a lot of potential for future research.

We can link this discussion forward to Chapter 4 by considering the implications of dynamism – of change through time. The metaphorical apparatus used by conventional discussions of social dynamism in social policy is Newtonian. The object moving – usually individual people, but it may be households or sub-localities – moves through a multi-dimensional state space in the classic Newtonian manner of incremental change, changes of degree rather than kind. And yet the crucial issue being addressed by dynamic analyses is not change of degree but change of kind – transformation of morphology or metamorphosis. Moreover, the conventional discussions of dynamism, working with a Newtonian conception of systemic change, consider changes in the position of individual entities but not in terms of the structure of available possible positions. That is, they do not address the key issue of transformations in the character of the social structure itself. If we deal with categorical data as in our time-ordered four-dimensional tables constituted according to Burchardt et al.'s (2002) specification above, then there is an inherent categorical distinction built into the description of trajectories. Cases are categorized at any given time point by the actual contingency table cell in which they are at that time point and we can map the movement of cases among cells over time. Here the categorical character is a necessary consequence of the level of measurement of the variables in the first instance – which necessarily means that changes in position must be changes of kind.

Here is an appropriate point to introduce an extremely important concept for the exploration of social dynamics. We are scarcely ever concerned with the trajectory of any individual case – what happens to any individual enumeration district, household or individual. Rather, we want to see what happens to lots of cases – to use the language of dynamics with what happens to *ensembles* of cases. Now we might map out the positions in a twenty-dimensional state (or phase) space, the position of all the enumeration districts in a given locality – operationalized conventionally as a journey to work area – in terms of their co-ordinates in that space at the three time points for which we have census data. What will result at each time point is a set of clouds of points in the multi-dimensional phase space. We could number code each case and see its position at each time point. If there is any 'structure' to the social system which is constituted by the ensemble of cases, then we will see neither a random nor an even distribution of cases at different time points, but rather that most cases will be in some different zones with relatively high densities of cases in them. We can call these zones attractors. Essentially, these attractors represent different kinds of cases. The set of attractors is a model of the social system and the movement of cases among attractors over time is a record of dynamic change. Moreover, the very attractor sets may themselves change over time with changes in social structure.

There has been a considerable emphasis on the introduction of a dynamic frame of reference into the examination of data relevant to social exclusion (see, for example, Leisering and Walker 1998). However, dynamic treatments have usually used essentially arbitrary specifications, often including simple cut-off points on a continuous measure of relative income, to constitute an Aristotelian polythetic categorization of social exclusion. So we find considerable, and essentially trivial, discussion of whether or not individuals or households remain in the lowest quintile of incomes or more into the next lowest quintile over a set of scans in a longitudinal study – actually a monothetic classification. The real issue for social science is understanding how there is a complex and recursive relationship among all of the social levels of macro, meso and micro. And in accessing this our classification procedures must always be relational – we have to look at how positions in the social hierarchy, whether for individuals or social areas, are related to other positions. This kind of relative location specification enables us to understand something about the social causation of exclusion in the strong sense.

Whereas at the individual and household level the problem of handling the complex and interactive character of exclusion has typically been dealt with by specifying a polythetic classification, when it comes to areas the approach adopted has been to generate a linear compound of a set of descriptive continuous variable measures in the form of an index. There is an important implication of measuring deprivation in terms of a single continuous index. The *National Strategy for Neighbourhood Renewal* asserts that: 'Deprivation is a spectrum and there is no clear cut off below which a neighbourhood can be described as deprived and above which it is not'

(Social Exclusion Unit 2000: 13). At a global level the United Nations Development Programme Human Development Index is a similar, if more socially extensive and sophisticated, single indicator measure for comparative purposes. Although 'targets' in governance are generally expressed in terms of uni-dimensional measures, both continuous compound indices and single targets actually serve to conceal the reality of real social discontinuities. This is important because it turns the real politics of governance into an administrative task. The political objectives of social transformation – extraordinarily important in popular politics at sub-national levels – become diminished into mere administrative achievement of really rather meaningless targets.

Conclusion

This chapter has been about both the political and technical language of 'social exclusion'. The central point to make in this conclusion is that the political and social scientific discourses cannot be separated. They come together in the domain of governance. It cannot be emphasized forcefully enough that the ways in which things are measured in the domain of social statistics is enormously important for the actual processes through which politics are mediated into everyday life. Let us now develop the discussion of dynamic perspectives in full.

4

Dynamic society – dynamic lives

This chapter will review three strands of dynamic thinking in contemporary social science in terms of their implications for 'social exclusion'. The first deals with the nature of the categorical transformation in the nature of the capitalist social order since the mid-1960s. This is usually described as a shift from Fordism to a post-Fordism. The post-Fordist thesis has already been reviewed in Chapter 2. Here we examine its essentially dynamic character. The next strand, empirical investigation of dynamic change, has been made possible through the development of longitudinal studies charting the trajectories of individuals and households through time. Although such studies are necessarily micro in character, the accounts generated, even when these have gone no further towards the macro than mere aggregation of individual case data, have forced us to recognize the dynamism of the social. This is an illustration of the realist premise that we know the world because it makes itself known to us as we develop the tools for knowing it – here the macroscopic instrumentation of computing-based data management. The last strand is the potential contribution of the conceptual vocabulary of complexity/chaos theory for understanding not only the dynamics of the social order and of individual biographies taken separately, but also as a way of integrating macro and micro trajectories through employing the idea of reflexively interacting nested systems.

Postindustrial, postmodern, post-socialist?: advanced industrial societies in the twenty-first century

Therborn's proposition of 'the Brazilianization of Advanced Capitalism' (1985: 32–3) is a good starting point for a consideration of the transformation undergone by contemporary advanced capitalism. For Therborn, what we are seeing is a tripartheid division of the social system into one headed by a super, and super exploitative, rich with a 'squeezed middle' of relatively but not absolutely secure workers and a large and emmiserated poor. Much of this book is concerned with an elaboration and qualification of this theme, but the idea is an important one even if reduced to its most basic element. We live in a period of change, usually indicated by the use of the prefix 'post' – after. There are a variety of 'posts': postmodern, postindustrial, post-Fordist – all implying that something has changed. Let us take them in order of declining simplicity. The term 'postindustrial' is straightforward at first sight. It is used to describe a transformation of the sort of work done in advanced industrial countries. The point of the description 'advanced industrial' is that the production systems of such societies are/were (this clumsy formation is meant to indicate that things have changed but not in a uniform way) characterized by the production and primary distribution of physical commodities by wage labour working under a factory system. Most of industrial employment is in manufacturing, but there are important related areas, notably mining, construction and the 'blue-collar' services of goods transport, the production and distribution of gas, electricity and water, and the manual component of information communication by post and telecommunications. Non-industrial employment includes agricultural production, secondary distribution through retail processes, and a range of private and public service employment including financial services and welfare state activities. The Industrial Revolution was precisely the process of the generalization of the production of commodities by factory-based industrial systems.

Since the 1970s, what had been continuous growth in both the absolute numbers of industrial workers and the proportion of all adults who fit into this category has gone into sudden and steep reverse in the countries that have had the longest tradition of this process of development. Globally, of course, the processes of both absolute and relative industrialization are proceeding apace. We must remember that the decline in employment in industry is far greater than the decline in the productive output of industry. In most countries decline in employment has been associated with actual large-scale growth in industrial output.

Deindustrialization has multiple causes. At the systemic level, there has been a massive growth in labour productivity based on both technological innovation and the development of new production management techniques. On a global scale, there is a 'new international division of labour', with the creation of industrial systems in previously peasant societies, much of which has been fuelled by the export of capital by transnationals from the original core zones of industrial capitalism. The collapse of the 'second' world of Soviet-style systems has opened up both the possibilities for such investment (especially in China) and brought into competition cheap producers of basic industrial staples, although it has also caused deindustrialization with the collapse of the Eastern European military–industrial complex.

In the UK, there has been a specific national factor in that public policy through the maintenance of a high exchange rate in the early 1980s and through a variety of meso-economic planning and development mechanisms, has privileged finance capital and the 'city' over manufacturing capital. In effect the revenues of North Sea Oil have contributed to the destruction of the UK's manufacturing system – the economic consequences of Mrs Thatcher and the policies of her chancellors which were both economic and concerned with the relative advantage of one section of capital, and explicitly political and intended to destroy the capacity of the organized trade union movement in its citadels of power.

The term 'post-Fordist' originates with the French regulation theory school (see Amin 1995) reviewed in Chapter 2. Whereas deindustrialization leading to a 'postindustrial' social order is an evident process, with the idea of 'postindustrial' representing a transformation of quantity into quality, the change from Fordist to post-Fordist is inherently qualitative. The term Fordist describes a mode of production organized around techniques of mass production and associated mass consumption. The macro-economic management of this system is geared towards maintaining employment in order to maximize the potential of wage-based demand as a basis for consumption. It is Keynesian both at the national level and in relation to the management of international economic relations through the institutions created for that purpose by Keynes himself. An important component of this process of regulation is the provision of universalist social welfare and particularly of insurance-based wage substitution benefits – the Beveridge element in the whole scheme. Post-Fordist production is a product of technological innovations and new management practices which permit 'flexible specialization' through batch production as opposed to the massive homogeneous runs of the Fordist era. Such flexible specialization requires a flexible labour market and is associated with the differentiation of labour and of its rewards.

Two important characteristics of the Fordist/Keynesian social order were the shape of its income distribution and the pattern of available social mobility. Lipietz described the change from the 'Montgolfier' society in which most people and households were in the middle – the shape of a hot-air balloon – to an hourglass society with what US commentators call 'the squeezed middle'. He remarked that in 'the homelands of flexibilization' (the US and UK) increasing inequality is the product of three broad tendencies: a shift in factor share of incomes from wages to property; a cut in cash welfare transfers to households; and increasing disparities in earned incomes (1998: 180). The other structural change that matters in this transition, indeed is fundamental to any dynamic discussion at the level of individuals and households, is the change in the possibility of social mobility. Leisering and Walker note that:

> Individual mobility is crucial to modernity. It is a functional prerequisite of change in social structures . . . Mobility is also a powerful means by which people drive forward their ambitions in life.

Irrespective of the actual mobility that occurs, the idea of mobility is fundamental to the legitimization of Western Societies. The promise of mobility allows 'open societies' to maintain a system of firmly established structural inequalities. The optimism about macro-dynamics, the belief in societal progress, translates at the micro-level into the belief in individual progress.

(1998: 4–5)

There is important evidence that the shift from industrial to postindustrial social structures involves a closure of mobility opportunities. Erikson and Goldthorpe (1992) noted that the history of mobility patterns may well involve changes of kind, the crossing of thresholds in which periods with relatively high levels of mobility are succeeded by periods in which mobility is much more constrained. This idea of 'developmental threshold' is very similar to the idea of phase shift and we will return to it in the discussion of complex dynamics which will conclude this chapter. Certainly, there is evidence that mobility is closing down in postindustrial societies. Aldridge (2001) reviewed the UK and related literature and debate in a discussion paper for the Cabinet Office's 'Performance and Innovation Unit'. This discussion reflects the contradictory position of UK government, a contradiction explicitly identified by Aldridge, between the promotion of a meritocracy based on equal opportunity and simultaneous concern that society should be inclusive in its general character. Of course, the worst possible scenario from the point of view of parties like New Labour, and indeed for any government concerned with social cohesion as a basis for social order, is a society which is simultaneously exclusive and closed, with upward social mobility not a realistic prospect for the great majority of the poor and the middle mass. Such closure is central to any consideration of social exclusion and it is particularly significant that spatial location may be a determinant factor in it.

Whereas deindustrialization is a descriptive term and post-Fordism is an idea from political economy, the notion of postmodernity is rooted in considerations of cultural form and reflection on the nature of ideas themselves. Here the 'after' is after modernity, after an era characterized by the general belief in the use of reason as the foundation of social progress. Therborn defined modernity: 'as an epoch *tuned to the future* [original emphasis], conceived as likely to be different from and positively better than the present and the past' (1995: 4). Postmodernism has no such optimism, seeks to deprivilege 'grand narratives' and emphasize differentiation in knowledge and in social practices. It is virtually universal in the academy, has some significance in cultural debates, and plays only the role of background (but not wholly insignificant) noise in social politics where the important debates are between liberal and collectivist interpretations of political economy.

The reality of deindustrialization is accepted by all. The idea of a transition from a Fordist to post-Fordist era is quite broadly considered appropriate. The idea that our era is postmodern is seriously disputed by those who, like King (1996), argue that we live in a period of late modernity which is certainly different from that which existed through the mid-period of the twentieth century but which remains profoundly affected by its basis in capitalism and by the role of arguments about the use of the results of 'reason' in the conduct of politics. Sayer (1995) notes pertinently that whilst the academy debates postmodernity, that oldest of modern conceptual sets, liberal political economy, is more important as a basis for political ideology and process than it has been for more than a century. It may be that the modernist idea of Soviet-style progress is fragmented and dissolved, but capitalism's version of modernist theory is alive and well, and kicking very hard.

Nelson (1995) employed the term 'postindustrial' in a more analytic way than the simple descriptive usage which it has had in preceding discussion. His arguments are important and convincing:

> My argument looks not to any crisis in capitalism but to a new vigor [sic] and resources – to the Schumpeterian concept of creative energy – that *activates* [original emphasis] the corporate quest for profits. . . . The centrepiece of my position is that in recent years corporations have acquired new resources, qualitatively different from those available in the past. These resources are organisational and knowledge based and are tantamount to a revolution in the inventory of tactics and strategies available to corporations . . . corporations have used these strategies to intensify competition, affect greater political control, and widen the gap between rich and poor in America today.
>
> (1995: 20)

The ideas which surround the description of 'postindustrial' and the analytical frame represented by 'post-Fordist' are complementary. However, even taken together, the descriptive accounts at best begin to deal with the implications of change for the lives of people and for the ways in which they act, both individually and collectively. 'Postmodernity' as a project is one of disaggregation and separation, and whatever the limitations of the idea set, its very existence is indicative of a change in relation to social action. Nelson's careful analytical account of 'postindustrial capitalism' brings explicit agency back in, agency against equality. There are two key determinist statements in the Marxist canon. One is that 'base determines superstructure'. Regulation theory is essentially a sophisticated gloss on that proposition. The other is that 'social being determines consciousness'. It is worth thinking about that as a way of understanding the relationship between social change and social exclusion because consciousness is the basis of action. The exploitative rich certainly act in their own interests. The interesting question is whether the rest of us will act in ours.

There seem to be two models for advanced industrial societies. One is represented by the USA, where a holding constant of the absolute value of wages has led to a relative emmiseration of blue-collar and routine white-collar employees associated with the development of a highly profitable new sphere of low-waged services, but a maintenance of overall employment levels. The fundamental basis of this is low wages. Low wages can only be maintained in a system with relatively low levels of unemployment if legislation is used to destroy the organizational capacity of workers. In the US, this is a function of civil suit. In the UK, it has involved both the criminalizing of picketing and the outlawing of sympathetic action. Union-busting is very important. The other type of system was the developed European norm of France and Germany, where institutional arrangements tended to preserve relativities in real wages and there are high levels of wage substitution benefits, but there is also a high level of unemployment, particularly among labour market entrants. This style is now under considerable ideological and political attack, with governments of all political complexions, including the German Social Democrats, attempting to reduce the value of wage substitution benefits in the interests of promoting a flexible labour market and higher levels of employment. In Poland, structural readjustment has been uneven and localized in its effects, with very high levels of unemployment among displaced peasant workers and women in particular places and sectors, but increasingly even highly unionized workers, for example in coal mining, are losing security. In the UK, high levels of employment have been achieved, although non-employment levels reflect the continuing transfer of many older men to the status of long-term sick rather than economically active.

The UK Liberal Democrat-initiated Commission on Wealth Creation and Social Cohesion described the situation thus:

> One side-effect of the new economic era is that a sizeable minority see their incomes rise and also enjoy a fair amount of security, but the majority have to struggle to keep incomes stable, and many experience declining incomes along with greater insecurity. More importantly, people no longer live in the same universe of opportunity; there are winners and losers, and the gains of the winners do not trickle down to the losers. Widening income differentials result in a serious disjunction in the commitment of different groups to the values and institutions of society.
>
> (Dahrendorf 1995: 15)

The report of this commission is succinct and clear, in marked contrast to the report of the Labour-initiated Commission on Social Justice (1994), and its identification of the social consequences of economic change is correct in terms of broad tendencies. However, as always, the devil is in the details, and it is in the details that the Liberal Democrat initiative got it wrong, in a most revealing and significant way by reasserting (1995: 15) the existence of a permanent underclass. The permanent underclass in postindustrial flexible capitalism is generally speaking a myth.

What matters is the combination of low wages, insecure employment, and dependence on means-tested benefit supplements to low incomes. Poor work is the big story in any flexible labour market. Social exclusion is an active process. Insecurity and low wages are the basis for a reconstruction of the relationship between labour and capital on a global scale. Things have changed (been changed by agents) for the worse, but they can be changed again for the better.

This is an appropriate point to identify a crucial issue in relation to social exclusion which is illustrated by a contradiction in the Liberal Democrat's examination of the general issue. They identify two very different minorities in their discussion. The first is a minority who have gained by social change, a minority located at the top of society and separated from the rest of us by increasing and heritable relative advantage. There is considerable evidence to support the existence of a separation of the ever more affluent few from the remaining static or actually becoming poorer many. In particular, and of considerable significance in terms of the support base for 'New Labour' in the UK, we should note the emergence of what Aldridge has identified as: 'a new, highly prosperous, largely private sector employed "superclass" within the middle class which stands in increasing contrast with the traditional middle class' (2001). The increasing divergence in salaries between managers and professionals in the public services means that this superclass is no longer so particularly private sector in character. Indeed, there is increasing and politically significant movement between private and public sector managerial positions.

However, social exclusion as generally discussed is not about the emmiseration of the many, of the majority. It is about a 'sloughed off' minority at the bottom of society separated by material poverty and increasingly characterized by negative cultural diversion. These people are not just poorer. They are different. There is much less evidence for a clear division downwards in terms of permanent condition. On the contrary, as we might expect if the poorest are a functional reserve army for postindustrial capitalism, there is considerable dynamism, with people moving into and out of material destitution and in and out of the segregated socio-spatial zones of exclusion.

If we consider exclusion to be about material circumstances, then the degree of dynamic change in those circumstances over time makes the notion of a permanently segregated underclass absurd. The spatial evidence seems to tell a somewhat different story. We will find evidence of the polarization of urban space in postindustrial capitalism, but of a polarization in which the very poor and the not quite so poor live in the same areas with considerable mobility within those areas between those statuses in contrast with the 'respectable' spaces which continue to display the social relations and forms of the Fordist era. There is some mobility between those two sorts of areas over time for individuals and households, and indeed neighbourhoods themselves can change their status through the opposing processes of residualization and gentrification. Material and spatial exclusion is very real, but for most of the excluded these are statuses that can be escaped from, just as for many of the non-excluded the combination of material and spatial exclusion is an ever-present threat.

Exclusion from power is a very different matter. Power is the most nebulous and most important of all social concepts. Measuring it is almost impossible. We tend to use proxies in terms of the consequences of the possession of power, measured usually by measures of material circumstances. In postindustrial capitalism the actual ability of the mass to influence political process is much less than it was under industrial capitalism. We really can talk about the exclusion of the many to the advantage of the few. The politics of urban development and urban policy provide a very clear illustration of this process. More directly the constraints imposed on the capacity of unions to act at the point of production by the legislative underpinnings of flexible capitalism are crucial to the disempowering of ordinary people.

Let me make absolutely explicit something that is inherent in the account of the development of postindustrial capitalism presented thus far. My argument is that advanced industrial societies are converging on a norm of social politics organized around a flexible labour market and structural social exclusion. One interpretation of the general post-Fordist account is that such a convergence is an inevitable consequence of the logic of contemporary capitalist accumulation, that base is determining superstructure. I think that kind of mechanistic Marxism for capitalism's interests, what Cleaver (1979) calls 'mere political economy', is wrong and that the convergence is very much driven by the ideology of liberal capitalism, by the manipulation of political processes, and by the subordination of policies to business interests. Nonetheless, convergence is happening. Gorzelak puts this well for the Polish case:

> It has been generally assumed that the changes occurring in the post-socialist countries result almost entirely from a shift from the centrally planned economic system supported by a mono-party regime to a market economy introduced in a democratic political system. This approach stresses the 'ideological' or systemic factors in post-socialist transformation. . . . If this approach is correct, the post-socialist transformation should be regarded as a unique phenomenon, specific only to the transformation from a communist (or so called 'real socialism') system to a market economy. . . . However, even simple reflection reveals that these assumptions do not hold true. In fact, the restructuring processes that dominate in the post-socialist transformation very strongly resemble the phenomena which shaped economic life in more advanced Western countries since the 1960s and specially during the 1970s. . . . With a great deal of simplification one may say that the post-socialist transformation is a shift from Fordist to post-Fordist type of organisation of economic, social and political life. This shift was not possible in a closed system, separated by economic and political barriers from global markets and therefore not exposed to economic and political international competition. Once these barriers were removed, the old patterns of economic production could not longer be maintained and

'imported' patterns of new ways of socio-economic and political organisation begun [*sic*] to shape the new reality.

(1996: 32–3)

It is true of course that we can easily identify the agencies that are forcing this sort of transition in Poland. They are the employers of what Poles call the Marriottsky, since these people jet into Warsaw, stay at the Marriott Hotel, and instruct the Poles as to how to reconstruct their economy and their society. However, we have to accept that this process is having an impact everywhere. There has been a massive industry of examination of different welfare regimes that has developed following Esping-Andersen's interesting book (1992) on that topic. It is ironic that this interest has become an academic growth industry at just the time when global pressures, which are primarily ideological, although they are represented as inevitable tendencies in the only possible reality, are leading to a massive reordering of all welfare regimes which do not prioritize labour flexibility. As we shall see, a consideration of complex social dynamics shows us that another social order is possible, but the flexible and excluding version is the one that is being made for all of us if things go on as they are.

The one thing that all commentators agree on, whatever their views on the desirability and/or inevitability of the kind of new social order that has come into being, is that there has been a qualitative change. Things are not the same as before – in the language of complexity/chaos, we have experienced a phase shift at the level of social order. Let us now turn to a research programme that is exploring the implications of that shift for individual lives.

The complex dynamics of social exclusion

Past theories, essentially static in form, are challenged by new ways of thinking.

(Leisering and Walker 1998a: xiv)

Leisering and Walker's important collection *The Dynamics of Modern Society* (1998a) is representative of a very rapidly developing programme of dynamic analysis which derives from the availability of longitudinally ordered data sets in which the trajectories of individuals and households can be followed through time by repeated remeasurement of the character of those individuals and households at regular intervals. This is not a new programme. The oldest still continuing UK longitudinal study is that initiated by Douglas in 1946 which is still pursuing the life trajectories of those born in one week of March of that year. However, the more recent studies, typified by the British Household Panel Survey, return to remeasure at much more regular intervals and tend to be household-focused rather than dealing with individuals.

The difference between the earlier cohort studies and the new longitudinal studies is not the product of arbitrary whim. Although Douglas's study was originally concerned with paediatric health, it rapidly became focused on educational attainment and social mobility. The study was embedded within a conception of life courses that reflected the social realities of the Fordist era, in which people were not absolutely fixed or ascribed by their circumstances of birth, despite the continuing significance of those circumstances. Instead, there was a considerable degree of upward social mobility, often but not invariably mediated through educational attainment, which reflected the changing occupational structure of developing Fordism, with its growth in more desirable white-collar employment locales. The tradition of mobility studies, typified in the UK by the Nuffield programme, was one that looked at change but conceptualized such changes as essentially single. People started off in one position and either stayed there or moved, but there was really only one key transition. Bauman (1998) notes that such mobility studies involved a theory of stratification rather than a theory of classes in which movement was by individuals in relation to the system rather than by collectivities through transformation of the system.

Although the notion of individual, once and for all mobility did fit the general reality of the Fordist era, it was a simplification even then. Now it is wholly inappropriate. Many people do have relatively stable life trajectories, but the proportion of those who do not, whose lives involve repeated personal phase shifts to radically different circumstances, is very much greater. The great value of the dynamic approach to longitudinal studies is that it enables us to chart the character of such shifts for very large ensembles of individual trajectories.

Leisering and Walker locate this new tradition precisely in relation to the phase shift in the whole social order described in the previous section of this chapter. They present an essentially Schumpeterian view of the inherent character of modernity:

> . . . the dynamism of modern society resides in novel institutions that display an intrinsic propensity to continued and unlimited change. It is this propensity, and not change as such, that we refer to as dynamism.
>
> (1998b: 4)

It is important to make absolutely explicit something that these authors do note in later discussion. One reading of their account of dynamism would present us with an understanding of change as a continuing and ongoing process, a process which could be described by ratio scale measurement of conditions. This is essentially the approach of time-ordered studies in economics. Leisering and Walker do recognize that social dynamism does not take this form, but that it instead involves abrupt qualitative changes. Their important discussion of changes of regimes of inequality (1998: 6) is exactly an account of qualitative change, of phase shift. This point is crucially important.

The weakness of the dynamic tradition as it has so far developed derives from the micro character of the data sets on which it is founded. For example, the three substantive empirical sections in the Leisering and Walker collection contain a series of interesting and important chapters describing the dynamics of people within societies, but not the dynamics of society understood as an emergent reality. The development of dynamic perspectives, using the enormous macroscopic range provided by longitudinal data sets, enables us to chart life courses, but we have to set those life courses within the complex and non-linear dynamics of changes in the whole social order and changes in socio-spatial systems which are contained within that social order.

More recent studies, notably the European comparative investigation surveying Austria, Greece, Germany, Portugal and the UK, reported in Aspari and Miller (2003), have added to our empirical account of at least the short-term income and asset possession of European households but have not got much beyond this. Micro-studies based on panel data sets, such as the European Community Household Panel, seem to find it relatively easy to deal with income levels and possession of material assets but much harder to access the other socially relational and political aspects of social exclusion. Indeed, the approach of Apospori and Miller's contributors, whilst certainly dynamic in that household conditions were examined through time across a range of time points, seems to be based on a dynamized version of a fairly traditional operationalization of poverty.

These accounts are crucial to any understanding of the character of social exclusion in postindustrial society, precisely because such exclusion must have a time component. At its simplest, this time component is duration. Short spells of poor condition can be handled quite well if these are set within a life trajectory which includes spells of better conditions. If we look at income alone, we might find some people who, measured at a point in time, had no income at all at that point, but who had quite high incomes and good standards of living if we used a different accounting period. This could be true of, for example, very highly paid freelance media personnel, who might have a flow of income very different from that of a salaried person.

We also have to bear in mind that there is a distinction between operationalizations of poverty, which are almost invariably based on a poverty line so that those below this line are in poverty and those above it are not, and a dynamic understanding of social exclusion. Middleton et al. (2003) argue that movement out of exclusion is not simply a matter of crossing a line, but of moving significantly upwards in the income distribution – in their case operationalized by moving at least five percentage points in the income distribution.

The issue is that there are types of trajectory that might describe categorized sets of experience. Within the set of such sets we might find one or more that we might decide describe the dynamic experience of social exclusion. The obvious one is long-term unemployment with dependency on low-level benefits. However, we might well find, and indeed will find, that a set of individual/household trajectories that involve low-paid work as the normal condition, with considerable experience of unemployment punctuating such low-paid work, is much more significant and represents the most usual kind of excluded life in our sort of society.

Is there a way to integrate the micro-level accounts of individual life trajectories with the macro-level of categorical or phase shift transformations? I will argue that there is, and that it is provided by the perspectives of complexity/chaos theory to which we will now turn.

Understanding the complexity of dynamics

The best way to present a short account of the 'chaos/complexity' perspective (see Byrne 1998 for a fully developed account) is by picking up the implications of the idea of multi-dimensionality and considering what happens when one of the multiplicity of dimensions is time. Poverty is a uni-dimensional concept. It is measured traditionally by comparing material resources possessed by a household – the unit of ultimate consumption which may contain only one individual – with some either absolute or relative standard. The measurement takes the form of a financial summary expressed in terms of income over a specific time period. Much of the evidence about poverty comes from snapshots, from studies conducted at one point in time. Even at the beginning of poverty studies there was an alternative understanding of dynamism. Rowntree identified his cycle of poverty in the early 1900s by looking at how a working-class family's ratio of resources to needs was likely to move them below and above a poverty line at different demographic stages during the family's life. We can think of the time line of individuals and households as being the life course. In a multi-dimensional treatment, we don't consider and measure just one attribute over time as poverty studies measure income. We measure whatever we think is significant. These measurements are the co-ordinates on a set of dimensions which constitute a multi-dimensional state space. If we measure a household's income, size, housing tenure, employment relation (say through an operationalization of Pahl's 1985 conception of work rich/work poor: see Byrne 1995), educational connection, cultural level, and health state, then we have seven dimensions on which we have scores. We can use numerical taxonomy procedures to generate a typology based on these measures, and we can allocate cases to the categories which constitute this typology. If we measure the variables at different points in time then we can plot the path, the trajectory, of the household as it changes over time. We can see both if there are changes in the nature of the social typologies and explore the movements of individual cases among the types in the typologies. The state space is the space through which we plot these changes over time, not just for one case but for a multiplicity of cases, for what in chaos/complexity theory is usually called an ensemble.

In real systems, significant changes are not gradual and incremental but sudden and discontinuous. They are non-linear. For example, the loss of employment produces a non-linear change in economic circumstances, whereas a wage rise produces only a linear change. It is the non-linear, qualitative changes that matter to us. Most of the empirical chapters in Leisering and Walker's edited text are about non-linear changes in the life courses of individuals and households. We must also accept the reality of changes in the actual social categories which constitute the social domain within which individual and household life courses are conducted.

The idea that duration of condition is crucial to understanding the social implications of any set of circumstances is plainly sensible. It has been implicit in benefit systems for many years and was taken up as an explicit theme in the US by David Ellwood. The theme is developed in many of the pieces in Room's edited collection dealing with 'the measurement and analysis of social exclusion' (1995). However, this dynamic literature has tended to see discontinuous change, the phase shifts, as nothing more than the boundaries of duration. The full implication of such non-linear boundaries has not been appreciated.

To understand why that should be so, we need to examine not individual cases but many cases, to look at the ensemble of trajectories. If we do, we find that as we map trajectories through time we do not find either an even or a random patterning of trajectories throughout the condition space. Instead, we will find certain areas of the condition space being occupied with sets of trajectories which, whilst they are not the same cycle on cycle, nonetheless stay within particular boundaries. The term used for such bounded domains is attractor. For a single trajectory the attractor is the limited part of the phase space within which it is contained. It is useful to think about the situation for ensembles of trajectories which have similar attractor paths. In other words, if we map all the trajectories in the condition space we find subsets of the whole ensemble in particular and different parts of the condition space. The use of numerical taxonomy procedures is a convenient way of identifying exactly these ensembles of attractors.

We are also likely to find instances where a case moves from one bounded set in the condition space to another, with that movement being determined by a change in one or more key control parameters which set its location in the condition space. For example, a benefit-dependent female single parent establishes a new cohabiting relationship with an employed man with reasonable earnings, finds it worthwhile to take a part-time job herself, on the basis of the new combined household income, moves from a poorly regarded social housing area to medium-priced owner-occupied housing, and experiences all the consequences – including perhaps more successful schools for her children, which are associated with that spatial change. This is a discontinuous change of kind.

People and households do not have life courses that are somehow separable from the society of which they are a part. People lead their own lives, but not in circumstances over which they have complete control. The kind of changes that are summarily described in this book as constituting the phase shift from industrial to postindustrial capitalism mean that the sorts of lives available to be led have changed. Of crucial significance here is the elimination of a middle-income lifestyle based on relatively well-paid male manual work supplemented by not badly paid female industrial or other work. There is a dynamic and non-linear trajectory for the social order as a whole. The system of society which has undergone non-linear change surrounds and contains the systems of individual life courses.

This is not to say that individual life courses are not important and do not represent a proper object of social scientific inquiry. They do, and the strength of micro-studies based on panel data is that they enable us to produce descriptions of individual and household trajectories which we can embed in accounts of broader social changes. However, the attention to causal processes in social policy studies tends to remain fixed on the individual rather than the social level. For example, the accounts of the large European comparative project presented in Barnes et al. (2002) and Apospori and Miller (2003) focus on key individual transition points in relation to the experience of young adults, lone parents, people experiencing sickness and disability, and people moving into retirement. It is absolutely appropriate to consider the contingent factors which produce outcomes in relation to individual cases, but attention to the individual level alone will always result in understanding social exclusion in weak terms. This has very important implications for policy and politics because accounts established solely at the level of the individual will result in policy proposals which tackle the situation of individuals without reference to the overall character of the social order as a whole. They stand in a long tradition of UK poverty studies which may well argue for redistribution to those who are poor and/or excluded, but do not address the way in which a social structure creates an excluding attractor set.

There are other levels of dynamic change besides that of individual/household trajectory. Spaces have dynamic trajectories. The globalization thesis is an account of the dynamic trajectory of the whole social world in space. There is an extensive spatial literature about the dynamic changes for regions and localities within that global space. Here the spatial level which will be considered most carefully is that of neighbourhoods within city regions considered as containing systems. In other words, we have a multiple set of nested systems. This idea is due to Harvey and Reed (1994). They conceptualize a series of systems in which, to use our example, the global social order contains regions, which in turn contain localities, which in turn contain neighbourhoods, which in turn contain households, which in turn contain individuals. It is very important to note that in this approach there is no hierarchy of influence. Causal processes can run in both directions. Nonetheless, it seems obvious that grand global changes and changes in the socio-spatial organization of the regions and cities and neighbourhoods within which people live have enormous influence on the possibilities available to them for developing a life course.

The idea of 'chaotic/complex' change, as opposed to the idea of catastrophic non-linear change in which there is a qualitative transformation but only one new sort of trajectory is possible, contains within it the idea of not one sort of possible future but of different sorts of possible futures – the plural is crucial. Complex systems are relatively robust and we have to distinguish them from chaotic systems in which very small differences in initial conditions can generate enormous differences in system trajectory through time. However, complex systems can and do change form in a qualitative fashion – a process for which the term metamorphosis stands as a good metaphor. They remain intact but change radically in character. Moreover, such transformational change can be the product of any combination of external impacts and internal interactions. In their seminal book on these topics, Prigogine and Stengers (1985) noted that in social systems where there was the possibility of reflexive social agency, that agency might be the engenderer of change. At the level of the individual/household, action can change life course. At the level of the whole social order, collective intervention can change the social system. In other words, the kind of miserable, divided, excluding postindustrial system that seems to be becoming generalized on a world scale is not the only form of social order available to us. Different actions might produce different outcomes. At last we have a glimpse of hope!

The concept of 'control parameters' is very important here. In essence, the term describes the way in which non-linear qualitative changes in the character of systems which are described in a multi-variate way are often not the product of changes in the values of all the parameters describing that system. System transformation may result from changes in a very limited number of those parameters, often only one of them. For single parents, the establishment of a two-parent household can be such a crucial change. This applies equally to whole social systems. Of particular significance for us will be the idea that the degree of inequality in a social system is a control parameter for its form. Highly unequal social orders generate the attractor state of social exclusion. More equal social orders do not have this attractor state.

There are three key points which emerge from the preceding discussion. The first is that 'social exclusion' is an emergent phenomenon that is constituted by the interaction among the life courses of the ensemble of individuals and households who for varying periods of time occupy a separated part of the condition space describing possible life courses, which in part is defined by categorically worse conditions as measured on a multi-dimensional basis. In other words, 'social exclusion' is not a label to be applied to particular 'socially excluded' individuals and/or households. We must get beyond nominalism.

The second is that the existence of this separate domain is a product of changes in the character of the social order as a whole. Contemporary social exclusion is a product of the phase shift in the character of contemporary capitalism. It is an inherent property of polarized postindustrial capitalism. In this context, the significance of age cohort is of particular importance. Those who established much of the basis of their life courses under a previous and more equal social order will be much less affected than those whose life courses are established under the new and less equal social order. The young cannot carry forward the advantages of Fordism, other than what they may inherit as assets from their parents, although in relation to social mobility through education and access to housing in non-excluded neighbourhoods such inheritance may be of great significance.

Finally, to express in a very preliminary way something that will be crucial for the conclusion to this book, we must carefully distinguish between actions that change the trajectories of individuals and/or households in terms of shifting them across attractors within a given condition space, and actions that change the character of the condition space and the attractor sets available within it. We will find policies which move people from excluded to non-excluded, whilst leaving exclusion as a domain. The real issue is how to get rid of the domain, how to create a social order that excludes exclusion.

We now turn to a discussion of the actual empirical experience of the dynamics of social exclusion in terms of income distribution, the organization of socio-spatial urban systems, and the experiences of exclusion in relation to education, culture and health.

PART TWO

5

The dynamics of income inequality

Income inequality matters for social exclusion because income is both the basis of social participation through consumption and a reflection of the power of people in their economic roles. During the Keynesian era, income inequalities in advanced capitalism became smaller (Goodman et al. 1997). The poorest people and households became better off relative to the rest of us. Likewise, the very affluent became less so in relational terms. Now things are different. In postindustrial capitalism economic restructuring and changes in policy have interacted to produce more unequal and excluding societies.

In Chapter 4 we identified two aspects of the dynamics of income inequality. The first was the macro level of the distribution of income within societies. The second was the micro level of the trajectories of individual (and/or household) incomes over time. It order to examine these linked processes, we need panel data describing the forward trajectories of individuals and households. This chapter will deal with each of these levels in turn and go on to review how fiscal, benefit and industrial relations policies have played a proactive role in creating both interlinked domains of contemporary social life.

From relative equality to inequality: the phase shift in income distributions

Three points have to be made before we examine changes in income distributions. First, we have to specify what we mean by a change. Studies of income distribution usually draw on the disciplinary frame of reference of economics which almost always works with continuous data supposedly measured at a level which corresponds to the full properties of general

arithmetic. Changes are understood as incremental and smooth. The chaos/
complexity approach suggests that what we look for when we examine any
change over time is not incremental change but rather sudden and abrupt
discontinuities, non-linearities, qualitative changes. Marx described changes
as a transformation of quantity into quality. The question is, have income
distributions changed qualitatively and thereby produced a different kind of
social order?

Second, we have to note the limitations of the data used in describing
income distributions. Typically, these are derived from income tax systems.
Thus they do not cover that part of income that avoids or evades taxes. At
the top end of the income distribution, this matters because there is an
entire industry of tax advisers whose whole purpose is to use legal tax
avoidance procedures to reduce the tax liability of their clients through
removing substantial income from the tax system. Illegal tax evasion
matters for income across the range, but is most significant at either end
for illegal workers on very poor pay in the shadow economy and for some
of the most affluent on high incomes, including incomes from crime. In
addition, income tax derived data can tell us about income before income
tax and after it but does not inform us about the effects of payroll taxes
unless collected along with income tax, indirect taxes, many income transfers from welfare systems, or the effects of non-cash direct incomes from
welfare systems and in particular education and health systems. We do have
data on these effects for the UK, but we cannot necessarily generalize from
them.

The third aspect is the relationship between the forms of income distribution in societies and the class structures of those societies. Income is
never irrelevant to any theoretical scheme of class, but it is only central to
Weberian approaches in which differentiated income is the basis of differentiated consumption. This book is informed by a generally Marxist
perspective, but I agree absolutely with Westergaard when, having defined
class very broadly as 'a set of social divisions that arise from a society's
economic organisation' (1995: 1), he remarks:

> . . . it is my aim precisely to clear away any assumption that close
> attention to distributive benefit and disadvantage is inherently out of
> tune with Marxism; and to uphold instead the contention . . . that the
> consequences of unequal economic distribution by way of unequal
> personal experiences and prospects in life must be central to class
> analysis of whatever theoretical persuasion.
>
> (1995: 4)

As Westergaard notes, empirical studies of inequality pay attention to
income because it is easily operationalized and income distribution data
are available. In contrast, power is difficult to operationalize and no data
are available. This also explains why contemporary discussions of social
inequality place so much emphasis on consumption, again a measurable
thing both in quantitative and qualitative terms, and thereby turn to

consumption as the domain of agency rather than the less accessible processes by which social orders are created.

There is a deal more to class than just income, but it will do as a dimension around which to explore inequalities. Interestingly, it is easier to explore income inequalities by dimensions of inequality – race/ethnicity, gender and age – than it is by class, precisely because they are operationalized independently of income. It is worth noting that race/ethnicity and gender are principles around which legislative programmes, derived from the liberal conception of possessive individualism, have operated for more than twenty years in both the USA and the UK. These programmes have reduced income inequalities by the categories of gender and race/ethnicity, whilst income inequalities within the categories have substantially increased.

Age is very interesting as a collective descriptor. Here, attention will be paid not to the old, who are so often poor but whose low incomes are not part of the process of social exclusion per se, but to the young. If we have had a qualitative shift in the form of the social order, then we would expect its effects to be particularly apparent among the young who are entering the new social world, and in particular its employment system, *ab initio*.

Ideally, we would like to consider both income and expenditure because of the dynamic instability of income in societies with relative insecurity of condition. If we examine data that cover both income and expenditure in a given week, we find a dissonance between location in the distribution of expenditure and income. The households in the lowest decile by income are not necessarily located in the lowest two deciles by expenditure. This derives from the instability of incomes. People can smooth expenditure over periods longer than a week when they have irregular incomes to contend with (see Goodman et al. 1997: 6). However, most data available do not enable us to take this into account, so, with the limitations recognized, we will work with what we have.

The changing pattern of income distribution in the countries of the North

Foster and Pearson (2002) conducted a review of the general trends in income distribution in the 21 member countries of the Organization for Economic Cooperation and Development (OECD) covering the period from the mid-1970s to the mid-1990s. In general, income distribution was relatively stable in the 1970s but since then there has been increasing polarization of incomes, starting in the 1980s in the Anglo-Saxon countries and spreading to Continental Europe during the 1990s. From the mid-1980s to the mid-1990s, income inequality increased in at least half of all OECD countries and in no country was there a clear decrease in income inequality. Foster and Pearson examined changes in both market income and disposable income (income after direct income taxation) for 13 OECD member countries (2002). In 9 of these, the top quintile of the income distribution experienced an increase in share of total income. Only in Ireland did the shares of both market and disposable income fall for this quintile. In none of the 13 countries did the income share by either measure increase by more than 1 per cent for any other quintile, and in general shares on both measures tended to fall, particularly in the UK.

A clear illustration of the impact of these changes is provided by data on the percentage of children in the UK living in households with less than 60 per cent of the median household income. In 1979, 12 per cent of children in relation to total income and 14 per cent of children after housing costs had been deducted fell into this category. By 1991–92 the respective figures were 26 per cent and 31 per cent. Family support measures under New Labour have made some difference to the first figure. By 2001–2002, the figure for children in low-income households in relation to gross income was 21 per cent. However, after housing costs were taken into account, the figure was 30 per cent and indeed this level was maintained throughout the 1990s regardless of which party was in power. Over the period 1997–2001, 16 per cent of children lived in households which had incomes below 60 per cent of the median for at least three of those years and 25 per cent lived in households which had incomes below 70 per cent of the median on the same basis. Child poverty was twice as prevalent in 2001 as it had been at the end of the 1970s.

Between 1979 and 2001–2002, the real gross incomes of the bottom decile in the UK increased by a third, whilst the real incomes of the top decile increased by 80 per cent. In 1979, the top decile had an average income three times that of the bottom decile. By 2001–2002, that ratio had changed to four times. Despite some important modifications to income distribution in the middle range, stemming from New Labour's tax credit innovations, there has been no change in this ratio since they gained office. The ends are drawing away from each other, and this is particularly true of the very affluent. Shepherd's (2003) review of trends in income inequality under the post-1997 New Labour government shows that the UK Gini Coefficient – a standard measure of income inequality – was at its highest ever level in the last 30 years at the beginning of this century. Despite an evening of income in the middle 70 per cent of the UK income distribution, there has been an overall increase in income inequality. The Institute of Fiscal Studies concludes that:

> . . . over the 40-year period, the incomes of the richest tenth have risen considerably faster than those at points lower down the income scale, and almost twice as fast as those of the poorest tenth (the income of the richest tenth grew 140 per cent in real terms between 1961 and 2002/ 03, whilst the income of the poorest tenth grew 86 per cent over this period).
>
> (Goodman and Oldfield 2004: 9)

Note the massive increase in the proportion of income received by those at the very top of the income scale.

> the top 1% in our sample have taken an increasing share of total income since 1979, with the sharp rise continuing over the 1990s. By the start of the 2000s, the top 1 per cent held around 8 per cent of total income, compared with income shares of around 5.8 per cent in 1990 and 3.5 per cent in 1980. Compared with these 'very rich' household incomes, the income shares of percentile groups within the rest of the top 10 per cent have stayed relatively constant over the 1990s.
>
> (Goodman and Oldfield 2004: 14–15)

During the 1990s, the share of total income received by the poorest 10 per cent declined, and the share of income received by all others except the top 1 per cent of income recipients remained much the same. This is a very important finding, and we will return to its implications in the conclusion. Here, let us note the characteristics of this group:

> . . . the top 1 per cent of individuals have incomes *after tax* of over £82,000 per year, expressed as the equivalent for a couple with no children. Almost a third of the top 1 per cent are in families with someone who is full-time self-employed (compared with less than a tenth across the population as a whole). Nearly 60 per cent of the top 1 per cent live in London and the South-East (whilst 33 per cent of the British population as a whole live in London and the South-East). Very few of the top 1 per cent are either lone parents or single pensioners; other family types are all fairly well represented at the very top. . . . the top 1 per cent receive a considerably higher proportion of their income from self-employment and from investments than do those lower down the income distribution. Earnings are also a sizeable source of income for this group, though less important than for other middle- and high-income individuals.
>
> (2004: 16)

US data is differently constructed, but shows that between 1979 and 2001 the real income of those in the bottom quintile of US incomes by household increased by 13 per cent, whereas the real income of the top 5 per cent increased by 80 per cent. The ratio between these two groups in 1979 was 1:6.7 and in 2001 it was 1:8.4. This means that the highest income recipients (and remember all these figures relate to taxable income) saw the ratio of their incomes to the incomes of the poorest increase by 25 per cent.

Braun, in a book with the interesting title of *The Rich Get Richer* (1997), describes US changes up to the mid-1990s. The crucial factor is the decline in real wages for most people in the bottom two-thirds of the income distribution. Braun, drawing on US Bureau of Labor Statistics, puts it like this:

> . . . since reaching its peak in 1972–1973 real average weekly earnings have fallen by nearly 19 per cent through December of 1994. . . . The

average American worker is worse off today than at any time in the past third of a century. In terms of real earnings, today's typical worker actually earns less pay than workers did in 1960.

(1997: 222)

In contrast to these declining real wages, profits have never been higher in US business, running in 1994 at more than twice the average rate for 1952–79 (Braun 1997: 188). In 1992, almost a sixth of US workers fell into the US Census Bureau definition of working poor and earned less than $13,091 in that year (Braun 1997: 238). The size of this group had increased by a third since 1979. In the USA, the poorest fifth of households saw a 13 per cent drop in real income over the period 1973 to 1992, although by 2001 this loss had been recovered to some degree in consequence of tax credit developments. Over the same period, the top fifth of the income distribution saw an increase of 11 per cent (Braun 1997: 257). Braun quotes figures from the Congressional Budget Office which demonstrate that the wealthiest 1 per cent of the US population has nearly as much after-tax income as the bottom 40 per cent and that the top fifth in the US income distribution receives as much income as the bottom four-fifths (1997: 263).

Atkinson (2003) documented the change in the real incomes of the UK's very rich, that is the top 1 per cent in the distribution, throughout the twentieth century. Their share of all gross income has more than doubled since 1978. The share of the top 0.5 per cent and top 0.05 per cent have increased even more. The result is that: 'top incomes are now broadly back where they were at the end of the Second World War' (2003: 20). In the UK, France and the USA, the proportion of income received by the top 1 per cent in 2000 was roughly the same at about 17 per cent of all recorded income. This was the same in the UK and France as in 1945 and the same in the USA as in 1929. The key point is that the UK in particular and the USA to a considerable degree became much more equal in the 1960s and 1970s and that tendency has now been reversed. France remained unequal throughout the period.

Westergaard summed up the position thus:

Even people up to mid-point incomes, and a number some way above that level, have gained quite little either by comparison with the rich or by past standards of rising prosperity. The poor are much less a minority by virtue of exclusion from benefit of radical-right market boom than are the wealthy by virtue of high-boosted privilege from it.

(1995: 133)

When considering the Polish situation, it is important to bear in mind Gorzelak's (1996) argument that what is happening in Poland is not different from the transitions experienced in the West. It is simply the same thing speeded up. What have been the effects on income distribution in Poland?

Weclawowicz (1996: 95) quotes from Domanski (1994: 55) and shows that a substantial gap has opened up in the pattern of incomes in Poland. In 1978, the average monthly income per person in households headed by 'managers and higher state administration officials' was 145 to a national average of 100. In 1993, it was 317 to a national average of 100. In other words, the relative incomes of the top group had gone from 1.5 times the norm to more than 3 times the norm. The non-technical intelligentsia haven't done badly either, with their relative incomes rising from 1.5 times the norm to 2.3 times the norm over the same period. All manual worker groups in industry and agriculture, and peasants as a category, saw a fall in relative incomes. Skilled workers who had had per person household income of 0.95 the national norm in 1978 saw this fall to 0.79 in 1993. The fall for all other manual categories was even greater.

Podkaminer (2003) considers that a new period in Poland's economic history began in 1995–96 with a radical liberalization of economic organization coupled with the establishment of a generally convertible currency and free capital movements. By 1999, farmers' and manual workers' relative incomes had fallen substantially from their 1996 level, whereas relative incomes for white-collar workers were sustained. Both expenditure and income inequality indicators increased in a way which clearly indicated developing social polarization. In 1999–2000, 23.8 per cent of Poland's population were below the national poverty line and 34.4 per cent of households considered themselves to be in poverty (Podkaminer 2003:761). Keane and Prasad (2002) confirm this account in general, and together with Podkaminer draw attention to the logic behind recent changes in transfer payments in Poland. As Podkaminer puts it:

> The very generous unemployment benefits and pension systems of the early 1990s had a purpose. The were intended to 'sweeten' the transition to capitalism and soften workers' opposition to privatisation (which usually implied massive labour cuts forcing workers to face unemployment or take early retirement). As privatisation progresses, that 'generosity' loses its usefulness.
>
> (2003:765–6)

The Polish experience is by no means the most extreme in relation to post-state-socialist restructuring, but it clearly illustrates the significance of institutional and political factors in such societies.

The trajectory of income distribution in France over the past 30 years is somewhat different from the UK experience. Atkinson (1999) notes that in the first half of the 1980s the share of overall income of the poorest decile continued to increase during the first half of the 1980s. The Gini coefficient rose only slightly from the mid-1980s to the mid-1990s. Although the: 'sustained period of equalization . . . came to an end around the mid 1980s; . . . the years since they did not show a marked reversal in terms of the inequality of disposable income' (1999:65).

Why have income distributions become more unequal?

In the mid-1990s the answer to that question in North America, Australasia, non-Communist Europe and the European 'second world' of former state socialist countries, was almost always given in terms of changing patterns of the relationships of household to paid work. The key driver was not simply non-employment. Just as important was the amount of employment income received by households. Essentially earnings net of tax have become much more unequal.

Hills (1995: 40) examined the changing shape of income distribution in the UK between 1979 and 1990/91. There were two interesting aspects to this. One was the separation between households with no full-time earners and those with full-time earners. Over the period, the modal income of the former set became much less than that of the latter set, having previously been rather close to it. The second was the shift in the distribution for those households that did have full-time workers. This became much more spread out with large disparities and an emerging bimodal form. This inequality of earned income matters a great deal because it is the simplest direct indicator of an overall change in the level of inequality in the social order. That level is a key control parameter determining the form of actual social order, from a range of possible social orders, which will exist.

The origin of this increased inequality, and of the changing characteristics of the poor, was unequivocally identified by Goodman et al.:

> The emergence of mass unemployment has had a major effect on the income distribution. Families with children now make up more than half of the poorest decile group compared with only around a third three decades ago, with the main reason for this change being the increase in unemployment between the early 1960s and the mid 1980s.
>
> (1997: 112)

However, in the USA employment levels in the early years of the twenty-first century are historically very high and yet income distribution has become substantially more unequal since the 1970s, and indeed gross real incomes for the lowest income group have changed relatively little. In the UK, we have seen a similar development with historically high levels of apparent employment, which are actually quite real for adults in the age range 20–45, which includes the majority of adults with dependent children. It appears that the role of mass unemployment in the 1980s was social restructuring – the creation of an indigenous reserve army of labour in order to weaken the power of workers and massively recommodify the wage–labour relationship. The medium-term effect has been the creation of masses of 'poor work'. In the USA unequivocally and in the UK somewhat more equivocally, work, albeit work with incomes subsidized from tax revenues, is now the basis of income for adults of appropriate age. This process is just now under way in Continental Europe and is almost complete in the former state socialist societies of Central Europe. Labour has been or is being recommodified by all of the processes of the massive weakening of organization through trade unions, a reduction in formal legal employment protection for workers, and a large reduction in the value and duration of wage replacement state benefits for the unemployed and increasingly other non-employed groups.

We would expect such changes to create a population of working poor. Strengmann-Kuhn (2002) used the data from the European Community Household Panel to establish the extent of working poverty in the member states of the European Union in 1996 using an income level of 60 per cent of the median as a poverty line. He found that for the EU as a whole, 13.3 per cent of the population living in an employed household and 9 per cent of the employed were poor. Rates of working poverty were highest in Greece, Portugal, Spain and Ireland; 17 per cent of the poor in the UK were employed, but 30.5 per cent of the poor lived in a full-time working poor household and 42.5 per cent in a household where there was some employment. In the EU as a whole, 22 per cent of the poor were employed, 50 per cent lived in a household with a full-time employee, and 61 per cent lived in a household with some employment. In the US, 15 million people are members of working poor families. Nearly two-thirds of the USA's poor work some time in a given year, and 15 per cent of them in 1996 worked full time. In 2000, according to US Bureau of the Census figures, there were 136 million people in the US workforce and 6.4 million of them were in poverty on the very restrictive US definition with its absolute basis. This refers only to legal and registered workers and not to illegals and off the books workers. There was a distinct influence of age, gender and race on the levels of US working poverty. The overall rate was 4.7 per cent. For blacks it was 8.7 per cent and for Hispanics 10.0 per cent. For men it was 4 per cent and for women 5.5 per cent. For persons aged 16–19 it was 9.2 per cent and for those aged 20–24 it was 8.7 per cent, whereas for those aged 45–54 it was 2.7 per cent. Some 14.8 million people in the USA were members of working poor families.

Why has inequality increased? Braun accounts for these developments in terms of the impact of global competition on the US economy. The new international division of labour has led to a massive deindustrialization, particularly in the mid-West, which as Braun notes (1997: 367) has had particularly dire consequences for white working-class males. However, he implicitly assumes a kind of common national interest which links working-class interests to higher service-class interests and the interests of the owners of capital, when he writes of a US interest as such. In reality, US capital has done very well and has been able to do so because insecurity, global restructuring and the disempowering of organized labour have enabled it to increase domestic rates of exploitation whilst maintaining effective nearly full employment. The massive deindustrialization of high-wage countries, typified by the shift whereby iconic Marks and Spencer's sourced 90 per cent of its clothing purchases in the UK in the 1980s and sourced less than 10 per cent in 2004, is dependent on the ability of capital to locate globally towards low-wage economies. This ability is inherently political. It reflects the massive weakening of governments' capacity for regulating the activities of business and the flows of capital in a globalized system.

Nelson's discussion of 'postindustrial capitalism' (see Chapter 2) explains how this has been achieved through economic and political intervention by large corporations. The ideological hegemony of classic free-market liberalism in US politics provides a covering gloss on extreme intervention and manipulation. In the UK, New 'Labour' is peddling the same sort of line, whilst acting as the rather open creature of global corporate interests. Crucial to the politics of postindustrial flexibility is the use of legal means to destroy the organizational capacities of workers at the point of production.

The effect on the 'class' structure of US society has been marked. In an article with the title 'The Incredible Shrinking Middle Class' (1992), Duncan et al. reviewed income panel data since the mid-1970s and concluded that:

> The good news is that late twentieth century America has offered abundant opportunity for the upper-middle class. The bad news is that at the same time, it has reduced upward mobility among the working class and produced persistently high poverty rates for families with children. These two opposing forces are draining America's middle class.
>
> (1992: 38)

The impact of political and institutional change is clear in Poland. Gorzelak argues that: 'The [Polish] working class had been struggling with communism for what could be called "socialism with a human face" . . . Instead of restructured socialism, liberal capitalism has now been imposed' (1996: 100). In contrast with the period of 'real socialism' when unemployment did not officially exist, by 1994 there were very nearly three million unemployed in Poland, that is 16 per cent of the civilian economically active population. Only 550,000 of these were unemployed as a consequence of redundancy (1996: 28). Many of the unemployed were young people coming from secondary technical schools and failing to get jobs in the contracting industries for which they had trained. Non-recruitment of the young coupled with job defence by those in work is of enormous significance in Poland. There is an important, if implicit, difference of emphasis between the accounts advanced by Gorzelak and Weclawowicz (1996) for the Polish situation. For Gorzelak, restructuring caused the problems in Poland and this has to be understood in terms of the imposition of the post-Fordist logic of capitalist accumulation facilitated by the recreation of a reserve army. In contrast, although appreciating perfectly the character of restructuring, Weclawowicz turned the focus onto the socio/political/cultural deficiencies of the Polish working class which, having brought down Communism through collective action, remained remarkably reluctant to accept its new role as the flexible labour force of a post-Fordist liberal capitalism. This can be seen in the Polish coal industry centred on the

Katowice industrial district in Upper Silesia. Here the miners, who were both the favoured aristocrats of 'real socialist' labour and a key part of the Solidarity opposition to 'real socialism', managed to retain their jobs and incomes in the early 1990s through the political influence of their trade unions. However, subsequently there has been massive restructuring and the mining labour force stands at 30 per cent of its original level. Poland is rapidly taking on the general postindustrial political and social forms.

However, we cannot account for the retreat from equality solely in terms of the inexorable operations of an anonymous and depersonalized global system, however strongly neo-liberal ideologues might assert that this is the only source of change. Global neo-liberalism as practical politics has weakened organized labour and facilitated the global mobility of both industrial and financial capital, but even that is not the whole story. We also have to consider the role of fiscal and welfare policies with welfare understood in terms both of the redistribution of cash and the provision of services in kind.

UK data charts the effects of tax and welfare provision on the income distribution. In 2002–2003 the poorest were better off than previously because of redistribution, whilst the most affluent paid much lower rates of marginal tax than in the Keynesian era *and* their basic incomes were much higher in relation to everybody else's. However, the poorest were only better off in relation to original income. If we consider final income, 25 years after Thatcher they too are worse off. In 1979, the poorest fifth got 10 per cent of all post-tax income, the middle three-fifths got 54 per cent, and the most affluent fifth got 37 per cent. In 2002–2003, the poorest fifth got 6 per cent, the middle three-fifths got 51 per cent, and the most affluent fifth got 43 per cent. This is the extraordinary unmentioned reality of New Labour's much-vaunted redistribution. The combination of their policies overall in the context of a postindustrial society is to have a situation where they have made the poor somewhat less poor but only in relation to original incomes. They have also done nothing to reverse, and indeed in important ways have reinforced, the policies of the Thatcher years, which have made the rich a great deal richer. And never forget that these figures do not take account of very affluent people's ability to hide their income from taxation.

UK direct taxation is marginally progressive, even though most taxpayers only pay tax at the standard rate. This is because of the existence of a system of allowances which means that the average rate of tax is not the same as the marginal rate across the wide range of incomes on which standard rate only is payable. However, the progressive element is much less than it used to be, particularly when income tax and national insurance are taken together. The UK's other taxes levied on individuals and households are primarily regressive. Both council tax, the local tax levied on domestic property, and consumption taxes in the form of VAT and excise duties, are highly regressive in relation to income. This is a crucially important point. Taxation as a whole and the provision of welfare do not redistribute from the rich to

Table 5.1 Income inequality by quintiles in the UK, 1979 and 2002–3 (percentage of total received by each quintile)

1979		2002–3
	Original income	
2	Bottom	3
10	2nd	7
18	3rd	15
27	4th	25
43	Top	50
	Gross income	
9	Bottom	7
13	2nd	11
18	3rd	16
24	4th	23
37	Top	43
	Disposable income	
9	Bottom	8
13	2nd	12
18	3rd	17
23	4th	23
36	Top	41
	Post-tax income	
10	Bottom	6
13	2nd	12
18	3rd	16
23	4th	23
37	Top	43

Definitions
Original income – All income other than from government transfer incomes

Gross income – Original income plus government transfer incomes

Disposable income – Gross income after direct taxation including council tax

Post-tax income – Disposable income after the effect of indirect taxation

the poor. Instead, in the UK today we have a system which is an excellent example of the postindustrial norm as described by Foster and Pearson:

> Benefit systems do redistribute income. But they do not primarily redistribute from rich to poor. Rather, they redistribute from young to old, from those who work to those who do not, and from childless families to families with children.
>
> (2002: 25)

In effect, cash transfers are largely horizontal. They transfer income through insurance and other systems in a way that renders the expression 'social insurance' meaningful – that is to say, they represent a risk-pooling arrangement for the middle masses and poor in relation to the contingencies of sickness and unemployment and the life stages of child rearing and retirement. The Speenhamland-style Clinton/Brown tax credits which we will examine in Chapter 8 work in exactly this way.

Let us consider the implications of cuts in the levels of taxation on those in receipt of high incomes. In the UK the pattern of taxation has been quite radically revised by massive reductions in the higher rates under the Conservatives which New Labour has not done anything significant to reverse:

> Income tax rates have been reduced markedly since 1977–78, particularly for those on higher incomes. The basic rate fell progressively from 33 per cent in April 1978 to 25 per cent in April 1988, and in 1992–3 a new lower rate of 20 per cent was introduced. The higher tax rates, which rose to a maximum of 83 per cent on earned income, have been replaced by one 40 per cent rate.
>
> (*Social Trends* 1995: 89)

In the USA the Bush administration has massively reduced the tax burden on the most affluent. Deaton sums up the position:

> . . . two-thirds of the benefits of the tax-cuts will go to the top ten per cent of tax payers, and fully a half to the top five percent. Over the next four years, someone in the top one percent of the income distribution will pay almost $100,000 less in taxes than if this year's changes had not been implemented. The corresponding figure of the average person in the bottom 20 percent is $36.
>
> (2003: 1)

Note that our discussion has been solely about the distribution of taxed income. We must at least note the scale of tax avoidance. In a letter to the *Guardian*, Prem Sikka, Professor of Accounting at the University of Essex, commented:

> Moore Stephens, tax partner says: 'No matter what legislation is in place, the accountants and lawyers will find a way around it. Rules are rules, but rules are meant to be broken' ('Be fair' plea as tax loopholes targeted, March 18). This shows the real morals of the tax avoidance industry. One wonders what kind of advice is given to those involved in money laundering, creative accounting or cheating on benefits. No wonder Britain is losing between £25bn–£85bn each year in tax avoidance.
>
> (20 March 2004)

It is not just that this change in tax regimes creates 'momentary inequality' – that is, inequality in income in the here and now. The differences in income facilitate investment by those with the highest incomes – investment in income-earning assets in all their forms, and of particular significance investment in the development of the human capital of their children so that they can earn more in future generations. In other words, inequality generates positive feedback down the years. Note that taxation on wealth in the neo-liberal societies is now minimal and very easily avoided. This is yet another reinforcement to the positive feedback of unequal trajectories.

Gender and income inequality

Anybody's position in any social structure is complicated by the effects of collectivities to which they belong. We are used to thinking of this as an issue for women because we have a notion of women as 'dependent' members of households to which they are not the main economic contributors. The massive growth in female employment in postindustrial capitalism has changed all that. The resources in a household have implications for everybody in the household, whether male or female, adult or child. However, dependency does remain significant and gendered (for adults).

Dependency is a crucial issue. At one extreme, it can be argued, from a possessive individualist position, that all adults must be treated as separate individuals. In the UK, the introduction of separate assessment for income tax purposes works on this principle to the great advantages of affluent households. Contrawise, poor benefit-dependent women are subject to a household test for incomes which actually predicates against them maintaining a legal relationship with their partners (see Parker 1989). If we do look at 'own right' incomes, then only about a third of adult women in the UK, almost all in full-time employment, have incomes higher than levels usually used to assess poverty.

There is considerable evidence of unequal resource distribution by gender within households, although it must be noted that much of this is somewhat dated and that the 'degendering' of social relations in general is likely to have had an impact on the pattern of intra-household resource distribution. However, studies that ignore this intra-household distribution, itself the product of complex and differentiated patterns of resource acquisition and allocation, and simply regard households as undifferentiated social atoms, are not describing social reality as it is. Likewise, the treatment of individuals as social atoms regardless of the resources of the household to which they belong is an invalid approach to social reality as it is. The only possible approach which would adequately address this issue would be a study based on detailed contemporary patterns of internal resource allocation in all forms. This is necessary, but it is not going to be done here. Instead, I am going to focus on the group of women who are the least complex to assess and who are often unequivocally socially excluded – single mothers.

There are two reasons for doing this. One is that the single mother is the limiting case of female dependency. There is no 'dominant' permanently resident male and the single mother acquires with motherhood all the liabilities of care which cause difficulties for full-time economic engagement, plus the liability to maintain her own dependent child or children. The other is that we need to address the new conservatism's obsession with the single mother as the generative mechanism of welfare dependency and underclass status. Overarching both these is the reality that many, if not all, single mothers and their children are plainly poor. I am going to use the position of single mothers as a basis for discussing arguments about the feminization of poverty in the societies being considered. Let me say straight away that here we will find differentiation both among societies and within them. The evidence is that in the UK poverty is less female than it was under Fordism/industrial capitalism, although there are far more poor women. In Poland, the proportion of the poor who are female has risen and this is a general phenomenon in post-Communist societies. Domanski (2002) shows that women in Poland were 98 per cent more likely to live in poverty than men. Russia, with a very large number of working single mothers, shows extremes of poverty in female-headed households. In the USA, 40 per cent of poor families were female-headed in 2001, compared with 23 per cent in 1959; 35 per cent of female-headed families with children were poor in contrast to 8 per cent of married couple households with children. In the USA a clear differentiation is developing among women. This is also a crucial phenomenon in the UK. Kodias and Jones put this well:

> . . . the slight improvements registered for women in general actually represent substantial gains made by a minority of women, primarily in the professions, and static or deteriorating circumstances for the majority of women who need to work.
>
> (1991: 161)

There are two causal accounts that argue that single parenthood is a generative mechanism for poverty. The first we might call 'weak and demographic'. This sort of account is not about the assignation of blame, nor does it argue that children's experience of single parenting per se does them any damage. It is a demographic/epidemiological account rather than one of causation for individuals. Essentially, it is based on the recognition that households headed by female single parents are likely to be poor. If there is a growth in the proportion of such households in a society, then there will be a growth in poverty/social exclusion which will take the form of a feminization of poverty because both the absolute numbers and proportion of the poor who are in female-headed households will grow.

There is an immediate statistically reflexive problem. If we see a growth in the time series in both poverty/social exclusion and female-headed, single-parent households we are observing merely correlation. Correlation is not cause. We can argue, and indeed should argue, that the causal chain may well be in the other direction – poverty/social exclusion based on the reduction of the wage-earning capacity of men, may well be causing households to be headed by female single parents. Given the existence of such reflexive relationships, the use of linear modelling techniques is always problematic, but Kodias and Jones conclude on their examination of US evidence that:

> . . . female-family formation explains only the pool, and not the poverty, of female families. Our analyses do show a strong relationship between family formation dynamics and female poverty growth. Beyond this, however, economic changes at the local level were found to be of significance. Growth in women's employment and the expanding female service sector were the most important correlates of female-family poverty growth in metropolitan areas. It is indeed ironic that the service sector, which provided the greatest increase in women's employment over the decade, is so strongly associated with female poverty. No support was found for the argument often advanced by conservatives, that welfare expansion is positively related to female poverty.
>
> (1991: 169)

This last point is of particular significance. The neo-conservatives whose ideas were discussed in Chapter 1 and who are represented in the UK by Green (1998), drawing on the ideas of Mead (1997), argue that the availability of benefits promotes single parenthood. In the more extreme forms, as expressed by Murray (1992) and in the crude version of the 'culture of poverty', benefit-dependent single parenthood is the generative mechanism for a lifetime trajectory of dependency and 'underclass' status, not only for the mothers but for their children, who lack the model of the male wage earner and perpetuate the poor female-headed family in their own reproduction. This old and lousy tune is the strong programme. Rowlingson and McKay's recent study of the dynamics of lone parenthood in the UK offers some interesting qualitatatively derived findings which are relevant here. These authors conclude that:

> . . . the growth of lone parenthood has occurred partly because of two sets of circumstances. For single women from poor backgrounds who get pregnant, lone motherhood is a relatively attractive option beside the alternatives of living with a poor man or staying as a single woman with a poor job. For women in couples with children, a different situation applies. These women are no longer so constrained, by economic necessity and social norms, to remain 'for better or worse' in a traditional two parent family.
>
> (1998: 206)

Some spatial data can cast some light on the actual causal mechanisms operating. In a study of Leicester as a divided city, I found (Byrne 1997) that there was a marked and emergent difference in the legitimacy status of children born to mothers with addresses in the affluent two-thirds and poor third of that historically prosperous locality. In the affluent areas, 96 per cent of all children were born to parents who were married. In the poor areas, less than 50 per cent of children were born to parents who were married, although the largest category of unmarried parents jointly registered their children from the same address. The emergence of the social divisions in Leicester were clearly established as originating in the deindustrialization of the locality. The growth in 'non-married' births, and the spatial pattern of such births, can be identified as a consequence of the same processes over the same period. This picture very much supports Rowlingson and McKay's general account given above.

The US experience is dispiriting. Kodias and Jones argue that the cause of poverty for female-headed families in the USA is not welfare dependency but rather the labour market positions available to them and forced upon them in a context where as Orloff puts it: 'the US is moving to require paid work as the only route for the support of households, whether headed by couples or single mothers' (1996: 55). So is the UK. This fits exactly of course with the logic of postindustrial capitalism as described by Nelson (see Chapter 3). Female-headed family poverty seems to be a function now of poor work.

Race/ethnicity and exclusion

When we turn to exclusion by ethnicity the limiting case is the historical experience of black US citizens.

> Until the 1960s, black Americans were virtually excluded from full and equal civil, social, and political citizenship rights accorded to the white native-born population and to naturalised immigrants. Thus, the boundaries excluding them were foremost racial, reinforced by social, economic, and political segregation. In the 1980s, blacks have gained formal citizenship equality. Yet, only middle class, and to a lesser extent working-class blacks have been able to benefit from the new legal equality. The economically weakest members of the black population remain excluded. The boundaries that exclude them are primarily socio-economic and secondarily racial. The socio-economic dimension reflects the limited nature and institutionalization of social citizenship in the United States.
>
> (Heisler 1991: 468)

Ethnicity is intimately linked with citizenship but different from it. The formal citizenship of black Americans was established with the emancipation of the slaves, but it took the civil rights movement of the 1950s and 1960s to turn it into anything approximating a reality. Catholics were nominal citizens in Northern Ireland, but a series of explicit mechanisms excluded them from the rights of citizens in a 'Protestant state for a Protestant people' at the provincial level, whilst, and ironically, the 'imperial' rights of citizenship of the colonizing power were fully available to them, and the imperial mechanisms were not discriminatory in employment and service provision.

In industrial and postindustrial capitalism, there is an additional confounding factor. Ethnicity is often associated with immigrant status. The two things are not the same. Neither Northern Ireland Catholics nor US blacks are immigrants in any meaningful sense. However, many (in the UK most) ethnically differentiated people are immigrants or the descendants of recent immigrants. In the UK, almost all immigrants were effective citizens on arrival, but in the USA this is not the case for Latinos, who form the significant part of recent immigration in relation to any discussion of social exclusion.

What position do people occupy in the system of stratification in the social order, if we look at their position by ethnicity? Note that there are two fixes on this. One, which underpins UK and US anti-discriminatory legislation, is individualistic and reflects the dominant motif of possessive individualism. We might see it as having achieved its objectives when ethnicity is essentially irrelevant to social position. This is becoming the case, for example, for people who self-classify as 'Indian' in the UK. The other is collectivist and considers overall position of those who self-identify with the group as a whole. Essentially, the second position is founded on group solidarity.

There are marked differences among the societies that are the basis of illustration in this book. Both the UK and the USA are multi-ethnic societies on a somewhat different scale, although the UK is much more multi-ethnic if the Irish descended are considered as an ethnic minority. In Poland, which before World War II was a complex and multi-ethnic society, the tides of world history and the criminal lunacies of the Nazi era, finished off by residual Polish anti-Semitism, have produced an effectively homogeneous population, although observation suggests that the Rom (gypsies) remain as a disadvantaged and significant group. France is a multi-ethnic society with a history of ex-colonial immigration similar to that of the UK but with a more restrictive approach to the allocation of citizenship rights. Despite France, the UK and USA's common status as multi-ethnic, the implications of ethnic minority status are very different in the three societies as a whole, and within them are very different for different groups.

In the USA, the key, continuing aspect of ethnic exclusion is represented by the position of black Americans, and this exclusion is generated by the continuing significance of the central residual element of the racism founded on the forms of chattel slavery, the continuing reality of ethnic segregation to a unique and intense degree of black from white Americans. This is a matter of racism rather than simple ethnic differentiation. The 'one drop of blood' basis for the identification of black Americans as not white – one drop of 'black blood' made someone black under the race codes which existed in many US states until the 1950s – was racially excluding rather than involving any of the cultural dimensions which are so significant for ethnic differentiation. In the US in 2002, 22 per cent of blacks, 20 per cent of Hispanics and 10 per cent of whites were poor, again on the USA's very restrictive definition of what constitutes poverty.

The situation in the UK is rather different from that in the USA. First, there is no specifically disadvantaged 'other than white' group. Rather, there are series of ethnicities with very different social relations surrounding them. Indeed, those who identify as black are the least separated from the UK white population. Peach notes in the introduction to a four-volume series describing *Ethnicity in the 1991 Census* (1996, 1997) that:

> The Black Caribbean population's position in Britain stands out in strong contrast to that of African Americans in the USA. Its structure is more working class than the population as a whole, but it does not differ dramatically in terms of housing tenure, jobs or residential segregation from the white population. It has an exceptionally high proportion of mixed Black and White households and in this way appears as the most integrated group.
>
> (1997: 23)

Karn summarizes the overall position of UK ethnic minorities thus:

> A particularly important point emerged in relation to occupations and lifestyles. *Within* each ethnic group there was a strong relationship between occupational level and lifestyle. However, *across* (original emphases) the ethnic groups, occupational level had far less influence on the quality of lifestyle. Other factors were contributing to the differentiation of the groups and giving advantage to the Whites. The same factors appear to have influenced the incidence of unemployment.
>
> (1998: 281)

In other words, at all occupational levels there is a real disadvantage for 'other than white' ethnic minorities as compared with 'whites' in their own occupational category. However, there are very different locations in relation to the overall social structure. People who self-classify as 'Indian' are on the whole somewhat better located in the social order than 'whites' as a whole. All other large ethnic minorities are not, with Pakistanis and Bangladeshis, being particularly disadvantaged.

The exclusion of the young in postindustrial capitalism

In considering the young, we should remember that as the social order changes then the people who begin key phases in their lives subsequent to those changes will find that their lives are very different from those whose lives were set on track in an earlier era. Hills summarizes the findings of the Rowntree Foundation's investigation of these issues, noting that: 'the stakes are higher for younger cohorts: as they enter the labour market, the difference between those who do well (linked to high qualifications) and those who do not is much greater than it was for those entering the labour market twenty – or even ten – years earlier' (1995: 48).

Schrammel (1998) demonstrates that young adults born in the 'baby bust' years of relatively low birthrates in the USA between 1965 and 1976 have been markedly less successful in terms both of earnings and other measures of occupational success than those born in the baby boom years of 1946 to 1964. This is particularly notable if we remember that the baby boom years produced 4 million children per year, which was nearly 20 per cent more than in the baby bust years. In other words, those entering the labour market from the early 1980s onwards did so with a much lower supply of citizen labour and on supply/demand criteria might have been expected to do better but actually did worse! This impact was particularly marked in relation to earnings. Real median earnings fell by 15 per cent for young adults between 1979 and 1996 and relative earnings – relative to all employed workers – fell by about 12 per cent. Schrammel considers that a major factor in this change was the general shift from secondary sector production of material goods to tertiary sector production of services in the US economy.

Changes in the UK have been equally dramatic. Bynner et al. (2002) note a similar decline in the relative incomes of young people by the mid-1990s which was plainly associated with a similar transition to a postindustrial labour market. In 1975 in the UK, 16-year-olds earned 45 per cent of national average wages and 25-year-olds earned 100. In 1999, the comparable figures were 38 per cent and 84 per cent, and in the UK as in the US this was against the demographic trend which had generated far fewer labour market entrants at the second time point. McKnight's (2002) review of the comparable experience of 1958-born and 1970-born longitudinal panels of UK children demonstrates that those who were brought up in poor families in both cohorts were suffering labour market and income disadvantage in their twenties, and this disadvantage was significantly worse for the later-born cohort. In other words, negative trajectories were more reinforced in the postindustrial period.

Employment prospects have substantially improved since the mid-1990s. However, Johnston et al.'s recent intensive ethnographic study of a deprived locale (2000) demonstrates that although individual life trajectories were varied and contingent, for most of those from a 'marginalized' (albeit itself internally differentiated) locale the postindustrial labour market offered insecure poor work with a pattern of benefit dependency both in and out of work. Bynner makes it plain that this shift is associated closely with the postindustrial character of the contemporary UK labour market for young men and with the credentialization of white-collar employment for young women:

. . . there has been a fall in the type of jobs available to young school leavers away from craft jobs for young men towards low-skilled occupations, and from administrative and clerical occupations towards sales and personal service occupations for young women. Many of these occupations tend to have more limited opportunities for advancement and are less likely to provide high quality training. It is evident that the vocational route into the labour market which provided high quality training to young people who left school at the age of 16 or 17 is rapidly disappearing.

(2002: 5–6)

The Polish situation is also dramatic. In urban industrial centres union pressure has often been effective in sustaining the jobs of those who already had them, but the mechanisms of transmission into work have broken down. There was in Poland a system of technical schools associated with particular industries and often with particular enterprises which channelled young adults directly into work. The collapse of recruitment meant that in 1993, 31 per cent of all Poland's unemployed were in the age group 18–24 (Weclawowicz 1996: 145). The problems that this poses are likely to be exacerbated by demographic factors which will inject even more young adults into the labour market. Educational differentiation is now emerging as a crucial factor in Poland. This is associated with both an expansion of state higher education and the development of a private (and semi-private) system of, in particular, business schools. Actually, the educational developments in Poland seem singularly suited to the provision of the divided labour force required for many postindustrial enterprises. Over 20 per cent of the Polish unemployed are under 25 years old, and in some Polish regions youth unemployment rates exceed 50 per cent (Mlady 2002). The US experience indicates that long-term developments are not to be understood in terms simply of a poorly educated helotry and an educated class with good and increasing levels of resource control. On the contrary, although there is a clear 'education premium' in life-time earnings, Braun (1997: 230) shows that real wages for college graduates have declined since 1987, albeit at a lesser rate than for non-graduates.

An important question which emerges from the development of qualification-founded social division, a social division exactly commensurate with the employment structure of postindustrial capitalism, is whether or not this is generating a cultural divide? Mead's insistence on the need to orientate welfare programmes towards workfare, to make welfare receipt conditional not on confinement in the panopticon of the workhouse, but on labour in a workhouse generalized to the society as a whole, is of course predicated not just on Benthamite utilitarianism, but also on a belief that a culture of anti-work exists among the citizen poor. Bluntly put, they want too much and will not put up with very little. The actual ethnographic evidence from the UK does not support this view. Indeed, security seems to be more important than wage levels. If anything, I think MacDonald is overestimating the aspirations of the dispossessed young when he summarizes the implications of the range of studies included in his edited collection:

There was one, inescapable conclusion which cut across all these studies. Both young people and adults wanted work. They would fail with flying colours the test Murray sets to prove the underclass's existence: 'offer them jobs at a generous wage for unskilled labour and see what happens' . . . They were extraordinarily dogged and enterprising in their search for work amidst the economic wreckage of their local labour market. They remained attached to remarkably durable, mainstream attitudes which valued work as a key source of self-respect, as the principal definer of personal identity, as a social (and in many cases moral) duty, as the foundation upon which to build sustainable family lives and respectable futures.

(1997: 195)

In my experience, young people don't need generous wages to induce them to work. They will work for any gain above benefit level. MacDonald's own study, whilst a convincing account of the situation of the marginalized young on Teesside, is not a complete account of young people's work experiences in even that limiting case of the social consequences of deindustrialization. There is another sort of work experience for the young which is predicated upon high-level qualifications and entry into another kind of labour market. However, this is not a work experience of historical advantage. The young adults with good formal qualifications who enter this labour market are relatively advantaged compared with the dispossessed working class. They are disadvantaged compared with their own parents.

This situation is well illustrated by the call centre industry. This is the top end of the generic labour market of postindustrial capitalism. Although there is a gender bias in the tele-sales/customer-services complexes, in that the staff of call centres are predominantly female, young men also work in these occupations. These jobs are clean, secure, require a good general education (many entrants are graduates), and are in contemporary terms relatively well paid, although they certainly do not offer a 'family wage'. They are remarkably supervised and managed, illustrating, contra Bauman's assertion (1998: 25), the continued significance of the 'panoptical drill'. There is a distinction between employment in this field and employment in the field of dispossession, but it is not a distinction of exemption from gross exploitation and powerlessness at the point of production. The main distinction is stability, although call centres may actually be rendered obsolete very quickly by the development of Internet-based information and purchase systems and the global transfer of jobs to low-waged Indian competitors.

The implications of social bifurcation for the young need spelling out carefully. The evidence is not for a situation in which some young people are much worse off than their parental generation of the Fordist era, and some are better off, with the divide being something on the lines of half and half. Rather, it is for a threefold division. There is a large dispossessed and casualized poor. There is a large better-qualified and better-remunerated in contemporary terms, but historically downwardly mobile, educated proletariat. Finally, there is a category, most of whom are inheriting privilege but some of whom are entrants from below, who get into the higher reaches of the service class as managers and private sector professionals. It is this elite whose situation is better. We seem to be developing a something less than 10 per cent, 50 per cent, 40 per cent society under postindustrial conditions.

Dynamics – the significance of life courses

The development of dynamic studies has provided some ammunition for those who dispute the significance of inequality. Pryke notes that if we examine the conclusions of the most important recent UK study of income distribution, that conducted by Hills for Rowntree, we find that Hills':

> . . . own estimates indeed suggest that when money income is measured on an annual basis, the top ten per cent are six time richer than the bottom twenty per cent but that when income is measured over a lifetime, the top decile has only two and a half times as much income as the bottom quintile.
>
> (1995: 22)

However, any lifetime data available in the 1990s describes the lifetime experience of those whose lifecourse trajectories had been under the conditions of Fordism. The whole point about the discussion of the phase shift from Fordism to post-Fordism is that future trajectories are likely to be very different.

Walker (with Ashworth; 1994) used US data and examined the life courses with regard to childhood experience of poverty (defined in terms about 25 per cent more generous than the official US poverty line) of all children in the panel born between 1968 and 1972 during the first 15 years of life. One group, comprising 62 per cent of the sample, never experienced poverty. Of those who did, more than half had a childhood of spells of poverty, punctuated by periods of moving out of poverty, although given the linear and single-dimensional definition of poverty we do not know by how much. Just over a quarter experienced only one spell of poverty of less than one year's duration. The rest experienced long spells of poverty or were always poor. The findings of this study certainly support the notion that the important group are those whose lives are characterized by movement to and from poverty, although we don't know the extent of the movement.

Hill et al. (1998) examined poverty processes in young adulthood using a sample who were aged between 8 and 13 in 1968. They use a linear model approach for analysis, with all the disadvantages of such techniques. The predictors of poverty transitions in young adulthood are personal behaviour, especially in relation to educational success and marriage/childbearing patterns and parental background. Hill et al. note that: 'the evidence of background being mediated by behaviours is weak, except . . . when the behaviours are taken to extremes' (1998: 99). This is distinctly pessimistic and supports an account of closure of mobility opportunities.

Goodman et al. (1997), using British Household Panel Survey (BHPS) data, examined household income movements for those who were in the bottom quintile of income distribution during the first three passes of this study in 1991, 1992 and 1993. Nearly half of those who were in the bottom quintile in wave one were there in both waves two and three. Of those who escaped between wave one and wave two, more than half made it only into the second quintile, so changes in income may have been marginal (see Goodman et al. 1997: 257–64). The categories of household most likely to escape the bottom quintile at some point comprised couples with no children and single people with no children (some of whom may well have been students who moved into work). The category least likely to escape was single parents with children.

Gosling et al. (1997) have used BHPS data to examine the relationship between low pay and unemployment, a crucial issue for the general description of postindustrial capitalism which is endorsed in this book. They have used data from the first four passes and note that whilst two thirds of all men aged between 18 and 60 and economically active in the sample were in full-time work continuously between 1991 and 1994, just 9 per cent were permanently unemployed during this period. In other words, nearly a quarter of men experienced episodic unemployment. So far as the relationship between wages and unemployment goes, their conclusions are unequivocal, if, as they remark, hardly surprising:

> . . . lower relative wages of individuals are associated with a higher probability that they will move out of work in the future. Among men over thirty per cent of those starting in the bottom quarter of the wage distribution spent some time out of work in the next two and a half years. This was true of just twelve per cent of those starting in the top quarter of the distribution. Similarly, looking at transitions into work 56 per cent of the men moving out of unemployment moved into a job with wages in the bottom quartile of the distribution. . . . movements into and out of work are overwhelmingly experienced by those who can obtain only rather low wages.
>
> (1997: 1–2)

Rowlingson and McKay (1998) and McKay (1998) have used BHPS data to examine the dynamics of lone parenthood. Here the crucial shifts are the entering of the condition by child bearing or break-up of partnership and leaving it by establishing a new partnership. McKay's conclusion that:

> Early lone parenthood appears not to be the result of rising labour market participation, but of growing inequality of opportunity among young women. Key factors are a disadvantaged background and low participation in education.
>
> (1998: 122)

supports the account of polarization of experience among the young argued for here.

Making it unequal: the role of postindustrial policy

Social policy as a field of academic study has traditionally been concerned with the way welfare systems distribute resources around the social structure. Sociology, and more recently geography, have had a disciplinary focus on the way in which the basal character of the social structure, by which is almost invariably meant the mode of production, however complex and qualified the description of that mode, 'determines' the character of welfare systems. Sure, there is scope for agency and contingency, hence the general interest across the social sciences in the idea of typologies of welfare regimes as originally developed by Esping-Andersen (1992). However, base is seen as determinant, even if the use of the word determine is the sophisticated version suggested by Williams (1980), that is to say the setting of limits. If the logic of welfare reform transcends the basis rules of capital accumulation, and in particular if it seeks to create equality on the one hand and challenges the notion that ownership represents a valid claim on social product on the other, then boundaries are being tested indeed.

All the above is true, but it is very far from being the whole truth. Welfare systems are not merely determined products of basal social order. There is an absolute and interactive reflexivity between the social arrangements of welfare, understood both as institutional forms and systems of distribution, and the social order. If the form of the mode of production (always capitalism, of course, but available in variants and marked by categorical transformations – changes of form which represent a difference of kind) limits and causes welfare, then welfare systems limit and cause the forms of production. Systems of welfare, understood in the broadest terms, are constitutive of the social order just as much as the arrangements of production.

With a vocabulary from chaos/complexity theory available to us, we can conceptualize the whole thing in a most useful way. We have to see mode of production as not simply the organization of the process of production. It must include all aspects of social reproduction. In chaos/complexity terms, we have a far from equilibric system defined by boundaries and constituted not by simple unidirectional causal processes, but by complex, reflexive and interactive causal processes.

The contemporary significance of the argument that social policies are constitutive lies in the ways in which a range of social policies make flexible postindustrial capitalism possible. Without them it could not be; they are fundamental to it. The development of welfare to work as an alternative to insurance-based wage substitution rights is simply the most recent, if also perhaps most important, development in a programme across the range of social policy which can best be understood as facilitating flexible postindustrialism. The implications of this new scheme will be elaborated in a moment, but a brief preliminary consideration here will illustrate the general argument.

Under principles of solidarism, as influenced by Keynesian specifications of the effective range of macro-economic policies, citizenship rights included the right to work. Note the difference between a right to work and an obligation to work. The right to work was a right to work of a kind which could be interpreted as acceptable in terms of a solidaristic definition of 'good work'. If such work was not available, and the offer of such work was the test of entitlement for those not working but fit to do so, then there was a right to wage substitution benefits paid at a solidaristic level. This remains the social/Christian democratic norm. Those in power had the task of managing the economics system so as to make work available to the potential workers. Solutions had to be demand led. Welfare to Work is supply side. The interpretation is that workers do not have work because they are defective, not morally or even rationally as was the understanding in the early nineteenth-century heyday of tutoring utilitarianism, but in terms of personal deficits. The obligation is imposed on them to redress these deficits, as a condition of benefit, in order to make themselves fit for labour. There is no specification of the conditions of that labour as having to represent 'good work'. The logic of the employment form of much of postindustrial capitalism is that the work will not be good work. However, people have to be made to do it, and in the personal services sector, which is not exportable, domestic labour (or immigrants without rights) have to be made ready to take on these tasks. Welfare to Work is a constitutive process for this.

The constitutive effects of welfare do not merely relate to the conditions and circumstances of the dispossessed. The allocation of large personal resources to the affluent through the reduction of their taxation levels is an essential precondition for the growth of the privatized consumption which is so central to postindustrial capitalism. Likewise the recasting in the UK of the form of state education away from egalitarianism and towards family-mediated individual achievement is constitutive for the differentiating processes shaping personal trajectory towards adult life. On the consumption side, the role of postindustrial planning in the shaping of differentiated urban space is another key constitutive element. Here, we have reviewed the impact of the tax system in terms of allocation of resources to the rich. In Chapter 8 we will examine the use of Speenhamland-style benefits distributed through fiscal and other systems as in sustaining poor work as a reality in postindustrial capitalism.

The new enclosure

The English Poor Law codified in the 43rd of Elizabeth of 1601 was a policy response to the problems posed for the reproduction of labour power and the maintenance of the legitimacy of the social order by the transformation of the rural economy towards a fully capitalist system of farming. This was achieved through the legal process of enclosure by which collective rights were transformed into personal property. The property of course went to the powerful, but the revenues derived from this transfer were taxed in order to provide a system of maintenance for those dispossessed by enclosure. By the late eighteenth century, technological innovations in agriculture coupled with competition from the factory system which devalued the domestic commodity production of agricultural labourers' families caused a crisis in rural social reproduction. The response was the Speenhamland system.

There is a very important parallel to be drawn between this process, what Polyani (1944) called the great transformation, and the present. Enclosure represented a massive transfer of common resources to the rich. It was legal robbery sustained by the law which: 'hangs the man and flogs the woman that steals the goose from off the common, but leaves the greater villain loose that steals the common from the goose' (Anon). The poor were emmiserated thereby: 'The affluence of the rich supposes the indigence of the many.' As Heilbroner reminds us: 'It is Adam Smith speaking, not Karl Marx' (1992: 27). The parallel with today is enormous. In 'flexible capitalism' we can see massive resource transfers to the most affluent, the capitalists and the comprador new superclass, including most politicians. This transfer is mediated not only by changes in employment and remuneration, but by taxation and benefit policies, which in combination represent a transfer of public resources on a major scale. This transfer, I am going to argue, represents a new enclosure, an appropriation of the commons for the benefit of the few at the expense of the many.

The political theory of possessive individualism was developed by Locke as a way of establishing a defined set of personal freedoms against domination by feudal and post-feudal elites. It was a revolutionary doctrine and is central to the development of modernity. It was not a doctrine founded to separate the interests of the individual from that of the community of the individual's peers. It was intended to define the freedom of the individual against the superior lord. Of course, in the Anglo–American world it became the justification precisely for elite appropriation of the commons. In Britain the elite was, ironically, drawn in large part from the old nobility and from Celtic chieftains transformed into nobles.

I am all for the reappropriation of the commons, but more immediately want to consider the revenues of tax as 'common' by an undeniably radical extension of Titmuss' idea of the fiscal component of the tripartite division of welfare (1959). Titmuss argued that a tax exemption granted to support a specific social purpose must be regarded as exactly equivalent to a direct public expenditure for any specific purpose. Forgone taxation was just as much a cost to the public revenue as any monetary expenditure funded from those revenues. Titmuss, however, confined fiscal expenditure to tax allowances which always were hypothecated, that is, had a specific and identifiable purpose. My proposal is that we should regard any cuts in taxation which apply not generally, but rather to the benefit of a particular social group, as a fiscal grant, even when these are not tied to any hypothecation. The basic understanding is that in welfare capitalism the public revenues represent the commons which are the birthright of all, and that giving up large chunks of them to the most affluent can be understood as exactly equivalent to enclosure.

This account equates a tax cut with a benefit increase so we have to examine carefully the way in which taxes and benefit interact. Treatments of the effect of taxation on the distribution of income can take two forms, that based on 'actual payments' and that based on the 'what if' approach. Goodman et al. explain the nature of these approaches and summarize their implications:

> The Jenkins (1995) study (based on the 'actual payments' approach) answers the question 'how much redistribution is the tax system doing now compared with a decade ago?' The answer to this is that it is doing about as much in the late 1980s as in the late 1970s. This is because the pre-tax distribution has become much more unequal, and so even with lower tax rates, the tax system is still doing plenty of redistribution. The Johnson and Webb study (1993) based on 'what if' approach is answering the question 'what would the post-tax distribution look like if the tax system had not been changed?', and the answer is 'much less unequal'.
>
> (1997: 206)

Hills makes the point somewhat more strongly:

> Without discretionary change, the direct tax system would have 'worked harder' and slowed the growth of inequality after 1978. In fact, substantial discretionary changes in direct tax structure have almost precisely offset the automatic effects, so that growth in inequality of post-tax incomes has matched that in gross incomes.
>
> (1995: 61)

In the United States the situation is even worse. Hills' comparative examination of income distribution led him to conclude that: 'In the USA taxes and transfers accelerated the effect of a widening distribution of market incomes: discretionary policy changes more that offset the automatic reaction to rising market inequalities' (1995: 72). This kind of development was not inevitable. In France and Canada over the same period, discretionary changes in tax and transfers operated as negative feedback and effectively cancelled out a rise in original market income inequality (Hill 1995: 72). Duncan et al., in a review of the causes of the 'shrinking middle class' in the USA, conclude that:

> . . . we consider it vital to continue to re-examine the Federal income tax and to reconsider wealth taxation – in particular capital gains taxation at time of death or transfer – as a source of meeting America's

human resource needs. Because the fruits of American economic growth are increasingly being concentrated among the privileged 10–15 per cent of the population at the top of the middle-age income and wealth distribution, serious consideration should be given to a modest sharing of this wealth.

(1993:264)

Their proposals are indeed modest. They argue for a raising of the top rate of US Federal taxation from 35 to 37 per cent and for a refundable child tax credit, of much more value to earners who pay low or no tax than an allowance. They also argue for targeted labour market policies intended to raise the qualification level of the low skilled. Their reference to wealth is of considerable importance. Reduction in wealth taxes in both the UK and the USA have made the inheritance of position and privilege even more important as a determinant of life trajectory at the upper end of the income scale.

It is salutary to consider the Institute for Fiscal Studies' conclusion as to the overall impact of New Labour's redistribution to date:

> Our analysis suggests that the redistributive measures of the present government have reduced the increase in inequality that we would otherwise have seen. But it is sobering to note that even the relatively large redistributive programme introduced by Labour since 1997 has only been sufficient to just about halt the growth in inequality, and certainly not to reduce it. The orders of magnitude involved are also instructive: the tax and benefit measures introduced under Labour have lowered the growth in the Gini coefficient by around 1.5 percentage points; this compares with the total increase in income inequality over the 1980s and 1990s (up to its peak in 2000/01) of around 10 percentage points, or around six times the magnitude.

(IFS 2004)

The reduction in the taxation of the affluent is a key factor in the reduction of the level of services in kind across the board. There are arguments that the absolute level of such services has been maintained, at least as measured by real expenditure upon them, but this is not the general public perception. That perception is of a decline in relation both to overall national income and in relation to need. Certainly, this is the general experience in relation to services provided in the UK by local government. This matters for two reasons. First, the provision of public services in kind is an important universalizing measure. The other side of public services is that they represent an alternative form of job creation to the traditional Keynesian macro focus of industrial production, which is now far less effective because of the combined effect of productivity gains and internationalization of production, and meso focus of infrastructure public works, again now far less job rich because of productivity gains. Social value derives from workers in health, social care, education and a range of other public services.

Cuts in higher tax rates reduce or eliminate the prospect for the employment in the public service, where there remains a trade union-based capacity for defence to some degree of the conditions, if not remuneration of work. The affluent are left free to spend on themselves alone and do so in the growing sector of postindustrial services, many of which are the products of privatization of the public sphere. The situation of workers in that sector is much worse than that of public employees.

In Poland, it is clear that large-scale tax evasion in the informal sector is a major element in the development of income inequalities, but there is a special problem which is typical of the experiences of post-Communist societies. In Poland in general and in Upper Silesia in particular, many public services were provided in whole or in part by enterprises. This was not uniquely Communist. It was in fact quite characteristic of carboniferous capitalism in general, in Western Europe as well. Even if the enterprises have not closed, as many have, they no longer are necessarily either directly providing or paying for public services of all kinds, including health clinics, social welfare services, subsidies to technical education, and recreational facilities.

Inglot notes of the restructuring period in Poland that: 'we witnessed an unprecedented expansion of social expenditure in proportion to the Gross Domestic Product' (1995: 362). Between 1989 and 1992, social expenditure doubled as a proportion of GDP. In particular, expenditure on pensions was increased in response to political pressure, with pensions being used as a way of easing the pain of industrial contraction. In general the post-Communist history of transfer payments in Poland demonstrated the then significance of real political pressures from below, which in any event accord with the actual, if somewhat undeveloped theoretically, solidaristic ideologies of the main political forces in the country. However, now things have changed dramatically. The 2004 fall of the Miller government, a government nominally of the centre-left, illustrates exactly the problem facing government in the neo-liberal and globalized world. The government fell over the issue of cuts in public spending designed to achieve a reduction in the overall budgetary deficit. Effectively, Poland was subject to what by third-world standards is a relatively mild social adjustment programme, but which has proved very unpalatable to the Polish public. The instability of contemporary Polish politics demonstrates exactly the common European dilemma of the contradiction between the task neo-liberalism asserts the logic the market imposes on governments and the political demands of electorates, which remain strongly collectivist in political belief and desires.

So we have unequal societies which are becoming more unequal. Social exclusion follows that as night follows day.

6

Divided spaces: social division in the postindustrial city

This chapter will examine the development and actual forms of socio-spatial division in contemporary postindustrial societies. As before, this examination will include consideration of the significance of class, gender and age. Here, we will have to think of class not only as some kind of uni-dimensional attribute derived from income or occupation, but instead as something which is expressed through spatial residence itself. We need to consider, not just nominalist attributes, but the reality of emergent social forms which are spatial in character. Spatial concentration of levels in the social hierarchy generates spatially distinctive cultural forms, especially when spatial concentration means that there is little social contact among the levels of the social order. If 'cultures of poverty' do exist, spatial concentration is a key element in their generation.

> . . . today's 'underclass' . . . inhabit a space characterized by a deficit of economic, social and cultural regulation. In such spaces older organized capitalist social structures – industrial labour market, church and family networks, social welfare institutions, trade unions – have dissolved or at least moved out . . . unlike the spaces of the city centres and the suburbs they have not been replaced by the information and communicative structure.
>
> (Lash and Urry 1994: 8)

Marcuse (1989) challenged the notion that there is a simple bipolar space with two separate kinds of social order within cities, but there is good empirical evidence to suggest that Lash and Urry are quite right in their general description of the emergent character of socio-spatial systems in postindustrial cities (see Byrne 1995, 1997, 1998). Their account fits very well with the idea of a bifurcation; the torus style space of the Fordist city (see Esser and Hirsch 1994) has become something qualitatively different with two very different types of social experience predicated on distinctive areas of residence. It is true, as Hamnett (2003) demonstrates, that there is a large and significant middle class, particularly in the core global cities. However, we have to ask ourselves is this middle class really very distinctive from the old 'aristocracy of labour' blue-collar working class of the industrial era? What is evident is that there is a mass of poor people and a mass of poor work. To the traditional dichotomy of blue-collar manual and white-collar non-manual workers, we must add the new collar colour of 'pink' – a useful way of defining the mass of personnel service, catering and related employees with low wages and poor working conditions. Pink collar equates with 'poor work'.

Wacquant (1999) proposed that the generative mechanism driving polarization has four dimensions. These were 'a macro-social drift towards inequality', 'the mutation of wage labor with both deproletarianization and casualization', 'the retrenchment of welfare states', and 'the spatial concentration and stigmatization of poverty'. Here it will be argued that rather than 'deproletarianization' an important component is 'proletarianization' as professional, para-professional and relatively secure public-sector worker groups become subordinated to managerial control and worsening of wages and conditions through privatization. We have to understand urban policies as drivers, not only of socio-spatial polarization, but also of the whole new globalized neo-liberal social order. Moreover, the complexity perspective which informs the argument of this book should always remind us that change is never the product of one process in isolation but rather results from the whole complex and interactive resultant of factors operating together. Indeed, the very specification of discrete elements may be overly analytical. However, with that caveat, we can certainly see increasing income inequality, the attack on the welfare state, the reduction in the power of workers as against capitalists in the domain of employment, and the character of urban planning and governance, as causal to the contemporary polarization which characterizes postindustrial urban space.

There is of course nothing new about the notion that cities are divided. Engels recognized the separateness of spatial life between the middle classes and the industrial proletariat in the Manchester of the mid-nineteenth century. However, the general tendency of the working-class project of respectability was towards the achievement of a social and spatial system in which, whilst inequality continued, its absolute range was much reduced and there were no dramatic and discontinuous breaks in the socio-spatial structure. The ideal-type of the urban for this project was represented by the British new towns of the 1950s, but in general in metropolitan capitalism, with the single but enormously important exception of the black American ghetto, socio-spatial systems under Fordism were much less polarized than ever before. That is not the case now. We can see this using multi-variate measurements of the character of social space. We can appreciate it from qualitative interpretative research. Callaghan (1998) has shown how detailed knowledge of the socio-spatial divisions of an industrial city forms a crucial part of the repertoire of everyday knowledge of those who live in that city. We utilize it in the practices of our everyday life.

There are two interesting aspects of socio-spatial division. The first is that, in contrast to division as expressed through household income, there is a rather sharp break located in the bottom half of the social order. With income, the rich are separate from the rest of us. With space, it is the poor who are separated off. Spatial exclusion is the most visible and evident form of exclusion. We know the 'ghetto' estates of the cities in which we live. The second is that there is a double dynamic of space. The first dynamic, scarcely researched at all in the new project of dynamic empiricism, is the actual movement of households around social space, and in particular from the spaces of dispossession to those that are 'normal', and from the 'normal' to the spaces of dispossession. Indeed, the actual expression of social mobility in terms of consumption is most marked precisely by change in area of residence. Callaghan's respondents (1998) envisaged their life courses as trajectories over time through the different residential spaces of the city in which they lived.

This is important because spatial location determines access to crucial social goods, in particular to different kinds of state education, which matter for future life trajectory. In other words, housing is not merely the largest element of privatized consumption and a crucial demarcator of lifestyle; for most of us, where we live determines what sort of schooling our children get and that determines much of their future life course. It is also extremely important for health, especially paediatric health. We will explore the implications of this in Chapter 7.

The other dynamic trajectory is that of the character of social spaces themselves. The transition from the industrial to the postindustrial is associated both with gentrification of inner city working-class neighbour-hoods, and in the UK and France with a transformation of social housing from being the zone of residence of the organized working class to its being the zone of residence of the poor and poorly employed. Space is not merely a demarcator with regard to social exclusion. A very considerable part of public policy in Europe has been directed through space by being targeted on spatially defined 'communities' and particular blocks of land with a view to the regeneration of land and the reintegration (and sometimes, in rhetoric at least, the empowerment) of the people resident on that land. The trajectories of spaces are determined by urban policies in interaction with the effects of other social policies. The evidence is that urban regeneration, far from reintegrating and empowering the dispossessed poor, has in general made their situation worse. Exclusive development is meant to exclude, after all.

The social implications of concentrated exclusion relate to the idea of 'community' (a term which for reasons that will become apparent will always be in inverted commas in this chapter). 'Community' matters not just because it is the key collective identity constituted through space, but also because 'community' development has been the only strategy of empowerment attempted, however half-heartedly and sometimes with a view to disempowerment rather than empowerment, in the whole repertoire of anti-exclusion policy. Gough makes a pertinent point in the regulation theory tradition in relation to this aspect of public policy. Neo-liberalism in the raw is intensely socially divisive. This is not just a matter of the generation of long-term social disorder. Raw neo-liberalism provokes opposition. What we might call mediated neo-liberalism, with its emphasis on community, may, as Gough puts it: 'achieve the essential aims of neo-liberalism better than "pure" neo-liberalism itself' (2002: 405). This will be a crucial point for consideration in Chapter 8, when we examine public policy initiatives directed, at least nominally, 'against exclusion'.

Having described space, and the dynamics of space in terms of the intimately associated processes of gentrification and residualization, we will examine the limited evidence available on the actual micro dynamics of people and households within space. Here, we will pay particular attention to the ways in which people use spatial relocation as a way of accessing collective consumption which is crucial for their own and their children's future life courses and to the related significance of space as consumption badge. We will also consider the far from trivial significance of space as immediate determinant of employment opportunities.

Finally, we will review the constitutive role of social policies in the creation of excluding and dispossessing space *and* the significance of urban policy processes as a crucial factor in 'political exclusion'. This latter element matters both in relation to a critique of 'anti-exclusionary policies' – the substance of Chapter 8, and in setting the terms on which a different kind of anti-exclusionary politics might be founded – the substance of Chapter 9 of this book.

Divided cities – the reality

Two sets of studies which have used numerical taxonomy for dynamic exploration over time in particular cities are my own examinations of Northern Tyneside and Teesside (see Byrne and Parson 1983; Byrne 1989, 1995) and the examination of the classical locus of urban social ecology, Chicago, by Morenoff and Tienda (1997). They found considerable social polarization, understood as a process which happens over time. In particular, transitional working-class neighbourhoods, which comprised 45 per cent of all census tracts in 1970, formed only 14 per cent of such tracts in 1990 (1997: 67). Hispanic immigration had modified the social ecology of Chicago, with concentration of Hispanics leading to the transition of many stable middle-class neighbourhoods to the transitional working-class category. In Chicago 'underclass' neighbourhoods were overwhelmingly (90 per cent on average) black.

Much of the scepticism about the idea of 'dual cities' has come from a largely justified critique of the over-simplistic application of the idea to 'world cities' (see Hamnett 1994). However, actual narratives of the history of socio-spatial systems over the transition to postindustrialism, whether quantitative or qualitative or both, across almost all advanced industrial cities, whatever the 'welfare regime' within which they are embedded, demonstrate social polarization. As Fainstein and Harloe note in their comparison of London and New York: 'similar economic processes have been accompanied by similar socio-spatial outcomes despite quite different political and institutional traditions' (1992: 2). We find this in British industrial cities, in Dublin (see Byrne 1984; Bartley 1998), Paris (Wacquant 1993), Chicago, New York, London and in Poland, in Katowice and Lodz (Byrne and Wodz 1997; Grolowska-Leder and Warzyswoda-Kruszjuska 1997). Fainstein et al. remarked that:

> If the concept of a 'dual' or 'polarizing' city is of any real utility, it can serve only as a hypothesis, the prelude to empirical analysis, rather than as a conclusion which takes the existence of confirmatory evidence for granted.
>
> (1992: 13)

The evidence is now overwhelming. It does not show that all postindustrial cities are polarized. It shows that they are polarizing, and that those which are fully subject to liberalizing postindustrial capitalism are polarized.

Hamnett (1996) argued that to see socio-spatial polarization as an inevitable consequence of economic restructuring is to neglect the significance of different welfare regimes. Madanipour et al. concurred:

> Urban socio-spatial structures vary. In some social exclusion and spatial segregation are virtually synonymous. Others exhibit a more fine-grained pattern of differentiation. In some places, ethnicity and race form fundamental dividing lines in socio-spatial structures. In other places, culture and kinship networks are more significant. Finally, specific patterns of local governance and welfare state provision affect local patterns of social exclusion.
>
> (1998: 8–9)

This ought to be true, but the reality is that existing variation seems to be much more a function of the different rates of progression of flexible globalization than of anything else. Here Smith (2002) demonstrates a fundamental distinction between industrial and postindustrial capitalism. He argues that in the cities of the industrial era the dominating systemic logic was that of social reproduction – of the organization of urban governance and the city in general towards the reproduction of labour power. In contrast, in the 'revanchist' postindustrial city the dominating systemic logic is the realization of profits from processes of urban development, and this is global reality across urban space. There is much to be said for this and MacLeod (2002) provides an excellent illustration of the logic in practice in Glasgow. However, systems do not operate in and of themselves. They require agents. Moreover, the general tendency is at least as much a matter of ideological hegemony as of inevitable systemic tendency. It is a consequence of policy choices as these interact with market forces. Actors make it happen, but actors in different places are acting in the same way.

Race/ethnicity and exclusion through space

There seems to be only one uniquely ethnic element in socio-spatial exclusion in metropolitan capitalism. This is the ghettoization of black citizens in the USA, generated by the racism derived from the history of chattel slavery; the continuing reality of ethnic segregation to a unique and intense degree of black from white Americans. Massey and Denton defined the situation in these terms:

> . . . racial residential segregation is the principal structural feature of American society responsible for the perpetuation of urban poverty and represents a primary cause of racial inequality in the US. . . . black segregation is not comparable to the limited and transient segregation experienced by other racial and ethnic groups, now or in the past. No group in the history of the US has ever experienced the high level of residential segregation that has been imposed on blacks in large American cities in the past fifty years. This extensive racial isolation did not just happen; it was manufactured by whites through a series of self-conscious actions and purposeful institutional arrangements that continue today. Not only is the depth of black segregation unprecedented and utterly unique compared with that of other groups, but it shows little sign of change with the passage of time or improvement in socio-economic status.
>
> (1993: 2)

Wacquant's comparison of the black American ghetto and the French urban periphery illustrates the uniqueness of the US situation very well. He noted that:

> . . . the colour line of which the black ghetto is the most visible institutional expression is so ingrained in the make up of the American urban landscape that it has become part of the order of things: racial division is a thoroughly taken for granted constituent of the organization of the metropolitan economy, society and polity. . . . the French banlieue remains a heterogeneous universe in which racial or ethnic categories have little social potency.
>
> (1993: 373–5)

In metropolitan capitalism, the French situation is the norm, although it may be a norm under challenge. A leaked French intelligence agency report formed the background to a *Guardian* story headlined 'Almost 2 million living in France's angry ghettos' (6 July 2004). This report did not simply comment on the social exclusion of such places – largely *banlieue* containing large immigrant originating populations – but noted their 'Islamicization', associated with white flight of those parts of the European-descended population who could afford to leave. In the wake of September 11th, this sort of polarization has considerable implications for security agencies, hence the report.

If anything, evidence from the UK shows that with two significant exceptions and the possible development of a third, the saliency of race/ethnicity is even less than Wacquant considered it to be in France. The evidence here comes from the series of studies carried out on the small area data available from the 1991 Census. Preliminary results from the 2001 Census confirm that this continues to be the case and there is a continuing lessening of ethnic concentration, although this remains very important. This data shows that there are series of ethnicities with very different social relations surrounding them. Indeed, those who identify as black are the least separated from the UK white population, as Peach (1997: 23) indicates in the passage already quoted in Chapter 5.

At the socio-spatial level, the important point is that with the exception of the situation of Bangladeshis in the East End of London in particular, but also in other UK cities (see Cameron and Field 2000), and Catholics in working-class urban Northern Ireland, there is no evidence of the existence of constrained ghettos (see Peach 1996). 'Black' British and Afro-Caribbean people are found in all social locations in UK cities, although they may have areas of relative concentration. People of South Asian origin are (with the exception of constrained Bangladeshi social housing estates) less likely to live in social housing, where there is evidence of a pattern of racial hostility towards them. However, there is no evidence of racial exclusion from middle-class neighbourhoods. This is a contradictory situation. 'Other than white' and 'other than black' ethnic minorities are spatially excluded, but only from the residualized and excluded locales. This matters because spatial segregation is so crucial for general social exclusion. As Massey and Denton remark:

> Because of racial segregation, a significant share of black America is condemned to experience a social environment where poverty and joblessness are the norm, where most families are on welfare, where educational failure prevails, and where social and physical deterioration abound.
>
> (1993: 2)

The significance of spatial segregation for social exclusion in the UK is immense, but, other than in the North of Ireland and for Bangladeshis, the fundamental principle of this segregation has been class, not ethnicity. The UK and the USA are the most neo-liberal of postindustrial advanced capitalist societies, but they are at opposite extremes, with the UK being the least and the USA the most ethnically segregated. Here, we do have a specific impact of a local factor – the US history of racialized chattel slavery. That said, the position of Bangladeshis is important and interesting. Likewise, there is evidence from UK locales with very high concentrations of Muslim populations originating in Pakistan for a developing ghettoization of the form that so concerns France's security agencies. This is particularly the case in towns in East Lancashire and in the city of Bradford, where dispossessed working-class Asian populations – dispossessed from the textile employment; which they were imported to undertake – are increasingly segregated from white working-class people by spatial area. This is not yet ghettoization, but it is beginning to look something like it. It also provides the basis for fascist political activity directed at white dispossessed working-class hostility expressed through a form of 'double closure' (Parkin 1979). In double closure, there is hostility directed upwards at 'superior' and exploiting groups and downwards at 'inferior' and excluding groups. That said, there is a high degree of local specificity to this process of segregation and there is little evidence for it outside Lancashire and West Yorkshire, although a careful examination of 2001 Census data, which is just becoming available, is plainly necessary to assess the overall extent of the phenomenon.

Poland, after the Holocaust and Stalin's reconstruction of European geography, is on the face of things an ethnically homogeneous society in which more than 97 per cent of the people are Polish Catholics. However, there are some quasi-ethnic differences, the most interesting of which for us is the distinction in Upper Silesia between autochthonous Silesians and post-World War II immigrants from elsewhere in Poland. Both groups are Slav and Catholic and have historically asserted a Polish national identity. However, in a series of studies, Wodz shows that the segregation of autochthonous Silesians in older workers' settlements, the *familioks*, and the very strong commitment of Silesians to a highly proletarianized culture of heavy industrial employment, may lead to this group being particularly disadvantaged by the processes of deindustrialization. These are exceptionally severe in this most industrialized of all Central European regions (Wodz 1994). Wodz places very considerable emphasis on the socio-spatial differentiation of the Katowice conurbation, which is in large part an almost accidental product of the phases of industrialization. Certainly, the intensely proletarianized autochthonous Silesians, who together with their near neighbours, the Czech and East German working classes, are really the only groups to have experienced both capitalist and Soviet industrialization, are 'ripe' for dispossession. This process is already under way through coal mine closure.

Gender and exclusion through space

There is a considerable and interesting literature on gender and space, but it seldom deals with the role of gender as a principle for segregation in residential space. Given the continuing predominance of heterosexual couples as the bases of households, gender segregation in residence is essentially a function of the spatial segregation of female-headed single-parent households. In the United States examinations of the phenomenon are inextricably bound up with considerations of different familial patterns by ethnic group. However, in the UK ethnicity is not the principal concomitant of single parenthood. On the contrary, the last 20 years have seen a massive increase in single parenthood, particularly among the overwhelmingly dominant autochthonous white UK population. In 1971, 8 per cent of families with children were headed by a lone parent. By 1994, 23 per cent of families with children were headed by a lone parent (Rowlingson and McKay 1998: 3). The 2001 Census shows that this figure has stabilized, with 22 per cent of families with dependent children being headed by a lone parent at that point.

Socio-spatial studies of divided cities show that whilst there is by no means an absolute segregation of lone parent-headed households, such households form a much larger proportion of all households with dependent children in the poorer halves of divided cities than they do in the affluent halves. For example, in 1991 in Cleveland and Leicester the proportions of all households headed by lone parents in the poorer halves of those urban areas were 28 per cent and 29 per cent respectively. In the affluent halves of both cities, the equivalent figure was 7 per cent in both cases (Byrne 1997: 62). All socio-spatial classifications of urban areas in the UK reveal a similar pattern. The origins of this pattern lie in the way in which households gain access to housing. The financial advantage that attaches to the owner occupation of dwellings means that since the early 1960s UK households that can afford to buy their own homes have generally sought to do so. This does not mean that all owner-occupiers live in the better halves of cities. The tenure is now so dominant that it contains a wide variety of housing, including some formerly privately rented older stock in the poorer half of divided cities.

The spatial segregation of single parent-headed households derives from their relative concentration outwith the owner-occupied housing stock and within social housing rented from local authorities or housing associations. Whereas three-quarters of couple households are owner occupiers, this is the case for less than one-third of single parents (Ford and Miller 1998: 16). This concentration results from the poverty of single parents, who are not excluded from access to social housing by low income but cannot afford to buy. It also reflects the dynamics of social housing in the UK over the 80-year lifetime of this tenure as a significant part of the general housing stock.

Social housing on a mass scale was originally built for the respectable working class, not for the poor. Indeed, the most important differentiation which operated in relation to it, right up until the 1970s, was not between it and other tenures but within it between those estates built under slum clearance legislation for the poor and those built to deal with general housing needs, usually to a much higher quality, which were a key location of the central working class (see Merrett 1979). This has changed in the last 20 years. First, much of the best social housing has been sold off into

owner–occupation through tenant purchase. Second, new couple households with reasonable incomes have considerable financial and social
incentives to purchase housing rather than rent it. The result is that much of
the social housing stock, particularly in cities other than London, is now
occupied by a mix of elderly people continuing to live in the family home
of their adult lives, people in couple households with low or no wages, and
single parents. Burrows (1999) shows how the movement of people into
and out of social housing reinforces the residualized character of this tenure.
The households leaving the sector are more likely to be relatively affluent,
employed, those aged 30–44, and couples with dependent children. Those
entering the sector are differentially likely to be poor, non-employed, aged
under 29, and single parents.

There is considerable dynamic movement between the household form
based on the poor couple/single parenthood. Single parents form new
unions. Single-parent households are formed by the break-up of couples.
The difference in marriage/cohabitation rates between the two halves of
the divided cities is of great significance here. In the typical and reasonably
prosperous UK city of Leicester, I found that in the poorer third of the city
less than half of all registered births were registered by married parents,
whereas in the more affluent two-thirds more than 90 per cent of births
were registered by married parents. Most births were registered by both
parents, but in the poorer parts of this divided city more births were
registered by two parents who were not married than by two parents who
were married.

It is conventional to comment on the strain imposed on couplehood by
the insecurity and low level of male wages for unskilled workers, a vastly
more significant challenge to the conventional family form than any change
in the character of sexual morality. In the concentration of single parents
in UK social housing, we are seeing the result of three dynamic processes.
First, and quantitatively the least significant, we see the consequence of the
housing of poor, young, benefit-dependent, never married mothers. Second,
we see the consequence of the downward drift of divorcees from couple
households in owner occupation who have lost their owner-occupied
dwelling on divorce for financial reasons. Third, we see the ongoing
dynamic movement from couple to single to couple to single and so on by
households. This is in aggregate a function of the wage and labour relations
of the dispossessed poor, whatever the contingent circumstances relating to
each individual household dissolution or formation.

Age and social exclusion through space

Now I want to examine the spatial significance of age separations, or
more precisely to consider the position of the young. Let me quote from
Wacquant, whose observation about the Parisian suburbs echoes absolutely

in relation to my own considerable (more than 25 years') experience as a community worker and inner city councillor in the north-east of England:

> If there is a dominant antagonism which runs through the Red Belt cité and stamps the collective consciousness of its inhabitants, it is not, contrary to widespread media representations, one that opposes immigrants (especially 'Arabs') and autochthonous French families but the cleavage dividing youth (les jeunes), native and foreign lumped together, for all other social categories. Youths are widely singled out by older residents as the chief source of vandalism, delinquency and insecurity, and they are publicly held up as responsible for worsening condition, and reputation of the degraded banlieue.
>
> (1993: 376)

Traditionally, these criticisms have been directed against male youths, but young women do also figure. Again New Labour has a specific innovative policy – ASBOs – Anti-Social-Behaviour Orders. Although these can be directed against people of any age, the prime target has been the young. An ASBO is a civil procedure requiring only the balance of probabilities level of civil proof. However, breach of an ASBO is a criminal offence and can be punished by up to five years' imprisonment. The logic behind ASBOs, coupled with a range of other initiatives, including the eviction of households from municipal and other social housing on the grounds of misbehaviour by some or all of the household members, is that of negative feedback. They are control mechanisms which seek to regulate the behaviour of the 'disorderly' young and to eliminate sources of disorder from particular social spaces. The imagery behind the ASBOs is a mix of the 'bad apple' which destroys a whole 'good' community and the 'stitch in time saves nine' logic of early deterrent intervention. They are always presented as targeted on a minority, especially a minority of the young, but youth workers have commented that they often seem to criminalize the normal early to mid-teenage behaviour of hanging around on street corners.

Communities?

Let us now consider the nature of social relations in the spaces of dispossession. In his examination of Red Belt cités, Wacquant reiterates a point made by Damer in an earlier study (1989). We are seriously in error if we treat locales like Glasgow's Wine Alley as internally undifferentiated. For those who live there, they are micro socio-spatial systems with a complex internal structure. It is the outward labelling that matters in relation to overall social location and social exclusion.

> . . . residents of the French cité and the American ghetto each form an *impossible community* [original emphasis], perpetually divided against themselves, which cannot but refuse to acknowledge the collective

nature of their predicament and who are therefore inclined to deploy strategies of distancing and 'exit' that tend to validate negative outside perceptions and feed a deadly self-fulfilling prophecy through which public taint and collective disgrace eventually produce that which they claim merely to record: namely social atomism, community 'disorganization' and cultural anomie.

(Wacquant 1993: 374)

Here, I want to examine the emergent social forms that derive from the common residence of people in excluded space. There are two terms which are used in discussing these, terms which are different but have a considerable degree of intersection. These are 'community' and 'culture'. 'Community' is a tricky word in every sense. Crowe and Allan (1994) note that although the term originally had a clear spatial referent, it is now being used to identify 'communities of interest' without a spatial basis. One of the most useful definitions was that given in 1944 by Glass when she distinguished between neighbourhoods which were simply people living in an area and experiencing the same things, from 'communities' which were conscious of the communality which derived from common spatial experience and were willing to act communally. The parallel with Marx's distinction between class in and for itself is clear. Here we are dealing with spatial 'communities', although the identification of specific 'communities' is much more likely to be a function of arbitrary dictat by administrative powers than to be the product of autonomous social action. At the same time, Wacquant's account of the atomized nature of social relations in excluded spaces, an account which argues against the existence of a clear coherent collective identity of interest *and* action, rings absolutely true. A turn to a consideration of the nature of culture may help us to understand this contradiction.

The most recent exponent of the idea of an emergent cultural differentiation of the poor is Wilson, although he explicitly disowns the term 'culture of poverty'. Wilson makes it clear that he is concerned with the 'ghetto poor' of the deindustrializing cities of the US frostbelt (1992). As Rose has pointed out, the Wilson thesis relates the micro level of neighbourhood to the macro level of economic forces through asserting that conditions in the one are a result of changes in the other (1991: 491–2). For Wilson, the primary causal process is deindustrialization, but he argues that this may create social situations through spatial segregation which lead to the reproduction of a new cultural order. Hence Wilson's concern about the single-parent headed family and the absence of successful middle-class black role models. Wilson sees the social atomization described by Wacquant as part of a cultural form. We might go further by employing a specifically dynamic view and see the antagonism between youth and elders as representing an emergent tendency, with the youth attitudes being at least the basis of the new culture. Note that the emergent culture is not constructed around spatially ordered solidarities. It is highly individualistic and self-centred.

Wilson and Wacqant's accounts of atomization are very different both from reactionary 'Calvinistic' blaming of the poor and from the rather optimistic original version of the culture of poverty proposed by the personally radical Lewis (1966). Harvey and Reed argue that:

> . . . the virtue of Lewis' thesis lies in the clarity with which it demonstrates that poverty's subculture is not a mere 'tangle of pathology', but consists, instead, of a set of *positive adaptive mechanisms* [original emphasis]. These adaptive mechanisms are socially constructed, that is, collectively fabricated by the poor from the substance of their everyday lives, and they allow the poor to survive in otherwise impossible material and social conditions . . . Unlike other explanations of poverty, it concedes that the poor have been damaged by the system but insists that this damage does not disqualify them from determining their own fate. This last judgement is something many social scientists of both the left and right have forgotten.
>
> (1996: 466)

This is an important point, especially when associated with Reed and Harvey's insistence on the development of a class-based politics of poverty. Both Reed and Harvey's and Wilson's accounts are class analyses. Wilson has asserted strongly, and in my view appropriately, that he writes as a social democrat. However, his account is one of absolute disempowerment, of disintegration under the conditions of externally mediated industrial restructuring, and of a social restructuring towards individualistic and anomic de-collectivized response to the impacts of such changes. There is a thesis of culture, but of disabling culture as a product of basal change. My own account of Teesside (1995) is broadly similar, as is Wacquant's of Chicago and Paris.

In contrast, Reed and Harvey, after Lewis, assert that the separate social identity of the poor can be a resource for collective action. Lewis's own work provides good evidence for this, although Harvey's (1993) study of white poverty in the mid-West describes collective strategies for survival rather than transformation. However, the point is important. Difference is not always disadvantageous. There is a complex argument here which hinges around the articulation of social and economic relations between the poor/excluded and the 'core' working class (although, as Reed and Harvey note, in an era of flexible employment that status is contingent for many of us). Here, we need to note that collective situation when recognized as such can be the basis of constructive collective action and equally note that such a situation will only produce collectivity if there is some degree of personal permanence in it.

Let me summarize this complicated but important argument. There are three versions of the cultural position of the poor. The first is that of those who blame the poor for their poverty. Even when there is a recognition of the historical construction of different social practices, the poor are blamed for their continued participation in this deviance. This argument holds little water in relation to, for example, the massive growth in non-marital parent-hood in the UK. This fits exactly with the second account, essentially Wilson's account, in which the combined effects of deindustrialization and socio-spatial segregation have engendered a new, atomized, and dis-organized deviant culture which exists because the poor are constrained into such a cultural form. For Lewis and for Reed and Harvey, the cultural forms of the poor are certainly a product of structural social relations which exclude and dispossess them, but they may represent a real resource for future social action. Freire would certainly agree with that proposition, and it will serve us here as a note towards the discussion in Chapter 9.

Traditional discussions of 'community' always emphasize not merely shared space but continued and long-term temporal stability. 'Com-munities' are made up of people who live together for a long time. I am actually deeply suspicious of the notion of absolute temporal stability even in the most remote rural locations. Urban 'communities' have a very high degree of spatial mobility into and out of them and always have had. What are the spatial dynamics of people in urban space in the postindustrial city? There are no micro studies I am aware of that actually document such mobility in detail, but we do have some gross aggregate data descriptions of movement derived from administrative records, census data and some *ad hoc* studies.

In Cramlington in the late 1980s, I found that the rates of household mobility from both 'difficult to let' estates and from ordinary owner-occupied areas were very high, with annual turnovers in excess of 20 per cent (see Byrne 1989b). Plainly, some households would stay put for a long time but many moved. Indeed, I found from administrative records that there was a quite substantial movement from ordinary areas into the difficult to let estates which derived from both marital break-ups and job loss. Like-wise, there was some less good evidence of movement out of the difficult to let estates back to owner occupation. There is a real need for studies of spatial movement through time. All the available impressionistic, anecdotal, and fairly minimal, flow studies suggest that this dynamic is an important part of people's life courses. A key problem for area-centred 'inclusion' policies which focus on the changing of individuals, usually through some programme of training, is that in atomized and anomic locales such people use the wages which training may bring them to get out.

This relates to one of the commonest observations made by residents of deprived and dispossessed spaces in describing their relations with the labour market. Wacquant's respondents in the Parisian *banlieue*, and people in the Chicago projects, residents of the Meadowell in North Tyneside and other UK 'outer estates', all assert that residence as signified by address operates as a basis for discrimination against them when they are seeking employment. They are badged by the space they occupy and that matters a good deal as a basis for excluding closure.

Making excluding space: the role of social policies

There are three sets of policies which promote exclusion through space. The first are those policies which, whilst not in any way spatial in inherent form, do have spatially differentiating consequences. Hamnett (1997) has written pertinently about the spatial impact of reduced higher levels of taxation in cancelling out the redistributive effects of regional policies. The same goes even more strongly in relation to intra-urban income distribution.

The second consists of those policies that provide differential social benefits on a spatial basis and thereby affect future life chances. By far the most important of these is the operation of public schooling systems. Massey and Denton (1993) and Bankston and Caldas (1996) have examined the enormous significance of ethnic segregation in the USA. Together with Rogers (Byrne and Rogers 1996), I examined the pattern of school success in relation to the social character of its spatially defined catchment area for England. The results of such studies all indicate that in general the character of schools reflects the character of the areas from which the children in them come. There are emergent properties (see Byrne 1998, Chapter 7) which derive from the interactions among children and socio- spatial location that have a profound effect on educational attainment. This matters a great deal, both in terms of inherent effect and because it leads to an atomized and family-only programme of action by people. They seek to get the best for their children, in the UK often by using 'parental choice' to insert their children into schools in 'better' areas (see Brown 1995, Byrne and Rogers 1996).

The third set of spatial policies that matter in relation to exclusion are those which constitute the form of socio-spatial systems. It is important to remember that these cannot be understood simply as reactive to the transition from an industrial to postindustrial system. On the contrary, they have played a crucial part in that very transition. Madanipour et al. (1998) note that we cannot understand the development of cities unless we understand the complex processes of public and private governance which manage the planning process. Here the words public and private must always be understood as containing a double meaning. They refer to both the public and private as spheres, that is to government and to private capital. They also refer to the actual conduct of processes of determination, to the public mode of democracy and the 'private' mode of corporatism. In contemporary cities much of the process of governance of urban space is conducted in private in a corporatist mode. In the UK an effort has been made in City Challenge and in its successor 'Single Regeneration Budget' to include 'communities' in this process through incorporated representative, but Geddes (1997) shows that such 'community' participation is at best confined to matters of the management of details of implementation and never has an influence on strategy where global imperatives of development are taken as a given. These instances matter a great deal both in substantive content and because they show us the actual exclusion from power which is a crucial part of social exclusion as a general process. Eversley's (1990) bitter condemnation of the direction of modern planning was exactly accurate. What we have seen with catalytic planning (see Byrne 2001) is the shaping of space to be unequal.

Swyngedouw et al.'s review of large-scale European Urban Development Projects (UDPs) demonstrates that these:

> . . . accentuate socio-economic polarization through the working of real-estate markets (price rises) and displacement of social or low income housing [and] changes in the priorities of public budgets that are increasingly redirected from social objectives to investments in the built environment and the restructuring of the labor [*sic*] market.
>
> (2002: 542–3)

These authors devote particular attention the actual non-democratic mode of governance of such projects and the extent to which popular participation in them is at best a matter of second-order consultation on details of implementation and far more often a mere façade to legitimize the way in which state revenues and processes are used to assist the realization of profits by development capital and capitalists. This is of particular significance because it means that the mass of people are systematically excluded from anything other than a symbolic role in the determination of urban futures. They identify the processes of specification and implementation of UDPs as dominated by elites outwith the normal processes of democratic government. This is governance by 'urban regimes'.

Swyngedouw et al. are very firm in their assertion that:

> Urban projects of this kind are . . . not the mere result, response, or consequence of political and economic change choreographed elsewhere. On the contrary, we argue that such UDPs are the very catalysts of urban and political change, fuelling processes that are felt not only locally, regionally, nationally and internationally as well. It is such concrete interventions that express and shape transformations in spatial, political and economic configurations. . . . UDPs are productive of and embody processes that operate in and over a variety of scales, from the local to the regional, the nation, the European, and the global.
>
> (2002: 546)

In other words, as with taxation and benefit policies, urban policies *and* processes must not be understood as caused by anonymous systemic globalization. They are causal to social change – constitutive in their own right. And here, in contrast with policies affecting the distribution of income per se, we can see raw power *excluding* the mass of people from any real power in urban affairs. We will return to this theme in Chapter 8.

In general, urban regeneration schemes, typified by the UK Urban Development Corporations, have been primarily about the regeneration of land. Indeed, in the UDC programme social development was specifically dismissed as an actual objective of policy. At best, benefits were to trickle down. The story of the impact of 'growth coalitions' on United States cities, including the archetype of Baltimore, is exactly similar. Fitch's *The Assassination of New York* (1993) explains the current state of the city in terms of the planning ideologies, interests and actions of the 'Finance, Insurance and Real Estate' (FIRE) elite who have dominated its planning processes. For Fitch, 'postindustrial' New York is a 'mutation masquerading as a modernization . . . a "Throwback" ' (1993: 235) to the preindustrial archaic urban form in which the city belonged to the elite consumers dominating and exploiting the producers placed outside it and somewhere else. Fitch's book is exactly and explicitly a history of agency, of active deindustrialization as a programme carried out by a coherent and identifiable elite.

In the UK, City Challenge and Single Regeneration Budget schemes that followed UDCs have incorporated both social objectives in terms of employment and housing, and a degree of public participation, precisely because the UDC programme had become identified both with private capital rooking the public purse for massive subsidies and with the absolute disregard of the interests of inner-city working-class 'communities'. The shift to partnership was supposed to redress the balance, but Geddes (1997) demonstrates that the benefits of partnership in terms of both outcome and process seem to have been minimal.

This is not simply because the interests of development capital have been given absolute priority. That has been possible only because in 'partnership' there has been no real countervailing power from the 'community' precisely because the 'community' is so fragmented and disorganized. Given the fragmented nature of 'community' and the logic of personal mobility in space, the proposals contained in the 1998 White Paper *Bringing Britain Together: A National Strategy for Neighbourhood Renewal* (Cm 4045) can only be described as vacuous. The authors of this piece seem simply not to know how people actually conduct their lives in the divided city. It is plain that organization is the key to any kind of re-empowerment of the dispossessed. In Chapter 8 we will review the actual experience of partnership – and of 'New Deal for Communities' in West Newcastle and find that far from an engagement of the dispossessed with the development of the future of their city, the 'urban regime' which did run Newcastle was proposing one of the most revanchist programmes of urban renewal since those implemented in the United States in the 1960s. We will return to organization in Chapter 9, but we must remember that it is process that matters most when we are dealing with issues of power.

Conclusion

The conclusion to this chapter cannot be optimistic. The creation of the postindustrial city through the combined and interacting effects of the global reorganization of capitalist production and the pursuit of fragmenting urban policy has disempowered the organized working class of advanced capitalism in the sphere of reproduction. This disempowerment has many aspects, but it is particularly significant in terms of the fragmentation of 'community'. The history of working-class politics of reproduction, a history much more 'hidden' than that of the working class at the point of production, is a history of action founded in the solidarities which emerged from common residence in the spaces of cities. This was, of course, to a considerable extent a politics carried out by women, which perhaps explains its neglect in formal history.

Wacquant's account of the way in which those spaces are now much less spaces of solidarity is accurate and extremely important. Crucial to that weakening of solidarity is the actual micro-dynamics of personal lives. People do not act with their neighbours. In the postindustrial city they act to leave their neighbours – to move to spaces of relative comfort and security. The spatial divides of exclusion are the most evident and real expression of the social division of postindustrial capitalism. They are the product of the dynamics of capitalist restructuring at the macro level. They are disempowered by the dynamics of personal strategies in the divided cities which that restructuring has engendered.

Divided lives – exclusion in everyday life

In this chapter we will examine evidence about the processes and outcomes of exclusion across a range of experiences in contemporary society. These will be those located in the domains of education, 'culture' and health, and we will deal with them in that order. Our focus on education will be closely related to what is generally called 'social mobility' but might better be understood as the ways in which formal educational processes generate a mix of 'human capital' and 'cultural capital' which are key control parameters determining the character of the trajectories of individual lives. That said, we will not just examine the complex systems of individual lives but will also consider the ways in which education serves to maintain the actual structural forms of postindustrial capitalism. Issues of individual mobility and structural maintenance are not really distinctive because the possibility of individual social mobility is one of the most important bases of legitimation in an unequal social order. Here we will focus on the broad general character of education in postindustrial societies but particularly in the prototypical case of the United Kingdom. In Chapter 8 we will examine educational policies that specifically focus on dealing with 'social exclusion'. With some relief, in Chapter 9 we will turn to the potential of radical educational practice – to Freire's dialogical social pedagogy – as one of the most important means through which social exclusion can be challenged by people in general.

'Culture' is one of the dimensions of social exclusion when social exclusion is understood as a multi-dimensional concept. Cultural exclusion is almost invariably understood in terms of deficits in cultural, and hence human, capital. The excluded poor as individuals lack the conceptual flexibility and general cognitive ability to participate in an appropriate fashion in a postindustrial society either as producers or as consumers. Even worse, they persist in adhering to collective cultural forms – to cultures as 'ways of life', to use an expression of Raymond Williams's, which are antagonistic to the logic of postindustrial capitalism and as 'unincorporated residual cultural forms' may even be the basis of collective opposition to that logic. The central argument here will be that cultural exclusion is not to be understood in terms of the deficits of excluded people and excluded communities, but rather as an active process of assault on the collective values, aspirations and institutions of working-class people as developed in industrial society. The neo-liberal programme is an ideological programme of cultural reconstruction and has to be understood as such.

There is an important link between our considerations of 'culture' here and the content of both Chapter 6, which dealt with urban processes in relation to exclusion, and Chapter 8, which will deal with 'policies against exclusion'. Urban regeneration is now explicitly a cultural project, but almost without exception it is a disabling and excluding cultural project. Since it is useful to draw on direct experience, this proposition will be demonstrated with particular reference to the (thankfully) abortive bid to make 'Newcastle/Gateshead' a 'European City of Culture'. Policies addressed at excluded collectivities, usually spatially defined 'communities', have often adopted a cultural agenda, particularly in relation to 'participation' in urban regeneration and educational programmes. We will devote considerable attention to these in Chapter 8. And of course a cultural programme is the essential foundation of any project which challenges the logics of postindustrial capital in a meaningful way. This theme will be the core of our considerations of ways of acting 'against exclusion' in the concluding chapter to this book.

The relationship between social exclusion and health has to be understood quite simply in terms of the most basic phenomenon. Being prematurely disabled by illness and dying before your time is excluding indeed. This section of the chapter will point readers to the copious literature on the social determinants of health, with health state being understood as, to a considerable degree, a consequence of exclusion. In an important respect health is different from education and 'culture'. Both of those sets of processes are essentially causal to exclusion. In health we deal primarily with the effects of exclusion. However, there is one important exception to this and that relates to the governance of health and the role of the private sector in health provision – to the related processes of re-commodification and de-democratization of health-care provision, again particularly in the prototypical UK. The governance of health demonstrates political exclusion in spades. This is an aspect we will consider in some detail.

Education and mobility in the industrial era

In the 1960s the sociology of education in the UK was concerned above all else with the relationship between education as a process, and in particular secondary education, and social mobility understood in terms of access to higher-level educational qualifications and consequent middle-class employment. This concern derived from a political project of social democracy which dated back to the beginning of the twentieth century and was summed up by the title of the important social reformer Tawney's pamphlet of 1922 *Secondary Education for All*. This project has to be understood as a reaction to the development of a stratified state system of education in the second half of the nineteenth century. At the top were the elite 'public' schools – public only in the sense that they were open to fee-paying pupils from anywhere rather than from a particular locality. The status of this group was recognized by government and other institutions developed in imitation of them. These schools were for the elite – both traditional and emergent. They were not exclusive in terms of access; money talked. One of their crucial functions was to convert the sons, and later daughters, of new money into acceptable members of an apparently traditional elite. They provided a channel for gentrifying people. Their curriculum was organized towards the production of the classically educated gentleman. The next level of education for those who continued beyond 18 – and many then did not – was ideally Oxford or Cambridge, where the style of education in classical mode continued. In practice, many public school pupils went on to acquire technical or professional educations at other universities, but the classical was the ideal.

Below that level were local day secondary schools – many, but not all, of which were ancient foundations as grammar schools. These had always been the local institutions for the education of the affluent and/or the able. The traditional curriculum had been classical but under the influence and funding of the Department of Science and Art, led originally by staff drawn from the Royal Engineers, there was a real turn towards science and technology in these schools in the later decades of the nineteenth century. They served a very important economic purpose as the source of skilled manpower – and womanpower, with particular reference to the teaching as an occupation itself – for the developing industrial and commercial structures of late Victorian and Edwardian capitalism. Although the main mode of admission was through the payment of fees, there were always some free scholarships which served to recruit the most able from below towards this level of education. Most graduates of secondary schools went into work at 16 or 18, although many continued with part-time professional or technical education thereafter. However, many also went on to professional or technical education in the 'red brick' universities or – especially important for women – trained as elementary school teachers for the next educational level down. These secondary schools were the avenues of mobility that mattered for the masses. It should be noted that these schools always imposed some ability test for admission, even on those who paid fees.

Below the secondary level were the elementary schools, which until the First World War had a leaving age of 12, which then rose to 14, and then after the Second World War to 15. These were brutally specific institutions intended to produce a population with basic literacy and numeracy, reasonable physical fitness and (for women) domestic skills who could serve as the labour force and social reproducers of industrial capitalism. Elementary education was for the 'hands' but not 'brains' of industrial capitalism. There was some possibility of movement at age 11 by competitive examination and free scholarship to secondary education. What Tawney wanted – and this was the policy of what was then a new Labour Party – was 'secondary education for all', access to more than a basic education for the entire population. This principle required both that secondary education should be free and that it should not be entered through competitive examination.

By the 1920s things were somewhat more complex than the above scheme indicates. There were intermediate schools between elementary and secondary, such as the 'Central School' attended by the author's mother, who was not allowed to sit for a grammar school scholarship in case she passed and her family had to pay for her travel and uniform! There was a large-scale system of technical education that could lead on to higher-level professional engineering and related qualifications. However, the great majority of people were still educated as hands rather than brains. Tawney and Labour's commitment to secondary education was always informed by two intermingled but different motives. One echoed the Victorian school inspector, poet and public intellectual Mathew Arnold's desire for a humanely educated public in general. The other was a rather pragmatic commitment to the potential economic contribution of a well-educated population – the human capital argument. This debate rumbled on through the Second World War and past a 1944 Education Act, which was supposed to provide secondary education for all but actually continued the elementary system under the guise of 'secondary modern schools', although it eliminated the fees element in state secondary schools and made entry a function of supposed ability alone. It was not until the 1960s that a Labour government moved towards something like Tawney's secondary education for all with the general development of comprehensive secondary education on a neighbourhood basis.

Throughout this period, social mobility was not simply a product of educational achievement in school and further full-time education but could be achieved in other ways. Many boys left school at 12, or later 14 or 15, served a craft apprenticeship, took technical education, and worked their way up into the most senior management levels. Many women left school young and either married up or worked up through institutions such as the civil service with its competitive and, for single but not married women, gender-blind examinations. Indeed, from the 1950s, with the elimination of the marriage bar, married women also had promotion prospects, at least in principle. Moreover, particularly in the post-Second World War years, many skilled manual occupations were highly paid and relatively secure, if physically demanding. The author went through a secondary and higher education in the knowledge that if he ever failed in education there was always a decent living to be made in the pit – as a coal-miner – and from the

1950s to the 1970s, coal-mining remained an available job which demanded male labour that could meet the physical requirements. Despite the apparent stratification of education in the industrial system of the twentieth century, there was both the possibility of mobility and, in the Fordist era, a decent living for many without it. Indeed, the availability of that decent Fordist living was one of the key sources of post-Second World War demand for more access to secondary and higher education. Most – but even then not all – working-class families could afford to support their children through secondary education and did not need them to go to work at the earliest possible age. Tertiary education in the UK was accessible through generous grants subject to a family income means test set at such a level that most working-class children received full maintenance support.

The Second World War itself was an enormous vehicle for educationally based social mobility in the USA under the GI bills, which funded veterans through tertiary education then and subsequently. In the USA, military service has always been an important basis for tertiary education for working-class, particularly black working-class, people and remains of great significance to the present day. In France and Poland, things were rather more stratified until at least the 1960s, with a real division between education for the mass of workers' children and the academic provision of lycées and gymnasia, although in Poland under 'real socialism' there was privileged access for workers' children to universities. However, at least in Upper Silesia, Poland's industrial heartland, the relatively high wages and other privileges of industrial workers, coupled with a specific system of technical schools associated with particular industrial enterprises, meant that many working-class children were 'steered' both by local cultural values and by the staffing needs of the industrial system away from higher education and towards early entry into work. That said, higher-level technical qualifications – for example as a mining engineer – had considerable status with the industrial working class. This seems to have been a common component of industrial value systems across Europe and North America. It is perhaps particularly important to stress that there were always part-time work-related routes available towards such technical qualifications.

The above historical narrative has been necessary for two related reasons. The first is that in discussing education and social exclusion in postindustrial society we need to know where we are coming from. The second is that it is absolutely vital to make the point that for all its stratification, when part-time education is taken into account, there was considerable educationally derived individual social mobility in industrial systems and that in the Fordist era there was often a very reasonable living to be made and life to be led without social mobility from the working class. Let us turn to the postindustrial condition.

Education and closure in the postindustrial era

The prophet of postindustrialism was Daniel Bell, who in *The Coming of Post-Industrial Society* (1974) forecast the kind of society that would emerge from advanced industrialism. This would be characterized by:

* Tertiarization – the shift from the secondary sector of manufacturing to the tertiary sector of services just as industrial society was characterized by a shift from the primary sector of agriculture to the secondary sector of manufacturing.
* The centrality of new science-based industries – this has been associated particularly with the rise of information technology.
* The development of a new basis for stratification. Castells has developed this theme with particular reference to the role of higher-level service-class workers in information technology.

Only the first of these prognoses can be regarded as unequivocally having come to pass, and an important argument of this book is that the third is flatly wrong. With regard to the second, it is important to realize that much service-based employment in postindustrial capitalism is in poorly paid 'pink collar' private sector services or in the health, education and social-care sectors, which are in the process of being transferred in large part to the private sector. Moreover, the economic driver of much of postindustrial capitalism is a financial sector which certainly draws on new information technology but is not qualitatively different in kind, although it is certainly quantitatively different in scale, from the merchant capitalism that has existed since at least the development of a sea-borne world system in the sixteenth century.

However, education – the acquisition through formal processes of higher-level credentials which represent some combination of human and cultural capital – is manifestly of massive significance in postindustrial capitalism. This is perhaps best indicated by the extraordinary increase in generational participation in tertiary education throughout the last quarter of the twentieth century. By 2001, across a range of advanced postindustrial countries, the typical figure for achievement of higher education amongst 25–34 year olds was around 30 per cent. Figures were much lower for former Communist European countries including Poland (15 per cent) but rather higher for the USA at 38 per cent. France and the UK stood at 29 per cent and 34 per cent, respectively. Interestingly, Ireland – which skipped the secondary stage in a direct transition from an agricultural to postindustrial society – had a level of 48 per cent (OECD 2003). In 1975, 4 per cent of French, 7 per cent of UK and 21 per cent of US 24-year-olds had a degree of some kind (OECD 1997). Plainly, the US prefigured the general trend, but the move towards higher education degree-level achievement figures of more than 30 per cent is now general in postindustrial societies and is indicative of a very different sort of relationship between education and social situation in such societies in comparison with their industrial predecessors.

The primary approach of government to education in the postindustrial UK is well expressed by Alexiadou in terms of an:

> . . . economic rationale that is seen to underpin social policy in general and educational policies in particular. This rationale binds together the discourses of modernization of the government, globalization, economic competitiveness and raising standards across the education and training system.
>
> (2002: 73)

Alexiadou is absolutely correct to identify education as central for New Labour both in relation to the development of economic competitiveness *and* as a method of combating social exclusion, but perhaps does not develop the potential contradiction between these two objectives. In the version of combating social exclusion which informs the New Labour programme and the operations of the Department for Education and Employment (DfEE) the focus is largely on the 10 per cent of young people who disappear from the systems of governance through education and training provision and do not enter the system of work (which in any event is of far less significance for those under 20 than was the case in industrial society). The management of a refusing and potentially (indeed often actually) anomic set of adolescents and young adults – a far more dangerous recreation of what Morse in the 1960s identified as the 'unattached' – is a serious issue for order, and that is not easily assimilated into a narrative of achievement as the basis of economic growth and development, although New Labour frequently attempts this rather difficult task. In this context, actual exclusion from school (see Cooper 2002) – the throwing of children out of the compulsory education process or at least out of the institution in which they are engaging with that process – can best be understood as simply the extreme end of a continuum in which many adolescents and young adults join the ranks of the non-included.

Let me identify two aspects which relate education in general to exclusion. The first is the relationship between education and achievement/mobility, and the second is the relationship between education/training and the 10 per cent who go missing from systems of 'inclusion'. We will examine the first of these in this chapter and the second in Chapter 8, when we examine policies and practices directed against exclusion.

In a system in which achievement through work-related/part-time technical training routes has been so curtailed as to have virtually disappeared, formal educational achievement on a primarily full-time basis is now fundamental, not so much for social mobility as for the retention of middle income and comfortable life courses by the children of everybody but the really rich. It is important to note that the part-time routes to professional status which for most of the industrial period were the ways in which the majority of engineers, accountants, senior local government officers and health administrators, and even many lawyers, acquired their occupational status have now to all intents and purposes been closed to non-graduates. At the same time, 'non-qualified management', which was the norm in industrial Europe at least in most non-technical areas, has itself been assimilated into full-time educational processes at the undergraduate level or through the normal requirement that MBA students should first have a bachelor's level degree. In practice in the UK, this translates into an issue of form of secondary schooling. In 2002, approximately 10 per cent of all secondary school pupils were in fee-paying secondary schools. Most of these are days schools or day pupils at boarding schools. The fees for Newcastle's Royal Grammar School – a former direct grant school which was partly in the state system but opted out in order to remain selective – seem typical at about £6500 per academic year. Such fees have to be paid out of final income as defined in Chapter 5. There are bursaries, but most pupils pay full fees. To set this in context, the fees for one child at this school represent more than 20 per cent of the final income of an average two adult, one child household. The fees for two children of secondary school age would be more than 33 per cent of the average income of a two adult, two child household. Private education is not generally accessible to the middle masses, but only to the top quintile or even decile of households by final income.

That said, access to it represents enormous advantages which are disproportionate to social status in relation to the standard of examination performances achieved. Whitty, drawing on a major research study, points out that:

> . . . attendance at selective private or state secondary schools gave only a limited advantage in terms of A-level scores, but this was translated into quite disproportionate benefits in terms of entry to different levels and sectors of higher education and the labour market.
>
> (2001: 290)

However, it is not only formally selective schools that matter – that is, there is more to selection than the operation of actual selective examinations, and under New Labour's current proposals this aspect of the process will become even more important than it is now. Byrne and Rogers (1996) showed how the original catchment area of state and state-maintained free comprehensive secondary schools had generated a positive feedback to create a fitness landscape in which schools were highly differentiated in relation to examination performance. The mechanism through which this has been achieved is 'parental choice' and developments in relation to choice have the most profound significance for the future development of the UK's educational system.

Choice is New Labour's mantra for the public services in general, but the process has particular salience in relation to education since successful choice in secondary education seems to offer the only realistic route for social mobility into the new elite for the children of the middle masses. As we shall see, 'choice' for the excluded poor/dispossessed working class is, mostly, a myth. Choice was introduced by the Conservative government in the late 1980s. Before that the major principle for the allocation of places at state-funded secondary schools was geographical. Essentially, these were neighbourhood schools, although often at one remove as they took children from sets of 'feeder' primary school places and it was the primary schools that used the geographical principle. There were all sorts of modifying rules – primacy given to children with siblings in the school and so on. There was of course considerable game playing with these rules, with aspirational parents stretching or breaking them in order to get children into high-achieving schools. At this time, the level of achievement of the school reflected both the social nature of the catchment area of the school and its previous status. Former grammar schools – selective secondary schools – in middle-class areas generally had high-achieving cohorts of pupils. The introduction of a principle of choice, itself open to all sorts of qualifying rules, introduced a massive positive feedback into this system and reinforced differentiation among schools.

In part, the exercise of choice has been a process drawing on pre-existing familial cultural capital. Ball et al. (1995) demonstrated how in a particular locality middle-class parents researched options and engaged actively with choice whereas working-class parents seemed to have a habitus of passivity which often took the form of letting children pick local schools in order to maintain friendship links. Even when working-class parents have sought actively to achieve choice, their real experience is of constraint despite a personal breach of passivity and localism.

However, choice has not just been exercised by parents. Central government has extended the range of options amongst which choices can be made. A variety of differentiated schools have been created by initiatives introduced by the Conservatives but continued in practice, if not always in administrative detail, under New Labour. The Conservatives permitted schools to 'opt out' of local government control and, although New Labour abolished this status, the previously opted out foundation schools remain differentiated from those under local education authority control in important respects. In addition, the Conservatives created 'City Technology Colleges'(CTCs), a policy continued in many respects by Labour with 'City Academies'. Here the private sector sponsors a school by paying a contribution towards construction and other costs, although approximately 80 per cent of costs are born from public funds. Several of these schools have been set up by a fundamentalist Christian foundation which teaches creationist science. The CTCs were able to operate a selective policy on an ability basis, although often selection was managed through interviews with parents. Academies have much more limited possibilities for selection in practice, although their ability to select a proportion of pupils for special relevant abilities, for example music, has generally favoured the aspirational middle classes. By 2004, more than half of UK state secondary schools were specialist schools of some kind with varying methods of selection of a proportion of their pupils.

New Labour's 2004 'Five Year Strategy' for education asserted that: 'We will never return to a system based on selection of the few and rejection of the many' (para 5.44 and elsewhere repeated). Essentially all secondary schools are intended to become specialist secondary academies with considerable financial and related autonomy from elected local government. Hattersley, the living disciple on earth of Tony Crosland, the Labour philosopher of a reformist socialism which accommodated with a Keynesian accumulation regime, considers that this strategy represents an uneasy compromise between Labour's traditions which go back to Tawney and Blair's concern for the aspirations of the middle classes who cannot afford private education for their children (*Guardian*, 13 July 2004). However, aspirations extend beyond the middle classes as traditionally understood. A study of higher education participation rates by UK postcode shows that the children of the traditional prosperous blue- and white-collar working class are increasingly entering higher education. In the very middle England Leicester suburb of Wigston, the rate of entry into higher education increased from one in ten of the age cohort in 1994–95 to one in three in 2001–02 (*THES* 2 July 2004: 4). Wigston is a locale that has made a relatively successful transition from industrial to postindustrial status. In contrast, in former mining areas, whilst there had been an increase in participation in higher education, it was still only one in ten in 2001–2. There have been some remarkable success stories by schools in poor postindustrial localities. For example, Walker City Academy in East Newcastle has pulled its performance rate at GCSE up from the miserable to above the national average in just four years without recourse to either selection or creationist science. However, despite this impressive and commendable performance, no more than a handful of its pupils will ever gain access to the high-status service-class employment that is regarded as the norm for the pupils of private schools in the same city.

The relationship between educational process and ultimate location is crucial to the legitimacy of a competitive postindustrial capitalism. What seems apparent is that the real social mobility through education occurred in the aftermath of the Second World War and through social democratic, albeit selective, secondary education forms in the 1950s and 1960s. All that is on offer for most children who achieve, even at the level of degree, is white-collar or semi-professional work which at best offers something like the remuneration and stability of skilled male manual employment in the Fordist era. So far as social mobility into the higher service classes goes, it remains true that of those who pass into the chamber of achievement, some go in through the door marked 'push' but most through the door marked 'pull'.

Cultural exclusion

When the term 'cultural exclusion' is employed in policy and related documents and discourses, it refers to the supposed cultural deficiencies of the excluded. It identifies those who are lacking in the cultural capital necessary both for gainful employment in the knowledge-based post-industrial economy and for the appropriately informed consumption of the high cultural products that characterize the postindustrial city as a cultural zone. Indeed, it generally goes beyond this – the culturally excluded are not simply deficient. They possess a set of values – the term 'culture of poverty' is the old expression, as we have seen – which is antagonistic to participation in production and consumption in the postindustrial world. In the policy literature associated with regional development it is common to find particular places, and especially the author's home region of the northeast of England, identified as problematic locales because of an anti-entrepreneurial culture based on a tradition of permanent employment in large enterprises and collectivist solidarity. This is general among populations with a strong proletarian tradition. Such criticisms are generally deployed in relation to the old heavy industrial zones of Europe, and particularly those with an established history of left politics. Understood in this sense, cultural exclusion is a problem to be remedied by the inculcation of new value systems and new forms of identity.

In any discussion of culture which is more than the use of the term as a gloss on the activity of property speculators and those components of urban governance in thrall to them in contemporary urban regimes, it is always useful to turn to the conceptual apparatus developed by Raymond Williams, and in particular to his lucid specification of culture as having three aspects. First, the word 'culture' is understood in aesthetics and other contexts, at least in the West in a tradition deriving from Plato, as describing artistic aspiration to the ideal of the real. Second, it describes representation of the world as it is rather than attempts to attain some ideal – Williams calls this 'documentary'. Finally, there is the social definition:

> in which culture is a description of a particular way of life, which expresses certain meanings and values not only in art and learning but also in institutions and ordinary behaviour. The analysis of culture, from such a definition, is the clarification of the meanings and values implicit and explicit in a particular way of life, a particular culture.
>
> (1962: 57)

In a discussion of cultural exclusion, we have to consider two processes. The first is an assault on the cultural values of the industrial working class in the name of flexibility and individualism – a combination of apparent economic imperative and the value systems of possessive individualism. The second is the sets of processes associated with urban regeneration in which the city is understood as a zone of cultural production and consumption. Here, as with health, non-democratic processes and forms of governance are an important component of the actual exclusion of people from political process itself.

In trying to understand the implications and potential of this situation, we can turn to Williams's (1980) discussion of 'residual' and 'emergent' cultures. Williams noted that in any cultural context: 'some experiences, meanings and values, which cannot be verified or cannot be expressed in terms of the dominant culture, are nevertheless lived and practised on the basis of the residue – cultural as well as social of some previous social formation' (1980: 40). This is 'residual culture'. By 'emergent culture' he meant the 'new meanings and values, new practices, new significances and experiences' which for him were 'constantly being created' (1980: 41). Residual and emergent cultures do not exist in isolation from dominant culture. On the contrary, dominant culture will incorporate elements of both into itself. Indeed, Williams considered that dominant culture 'could not allow' cultural practice of any other kind outside itself and that the agents expressing dominant cultural values actively engaged in the incorporation of elements of both residual and emergent culture. For Williams, the unincorporated – because unincorporable – elements of both residual and emergent culture were crucial sources of potential social transformation. We will return to this idea in Chapter 9.

We can I think readily see that the collectivist solidaristic component of industrial culture and the antagonistic view held of capitalism and its works expressed in the proletarian component of industrial culture are not readily incorporable into flexible postindustrial and post-democratic capitalism. That system can incorporate structures and some documenting of processes as part of 'heritage'.

Let me make something absolutely clear. For anyone who adheres to a strong version of social exclusion, who understands social exclusion as an active process in which people are excluded, then the assault on the collective value systems of working-class people – on culture as a way of life – is the most important element in the process of cultural exclusion. The active renunciation of this value system by New Labour, both in political expression and in policies, is crucial to social exclusion in the contemporary UK.

Cities of cultural exclusion

Zukin has identified:

> ... the seductive influence of the arts in political economy. With a continued displacement of manufacturing and development of the financial and non-profit sectors of the economy, cultural production seemed to be more and more what cities were about.
>
> (1995: viii)

Thus we have the postindustrial industrial city now identified as a zone for cultural production and consumption. This is not the old social democratic approach to cultural facilities and processes – the proud and defiant claim that nothing is too good for us and only the best will serve us which informed the relationship between culture and the post-World War II development of cultural institutions and forms, not least in Gateshead. Rather, it is about culture which draws on the debased contemporary versions of artistic forms which were originally developed as rejections of the commodification of art as both icons of consumption and as consumer goods in their own right. This is the core of the 'European City of Culture'. The reality was rather well described by Jones in a polemic reflecting on the bid by UK cities to be European City of Culture in 2008.

> Glasgow is the one City of Culture everyone can name. It made a big international eye-catching event of the opportunity. But to be a successful City of Culture – to be a successful player in the new global economy – you have to suppress your real culture and sanitise yourself for others' eyes. The Glasgow celebrated by the City of Culture was all art-nouveau tea shops and Peter Brook, with little reference to the actual culture of the city, which in 1990 included James Kelman's splenetic Dostoevskian novels of working-class life and Jerry Sadowitz's vicious comedy, cultural phenomena that reflect the city's texture. . . . Being City of Culture does not change real social conditions. It replaces them with an illusion: the dream that any city, however poor its suburbs, however dilapidated its infrastructure, can be 'regenerated' by culture. What this does is produce two cities, one city for business travellers, weekenders and cultural connoisseurs and another for the people who live there. Culture is Europe's answer to Starbucks. Rioters in Seattle smashed branches of Starbucks because the cosy coffee empire was a symbol not just of the global economy but of the vacuous post-grunge culture of Clinton's USA. In European cities the idea that culture is the way to bring in businesses by making your dingy town more habitable means that art and theatre are no longer valued for themselves but as assets. This is why the actual contents of this year's celebrations in the nine Cities of Culture are so nebulous. It doesn't matter what precise artistic happenings you have, so long as there are enough of them over the year to justify that precious title. It's culture in the abstract that is being celebrated, the one thing every European can get behind.
>
> (Jonathon Jones, *Guardian*, 8 January 2000)

Glasgow remains one of the most socially divided places in the UK, with its dispossessed working class systematically excluded by insufficient income from participation in the culture of a city which may be 'miles better', but for the residents of the outer estates – schemes in Scottish parlance – is also miles away.

Part of the area in which I live – the estuarine conurbation of Tyneside – the two municipalities of Gateshead (where I live and have been a municipal councillor) and Newcastle – were bidders for the 2008 European City of

Culture status and, to my not inconsiderable pleasure, lost. The bid was founded around the development of the Baltic Gallery of contemporary art – originally a wholly appropriate effort to retain a well-liked industrial landmark – the Baltic Flour Mill – in keeping with an established social democratic tradition of art for the people. However, the bid was not run by elected local representatives and did not involve any real participation by local communities. Instead, it was taken over by a business-led consortium headed by a property developer. It served as a façade behind which former industrial river front land was transformed into 'quayside' developments of extremely expensive flats. Word of mouth has it that the failure to engage communities and local people was the reason that the bid, which had been favourite, lost. Too many of the committee awarding the prize, including the committee chair, retained some of the old social democratic values themselves.

It is not the cultural content of the icons of the new commodity culture that are excluding. Indeed, many of the exhibitions at the Baltic have been very inclusive both in production and in content – some of the old social democratic tradition survives. Rather, it is the representation of central city space as a zone for expensive consumption serviced by a poorly paid, insecure army of pink-collar workers. And it is the process of determination – the substitution of business-led elite determination of strategy and tactics – in the Newcastle-Gateshead case very inept determination of both – for either traditional representative democracy or any form of participatory democracy. We do not have partnership, but the handing over of governance to private capital and its interests. This theme will be developed in Chapter 8. Let me conclude this chapter by a brief reference to the development of similar processes in health.

Exclusion and health

The obvious and apparent expression of exclusion in health is the differential rate of premature mortality by social class. This is most simply expressed in terms of differential life expectancy at birth. The most recent figures indicate a gap of five years between the life expectancy at birth for men and three and a half years for women between social classes I and II at the top and social classes IV and V at the bottom. This picture is repeated for morbidity (ill health):

> The findings vary by age and gender, but in general show that in the 1990s the socio-economic pattern of increasingly poor health with declining socio-economic position was not confined to mortality, but was reflected in measures of self-reported chronic sickness, and for several major diseases and causes of disability. Evidence from consultations in general practice supported this interpretation. There were, for example, strong socio-economic gradients in consultations with GPs for conditions classed as serious for both boys and girls, particularly

when children living in council housing were compared with those living in owner-occupied accommodation.

(ONS 1997: 230)

A summary of available evidence is given in Shaw (1999), Gordon (1999) and Bartley (2004). The literature on health inequalities and their social determinants is voluminous, and there is no space to explore it in detail here. Instead, I want to deal with the governance of health as an example of a process of political exclusion which typifies a very important component of postindustrial social policy. This is the privatization of the delivery of publicly funded services.

Health care has never been fully under direct democratic control in the UK. Between 1929 and 1948, there was a system of municipal hospitals which had developed out of the old Poor Law infirmaries, but this was incorporated into the National Health Service and changes in governance since then have removed all automatic local authority representation in health service governance. Originally the issue was the desire of the prestigious medical profession to remain autonomous and not be subject to the control of local councillors. Now the issue is the very general tendency in postindustrial capitalism for corporate involvement in the delivery of public services funded from direct taxation. This tendency is described in Whitfield (2001) and is of profound significance in that it involves a recommodification of what had been decommodified labour. In other words, profits will now be made from the labour of workers who work directly for the public on a not-for-profit basis.

The most important implication of this for us here is that the engagement of corporate capital in public service delivery requires – and that word is used very deliberately – the exclusion of popular and local politics from any decisive role in the strategic planning of services and determination of their mode of delivery. The key phrase is 'public private partnership' and there is a whole apparatus of consultancy, professional advisers and corporate finance which supports what is now one of the most profitable of all corporate activities. The UK is again prefigurative here, but the implications of the General Agreement on Trade in Services is that this tendency will spread throughout postindustrial capitalism. Crouch has described the implications thus:

Firms are not simply organizations but concentrations of power. . . . They become even more powerful as government concedes to them the organization of its own activities and bows to the superiority of their expertise. In addition to dominating the economy itself, they become the class which dominates the running of government.

(2000: 32–3)

Yet again, as with the processes of urban development, we see political exclusion. Moreover, this exclusion is not confined to health. The business model of control over delivery has been extended to the operation of schools, not just through the academy model, but by the wholesale replacement of democratic local governance of education by business management in some 'failing' local education authorities. The record of such business management has been risible and miserable, but the principle has not been abandoned. These are very profound changes and we will return to their implications in Chapter 9. Now we turn to policies directed 'against exclusion' – again using the UK as the prototypical example.

PART THREE

8

Including the excluded: the policy agenda of the third way

In Chapter 2 of this book we reviewed the approach to social politics developed by order liberals in Germany after the Second World War. This was a third way between the demands of a transformative socialism committed to the replacement of capitalism, whether by revolutionary or reformist means, and unbridled market capitalism. The term 'social market economy' was coined to define this approach. Crosland in *The Future of Socialism* (1956) adopted the same perspective, although without its formal grounding in Christian ethics. Now we have a new 'third way' as proposed by Giddens (1998, 2000) and endorsed by Blair (2001), but this is not at all the same thing as the original effort to establish some means by which the political aspirations of the many could be used to tame the inegalitarian and socially disruptive forces of market capitalism whilst retaining the capacity of that system for the generation of resources as the basis for social progress.

Instead, the new 'third way' must be understood as an effort to establish what is at best a compromise between neo-liberalism and the traditional objectives of Christian/social democracy and at worst, and probably correctly, as a verbal gloss on neo-liberalism in an effort to make that programme acceptable to publics as voters, and even more importantly to the activist members of traditionally reformist political parties. If the intellectual guru of the third way is Giddens, its true political progenitor was Bill Clinton through the Democratic Leadership Council which moved the US Democrats from the centre ground towards the neo-liberal right in the 1980s. The key themes of the third way are accommodation (seen as inevitable) with the agendas of globalizing corporate capitalism, equality of opportunity rather than outcome, and a concentration on the creation of wealth rather than its redistribution.

Even neo-liberalism with a smiley face cannot fool all of the people all of the time. The neo-liberal project in postindustrial, and what are in reality post-democratic, societies still has a fundamental problem of social order and has to cope with the day-to-day desire of politicians to be elected to office. The majority of politicians and political parties may well be the political whores of corporate capital but they do care which of them gets office. 'Social exclusion' poses major problems for the governance of the capitalist social order at the abstract level and for the day-to-day management of government on the ground. These problems are:

- The potential pauperization of a large section of the citizen population who cannot (in Europe, although this probably does not apply to the USA) be excluded from the receipt of benefits which are at least as adequate as the wages available for low-paid work in postindustrial economies. To use the language of the 1834 New Poor Law, we have a failure of less eligibility.
- A massive increase in social inequalities which has restored the inequality levels of a previous (pre-Fordist) era.
- A curtailment of opportunities for social mobility with a relative closure of access to the real elite and a widening gap between that elite and an increasingly proletarianized employed 'middle class'.
- The 'dropping out' of a residualized element of the young at the bottom of the social order who provide the man- and woman-power of a disorganized criminality.
- A developing ghettoization based in Europe not on ethnic criteria but rather on the spatial concentration of the excluded and poorly employed in specific locales in urban systems with consequent inferior access to spatially distributed public resources and especially schools.
- The disengagement of the dispossessed working class from the institutional forms and social practices of 'industrial community' and formal politics.

The policies reviewed in this chapter, drawing primarily but not exclusively on the policy agenda of the Blair government in the United Kingdom, are intended to address these issues and have done so with varying degrees of success. However, the tackling of social exclusion is important not just in terms of the substance of interventions but also because it has involved distinctive innovation in the forms of governance which illustrate the centrality of a business model of practice for New Labour and the third way.

The Social Exclusion Unit: the new forms of policy development and implementation

In 1997 Blair set up the Social Exclusion Unit located outwith traditional departmental structures. The Unit is staffed by a mixture of civil servants from a range of departments and secondees from local government, the voluntary sector, and business. There is an emphasis on 'joined-up thinking' which demonstrates a recognition of the complex character of exclusion as process and condition. Eighteen Policy Action Teams (PATs) were established drawing on personnel across departments and from outside central government with the brief of identifying issues and coming up with preliminary proposals for action. A key theme was that of the 'New Deal' – plainly with reference back to the New Deal of Roosevelt's USA in the 1930s. There were to be 'New Deals' for the unemployed, lone parents, the disabled and communities. Percy-Smith considers that the work of the teams was organized around five broad themes:

1 Getting the people to work: focusing on maximizing the contribution of the New Deal in the poorest areas; addressing barriers to employment; and developing innovative ways of assisting re-entry into the labour market.
2 Getting the place to work: focusing on effective neighbourhood and housing management so that issues such as crime and antisocial behaviour are addressed.
3 Building a future for young people: focusing on Sure Start to provide more integrated help for children at risk and other measures to motivate children and young people in relation to education.
4 Access to services: focusing on ensuring access to services in the poorest areas.
5 Making the government work better: focusing on improving the way government at all levels responds to social exclusion.

(2000: 3)

One aspect of the whole approach has been the emphasis on spatially distinctive locales – that term is used deliberately to indicated smaller sub-areas of the geographical division of locality – which are distinguished by their level of deprivation. So we have Education Action Zones, Health Action Zones, Employment Action Zones, New Deal for Communities, Sure Start areas, with geographical specification informing the policy agenda as a whole. The idea of distinctively excluded spaces is central to the whole approach.

The key point is that the operations of the Social Exclusion Unit are based on an apolitical application of technical expertise. Of course, there is some recognition that issues derive from the transition from industrial to postindustrial capitalism. However, there is no macro-political engagement with that process as a whole. In characteristic third way mode the transformation is taken as inevitable. It is the job of governance – since the actors involved extend beyond formal government, governance is the appropriate term – to micro-manage the crises emerging from that process of transformation so that it can proceed as smoothly as possible.

Let us turn to specific policy areas, beginning with the largest and most successful – the combination of low minimum wage and fiscal subsidies to families with children dependent on low-waged poor work which has recreated a rational engagement with employment for many households.

Speenhamland come again – fiscal redistribution and Welfare to Work

In 1795, the magistrates of the county of Berkshire concluded at a Newbury quarter sessions that the wages of an agricultural labourer were no longer sufficient 'to support an industrious man and his family'. A meeting was held at the Pelican Inn in Speenhamland and a policy was worked out which resulted in the subsidizing of labourers' wages from the poor rates on a sliding scale depending on family size and the price of bread (see Inglis 1972: 81). The 'Speenhamland' system was simply the best known of a range of similar local schemes devised around this time.

The background to these developments was complex. In part it was a function of enclosure. The elimination of common rights turned the cottager into a pure wage labourer. In part it was a function of rising prices in consequence of the French wars. In part it was a function of economic competition by factories against domestic labour. The development of factory spinning eliminated a significant source of income generated by the labourer's wife and children. The family was being transformed from an economic resource into an economic burden.

The magistracy was drawn from the English gentry, a class composed of as hard-faced a bunch of rural capitalist exploiters as has ever been assembled anywhere at any time. They were influenced to some degree by moral motives, but their prime concern was the collective as opposed to individual interests of capitalists as a class. At the local level they were, as Marx put it, acting as the executive committee of the whole bourgeoisie. Every individual capitalist farmer wanted to pay as low wages as possible. If such low wages were paid, there was no guarantee of the long-term reproduction of labour, since labourers would avoid marriage and the production of children. In the short term, there would be a seasonal problem of labour required at harvests, since additional labour was always drawn from families at these times. If the poor were emmiserated they might revolt. The French poor had just done exactly that. The magistrates devised a workable scheme for handling these problems, which scheme persisted until the introduction of machine threshing reduced the long-term demand for agricultural labour in general, and resulted in the New Poor Law. It should be noted that this later transition was also dependent on the extraordinarily severe suppression of workers' resistance and efforts at union organization (see Hudson 1981).

Let us turn to 'welfare to work', the new policy programme of liberalizing US and UK governments committed to the development and sustaining of flexible labour markets. Brown's budget of 1998 was concerned exactly with the promotion of welfare to work. Critics, not least the former Tory Chancellor of the Exchequer Kenneth Clarke, noted that Brown had presented a budget with no macro-economic content whatsoever. There was no sense that one of the purposes of government financial policy was to stimulate demand in order to create employment. Keynesianism was dead.

All the innovations were institutional rather than systemic. They were intended to increase the financial returns to employed work for people who had access only to low wages and thereby get them off benefits. There was a radical reform of employers' national insurance contributions to encourage the hiring of more low-paid workers, a tax credit for the child-care costs of parents with lower incomes, a US-style working family tax credit which replaced and extended existing family credits, and a subsidy paid to employers who take on the long-term unemployed. In addition, there was a massive extension of counselling and training provision for all the non-employed poor – New Labour's 'New Deal'. The thinking behind this approach was explained in the first 'forecast for the UK economy' issued by the Treasury: 'The Modernisation of Britain's Tax and Benefit System – Employment Opportunity in a Changing Labour Market' (Treasury 1997). The account given of the source of the problem reproduces the account given at Speenhamland two hundred years ago:

> Evidence on the dynamics of the labour market shows a clear link between unemployment and low pay. This low pay–no pay cycle means that, for many groups, income mobility is low. Relative poverty, defined as the proportion of the population living below half average income, is increasingly a problem for people below pension age, mainly through lack of work, but also through low pay. Many of those who suffer most are families with children.
>
> (HM Treasury 1997: 2)

This corresponds rather well – in a negative sense – with the useful concept of 'employment sustainability' suggested by Walker and Kellard. They define this as: 'the maintenance of a stable or upward employment trajectory in the long term' (2001: 7). The cycle of low pay–no pay is the exact opposite of employment stability with its three dimensions of job retention, job stability and opportunity for career advancement. This is the key demarcator between acceptable work and poor work.

For the Treasury pundits: 'the focus of reform must be microeconomic' (1997: 17). It is true that they do recognize the significance of the macroeconomic background, but the key processes must be supply side and directed at the quality of labour. In the language of complex dynamics, they are intended to move people between attractors, not to transform the phase state as a whole.

The effects of the tax credits, coupled with the introduction of a minimum wage, have been similar to those of the package introduced by Clinton in the USA in 1996. The UK measures are not so coercive, but in the USA the Welfare Act both shifted long-term responsibility for mothers with dependent children, the USA's only 'funded dependent group' of working age, to the states from the federal level, and imposed a time limit of two years on benefit receipt. This was sweetened by a rise in the minimum wage and a guarantee of protection of health benefits for workers who change or lose jobs. The other main foundation of the Clinton welfare programme is the

Earned Income Tax rebate which exempts the working poor from income tax until their incomes are well above the poverty level. Martin Walker commented: 'the gap is clear in the Clinton ideology, between those in work, who receive the state's help, and the undeserving' (*Observer*, 25 August 1996: 17).

The impact of these developments in the USA is profound. Ellwood (1999) identifies them as a quiet revolution. Federal spending on low income families not in receipt of cash benefits has increased by a factor of eight over fifteen years to reach $52 billion in 1999. The two important and linked developments have been the Earned Income Tax Credit which can boost income by 40 per cent in money terms and the eligibility through Medicaid and the Children's Health Insurance Programme of the health-care costs of children in working poor families. These developments have had a particular impact on the employment rate of female single parents with an increase between the early 1990s and 1998 from rates of 50 per cent to over 67 per cent. In the UK persuasion rather than coercion is the mechanism employed but the target is the same – to get lone parents working rather than passively benefit dependent – and to achieve a 70 per cent employment rate for lone parents by 2010. This is not a matter of elimination of benefit dependency because the working poor will remain dependent on direct cash-and-kind transfers and tax breaks. However, it means that benefit receipt will be associated with work instead of an alternative to it.

What these schemes guarantee is subsistence wages, in relative terms, of course, but not more than that. They are literally Speenhamland come again. This programme has two beneficial effects for globalizing flexible capitalism. First, it subsidizes the wage costs of the apparently necessarily low-wage service pink-collar sectors of postindustrial capitalism. Note that these costs are born by the rest of us, the middle income earners who have not had major tax breaks. The low paid have higher net incomes, but this costs those employing them nothing above the minimum wage. The fiscal employment subsidies are horizontal transfers within the working class. Second, the programme maintains both the work ethic and the general social order. Work remunerated below the level of social reproduction, and at a level no better than state benefits, corrodes the work ethic. Rationally people are 'stupid' to work for wages at such levels. Of course, they do work for such wages because there are many trans-economic reasons for working, not least self-respect (although working whilst greatly exploited is, of course, not a source of self-respect). Nonetheless, the actual logic of possessive individualism as expressed in economic rationality tells them they are daft for doing so. The restoration of the economic rationality of low-paid work is important.

And work is a great source of social order. Wages provide an income without resource to crime. People who go to work don't have the time, or energy, to be disorderly and criminal. The threat of job loss is an important order-maintaining sanction. These factors do not apply to work in the irregular economy. On the contrary, the expansion of the irregular and marginal economy is a challenge to formal order. It is interesting that the

US experience has been one of job creation within the formal and order generating economy, rather than marginalization and the expansion of the irregular economy on the Latin American model. The UK is seeking to go the same way as the USA.

'Welfare to Work' has had considerable success, although it has not worked as well in the UK's peripheral regions as in the USA's more employment-centred system where the Federal Reserve does pay attention to employment levels as well as interest rates. In particular it has not succeeded in getting the older non-employed of working age who are in receipt of long-term incapacity benefits back into the labour market. The UK Low Pay Unit praised the measures saying of Brown that: 'By allowing them to keep what they earn and support their families through their own pay packets he has given them back their dignity and self-respect' (*Guardian*, 18 March 1998: 15). There is an element of truth in this, but the long-term effect of these fiscal measures is that low pay will be even more institutionalized as an aspect of postindustrial capitalism, whilst the affluent who benefit as managers, service class workers, and owners of capital will continue to enjoy the fruits of exploitation without paying much tax on them. Well, New Labour is definitely post-socialist, and real redistribution and the promotion of relative equality are not part of the 'third way' agenda. The reintegration of younger adults with children into work has been extensive, but it is difficult to disagree with Grover's description of this process as being intended to:

> . . . re-regulate the reserve army of labour to increase its size and increase its closeness to labour markets by making it more 'employable'. In this context 'employable' actually means making labour cheaper to hire through the direct and indirect subsidy of wages.
>
> (2003: 17)

I will simply add that the direct economic purpose is not the whole story but that the maintenance of social order through integration into work is at least as important.

Catch them young and give them a chance – Sure Start

In the 1960s, the US Johnson administration's 'War on Poverty' introduced the 'Headstart' programme of making pre-school education available to children from deprived backgrounds. This was intended to take the children of the poor and give them a compensatory access to programmes of learning which would enhance their cognitive development. The compensation was to be for the linguistic and other cultural deficits which they experienced through their exposure to a 'culture of poverty' in their home environments. The imagery was of these children coming up to the starting point in the competitive race of life already running and ahead of children with no deficits from 'normal' home environments. Although the cognitive gains of

the 'Headstart' children disappeared during childhood, those who partici-
pated in the programmes have demonstrated greater scholastic and
employment achievements and less criminality as young adults than the
control groups who did not participate. Catch them young is a powerful
idea.

Plainly, the UK government's programme of 'Sure Start' was modelled
on Head Start. The programme derived from the Treasury-driven Comprehensive Spending Review process and is intended as a generic and
coordinated strategy with local variations in implementation. and has been
rolled out across the UK. By June 2003 there had been four rounds of the
programme and 260 programmes had been developed in England alone.
The areas selected for Sure Start programmes were locales of relatively high
deprivation. In particular, 45 per cent of children in Sure Start areas lived in
households which did not contain a working adult, which is twice the
national average rate. In all, some £300 million has been spent on Sure Start
since 2001 and up to 400,000 children living in disadvantaged areas, about a
third of all children living in poverty, are in some way engaged with the
programme.

Sure Start is not just a pre-school programme, but the pre-school and
related child-care aspects predominate in delivery. The principles of Sure
Start programmes are that they should be:

- two-generational: involve parents as well as children
- non-stigmatizing: avoid labelling 'problem families'
- multifaceted: target a number of factors, not just, for example, education
  or health or 'parenting'
- persistent: last long enough to make a real difference
- locally driven: based on consultation and involvement of parents and local
  communities
- culturally appropriate and sensitive to the needs of children and parents.

Sure Start is the classic example of joined-up thinking at the level of
central government in strategy and locally in terms of tactical delivery. It
addresses educational needs, provides child care which is central to the
strategy of getting parents, and particularly single parents, into paid work,
and has a participatory element which is important in terms of developing
community civic engagement.

There is an extensive evaluation programme under way in relation to
Sure Start. This is based around the Sure Start programme model of:

Changing existing services ⇒ Delivering improved services ⇒
Enhancing child/family/community functioning.

In practice evaluation so far is confined to establishing local contexts for
programmes and examining the character of service implementation and
change. There does not seem to be a very coherent operationalization of
what 'enhancing child/family/community functioning' actually means, and
one has to have some sympathy with the difficulties such a conceptual

framing poses for measurement! The one area of Sure Start where we have some knowledge about experience is in relation to the actual character of participation. Here there have been some difficulties which amount to a conflict between professional objectives and interests and those of parents involved in the development of schemes. On the surface Sure Start is not a controversial project but, despite the perfectly genuine effort at avoiding stigmatization, it is still founded around a rectifying deficits model of the parenting practices of the children who engage with the schemes. This is quite complicated because at one level Sure Start is redistributional – an unequivocal example of positive discrimination in New Labour's policy practices. However, there is a tension built into this since receipt of benefits is not universal. Only the children of the poor are meant to be in Sure Start. We will return to this issue of a tension between universalism and practice in the conclusion and will have more to say about participation in the rest of this chapter.

Rescuing the drop-outs – Connexions in practice

We have noted in Chapter 6 Wacquant's comment that if there is a crucial dividing line in the Parisian *banlieue* it is not racial but generational – running between settled adults and a disorderly young. This specific example of what Cooper (1998) has seen as New Labour's division between a cultural majority which is to be protected and a dispossessed other – the division between the majority of the orderly and a minority of the young who are disorderly and dangerous – is central to UK anti-exclusion policy. The Social Exclusion Unit turned its attention very early to those who are excluded from school in one of its first reports in 1998. The issues were identified very clearly:

> **The problem** – Truancy and exclusions have reached a crisis point. The thousands of children who are not in school on most schooldays have become a significant cause of crime. Many of today's non-attenders are in danger of becoming tomorrow's criminals and unemployed.
>
> **Why it matters** – This damages the children themselves and everyone else: the children themselves lose out because they stop learning. This is self-evident for truants, but it is also a problem for excluded pupils. . . . These lost years matter: both truancy and exclusion are associated with a significantly higher likelihood of becoming a teenage parent, being unemployed or homeless later in life, or ending up in prison; the wider community suffers because of the high levels of crime into which many truants and excluded pupils get drawn. Time lost from education is a direct 'cause of crime'. . . . The police and the public are paying a huge price.
>
> (1998: Introduction)

In other words, excluded and long-term truanting children were the potential recruits for a new criminal and disengaged underclass. In 1999 this report was followed up by another addressing the absence of some 160,000 young people between the ages of 16 and 18 from any of the systems of education, training or employment. In consequence, the 'Connexions' service has been established. This links the work of six government departments together with private and voluntary sectors groups and the youth and careers service with a view to offering guidance to all young people aged between 13 and 19 in relation to the transition into adult life. Connexions is managed by local partnerships including representatives from local government; the youth, careers and probation services; the voluntary sector; business; the police; Learning and Skills Councils (the quangos which oversee post-16 education and training); the health service; local youth offending teams; and further education. The key agent is the personal adviser available to all young people who can offer advice and support in relation to all aspects of transition but particularly in relation to training and employment. Connexions is a universal service, but there is evidently a targeting of interest on NEETs – young people Not in Education, Employment or Training.

This is indicated by the presence in the Connexions partnerships of the police and Youth Offending Teams. The latter were established under the Crime and Disorder Act of 1998 with the specific remit of reducing crime and disorder by disaffected youth in their areas of operation. They are involved with a range of activities including youth sports projects directed at the most difficult young individuals in particular areas. This emphasis on early rescue of the young disaffected is central to their operation. Of course these things are not new. Much of what is done by Youth Offending Teams descends from the development of 'Intermediate Treatment' in the 1970s as a way of handling children and adolescents who were seen as deprived but in consequence had the potential to become depraved. What is significant is the central role they have in policies directed against social exclusion. Being poor and orderly is not a problem. It is the anomic disorderly poor who matter.

There is an interesting question to be asked as to whether it is possible to draw a sharp line between the 'other' young – the NEETs who are potentially if not already actually a key source of social disorganization and disorder, and the generality of young people. Ferguson (2004) has challenged this distinction on the basis of an empirical examination of the actual trajectories of a sample of young adults into adult life. He set this account in relation to what he identified as three policy discourses operating in relation to 'failed transitions', a discourse of social exclusion, a discourse of disaffection, and a discourse of marginalization. In practice, these intersect but heuristically there is value in the distinction. The exclusion discourse carries all the complex and contradictory meanings we have already discussed in relation to that term. Ferguson pulls out the 'underclass' – Levitas's MUD – version of the exclusion discourse and identifies it as a specific discourse of disaffection. His marginalization discourse we might equate with the strong version of social exclusion associated with the structural determinism which informed the work of Willis (1977) when he considered 'how working class kids get working class jobs'.

Ferguson's discussion is subtle and important. He emphasizes the significance of agency by many young adults who can construct a different form of lifestyle which combines part-time work and study but represents, as he puts it, 'ephemeral participation'. The crucial point for us is that the study demonstrates that a simple binary divide between participants/non-excluded and non-participants/excluded is not the reality of young adult trajectories. Instead, we find a much more fluid and complex set of trajectories with very different approaches to the transition to work and an interesting possibility of the individual refusal to engage with the demands of inclusionary policy on its own terms. To use complexity theory's terminology, the projects directed at NEETs – and despite its universal claims Connexions is NEETs-focused – are negative feedback attempting to regulate complex and emergent processes. This raises the interesting possibility that they might have precisely the opposite effect to that which was intended and may be destabilizing rather than stabilizing, at least in the medium term.

Getting the place to work through getting the people involved – New Deal for Communities and Local Strategic Partnerships

New Deal for Communities was a consequence of the Social Exclusion Unit's remit to report to the Prime Minister on how to:

> develop integrated and sustainable approaches to the problems of the worst housing estates, including crime, drugs, unemployment, community breakdown, and bad schools etc.
>
> (1998: 1)

The result was *Bringing Britain Together: a national strategy for neighbourhood renewal*. New Deal for Communities took the form of the provision of £800 million, initially over three years, to:

> . . . support plans that bring together local people, community and voluntary organisations, public agencies, local authorities and business in an intensive local focus to tackle problems such as:
>
> • poor job prospects;
> • high levels of crime;
> • a rundown environment; and
> • no one in charge of managing the neighbourhood and co-ordinating the public services that affect it.
>
> (1998: para 4.4)

As with the Tories' urban regeneration schemes, New Deal for Communities was based on bids made by local partnerships. However, there was an indication of dissatisfaction with previous regeneration processes, including 'City Challenge' which had been intended to 'bring people back in' in the expression of a hope that some at least of the New Deal bids would be managed by groups not previously engaged with regeneration strategies. In other words, central government had started to hear the criticisms of developer/local authority 'urban regime'-led regeneration and recognized that the exclusion of the public at large and deprived communities in particular from any meaningful role in such developments was important both as an exclusion from political process and as a source of considerable public discontent. New Deal for Communities was associated with a range of other initiatives, including:

• Local Strategic Partnerships (LSPs), normally spanning local authority districts, which bring together a wide range of agencies and members of the community in order to plan the neighbourhood renewal agenda;
• A targeted Neighbourhood Renewal Fund (NRF) addressing deprivation in the 88 most disadvantaged local authorities; and
• The formation in 2001 of the Neighbourhood Renewal Unit (NRU) to join together these strands of work and to drive forward the overall strategy.

As of 2003/4 there were 39 New Deal for Communities partnerships in place covering about 1 per cent of the deprived neighbourhoods in England. The term 'partnership' itself is indicative and requires elaboration. Powell et al. have noted that: 'Partnership is the zeitgeist of the Labour Government and one of the essential features of the third way' (2001: 39). However, as Balloch and Taylor show, the term 'partnership' is unclear and contradictory:

> Partnership reflects ideals of participatory democracy and equality between partners. It assumes overarching common interests between different players and it can underplay the difficulties in bringing together different interests and different cultures.
>
> (2001: 2)

'Underplay' is putting it mildly indeed! New Deal for Communities partnerships, and Local Strategic Partnerships which operate at the whole locality level, are examples of the turn to the local in governance which Brenner and Theodore describe thus:

> Paradoxically, much of the contemporary political appeal of the 'local' actually rests upon arguments regarding allegedly *supra*local transformations, such as globalization, the financialization of capital, the erosion of the national state, and the intensification of interspatial competition. Under these conditions, in the absence of a sustainable regulatory fix at global, supranational, or national scales, localities are increasingly being

viewed as the only remaining institutional arena in which a negotiated form of capitalist regulation might be forged.

(2002: 341)

I think there is more to this. Certainly, 'urban regimes' in particular places seek to position their city-region in an advantageous position in the global hierarchy of localities, the purpose of projects like 'city of culture' as outlined in Chapter 7. However, the assertion that local 'inclusionary' projects, of which 'New Deal for Communities' represents the prototypical example, are about negotiating a local regulation of capitalism, seems to me to be too generous an interpretation. The political background to regulation, almost wholly ignored by the structuralist accounts which underpin regulation theory, was the compromise between social democracy and Christian democracy and the mutual agreement of those two political strands (of which one nation Conservatism in the UK was a variant) that the role of government included genuine regulation of capitalism – the real social market economy project. There was a genuine moral economy behind the politics of this era, however compromised that might have been in practice.

Inclusionary localism in the postindustrial era is not informed by any conception of a moral economy. Rather, it represents an exercise in controlling and manipulating by incorporation. In relation to urban regeneration, partnership's logic can generally be understood at best thus:

> The community hasn't got many skills so they don't bring much to the table. They are here to be consulted, negotiated with, but they don't help much.
> (A leading actor in the North Tyneside City Challenge, quoted in Geddes 2000: 793)

In other words, the community has to be jollied along and may offer some useful intelligence in relation to processes of implementation but has no strategic role in relation to the determination of overall regeneration objectives. Councillor John O'Shea of Newcastle City Council is on record as saying, in relation to the West Gate New Deal for Communities Partnership: 'Community Involvement was a window dressing to get the money' (quoted in McCulloch 2004: 133). McCulloch's accounts of 'partnerships' in Newcastle (2000, 2004) provide us with one of the few real ethnographies of these kinds of engagement. The original protocol for the West Gate NDC partnership asserted:

> Local residents will control all aspects of the New Deal programme including planning, delivery and finance. Any subsequent statements, clauses, or implications which contradict this protocol in fact or in spirit will be deemed invalid.
> (quoted in McCulloch 2004: 133)

The actual experience was very different. Not only did the community representatives interpret the actual processes of partnership decision-making as being given the run around by local politicians and employed community workers who seemed to be 'in and for the state', but during the life of the partnership New Labour-controlled Newcastle City Council initiated a programme of 'urban regeneration' under the title of 'Going for Growth' which involved what community participants in the West Gate partnership referred to as ethnic cleansing (see Byrne 2000; Cameron 2003). This was intended to be the largest programme of actual gentrifying displacement of poor working-class people attempted in the UK since before the First World War! In 2004, New Labour lost control of Newcastle to the Liberal Democrats, who are committed to cancelling this project – representative democracy has some gasps of life left in it.

There is no evidence whatsoever from any 'New Deal for Communities' project that there has been a systematic engagement with structural inequality. Newcastle is an extreme case, and the New Labour administration in that city has received a well-deserved boot up the backside into political oblivion, but it does represent the general tendency in projects engaged with urban regeneration.

One of the key problems with 'New Deal for Communities' was that it focused on particular components of urban systems without attention to the urban system as a whole. In other words, it was separated from the management of policy at the level of locality. The introduction of Local Strategic Partnerships following on from the publication by the Social Exclusion Unit of a *National Strategy for Neighbourhood Renewal* in 2001 was meant to address the urban system, at least at the level of local authority.

A Local Strategic Partnership (LSPs) is a single non-statutory, multi-agency body, which matches local authority boundaries, and aims to bring together at a local level the different parts of the public, private, community and voluntary sectors. LSPs are key to tackling deep seated, multi-faceted problems, requiring a range of responses from different bodies. Local partners working through a LSP will be expected to take many of the major decisions about priorities and funding for their local area.

In Newcastle, the LSP board is made up thus:

Chair – the Leader of Newcastle City Council
Community sector – 14 representatives
The voluntary sector – 3 representatives
The private sector – 10 representatives (7 representatives from the Chamber of Commerce, 2 from higher education and 1 from further education)
The public sector – 10 representatives (Newcastle City Council, Northumbria Police, Primary Care Trust, Learning and Skills Council, JobCentre Plus, Small Business Service, Registered Social Landlords' Forum)
Regeneration partnerships – 4 representatives from area regeneration partnerships

The noticeable absence is of any representation by organized labour, although the Chamber of Commerce is present. Newcastle's draft community plan was produced in 2004. There is absolutely no mention of potential conflicts of interest anywhere in this document. There is an issue of major substance here to which we will return in Chapter 9. In the local strategic partnership, as in the New Deal for Communities, we find 'the community' represented as an interest in the way that we might have found organized labour represented in traditional corporatist arrangements. Organized labour has a reality and representative structures. The issue of just what is 'the community' will be of central significance for us.

So far as 'New Deal for Communities', LSPs and other related area-based activities are concerned, they seem to fall well within the description offered of partnership on a Europe-wide basis by Geddes:

> . . . while the discourse of 'partnership against social exclusion' is one of a holistic response to a multidimensional problem, this is a discourse based on weak rather than strong conceptions of exclusion. With few exceptions, local partnerships studiously avoid engagement with the question of 'who are the excluders?', and with the structural, social, economic and political implications of a thoroughgoing assault on social exclusion, preferring easy assumptions about the possibility of an inclusive society. The dominant practice of local partnership – as opposed to some of its rhetoric – enshrines elitist, neocorporatist or neopluralist principles, and excludes or marginalizes more radical egalitarian and solidaristic possibilities.
>
> (2000: 797)

Partnership can best be understood as a mechanism directed at effective and 'joined-up' governance, but participation addresses the issue of political exclusion. It represents a postindustrial alternative to the political engagement through parliamentary and local democratic politics of industrial democracy. Participation – engagement of representatives of what is now generally defined as the 'community' in processes of decision-making – is a crucial component of New Labour's policies in a range of areas. Jones (2003) combines a review of the literature on participation-based policy with an empirical study of an instance on Merseyside. His summary echoes the views of Taylor (2000) to the effect that: 'there is a consensus among successive studies of community participation that communities, by and large, remain on the margins of power in most partnership programmes to date, even when they are relatively well organised' (Jones 2003: 582). Perrons and Skyers extend this point:

> . . . in the urban sphere in the UK, the formal devolution of responsibility to the local community often occurs in parallel with a centralization of effective control as well as real cuts in expenditure which directly affect jobs, and social, health and welfare services. Therefore, although local groups may be formally included in discussions over

local issues, the main agenda in terms of allocating resources to urban areas and determining overall priorities, is decided outside the immediate regeneration areas, either at national or local authority district level.

(2003: 265)

I propose that what is usually described as 'participation' where neo-liberal policy agendas are implemented on some sort of third way basis should be given its proper name, which is 'incorporation'. In industrial capitalism there was an extensive literature on the incorporation of the leadership of organized labour in corporatist tripartheid institutional forms at all of the national, regional and local levels. In other words, the leadership of organized labour was drawn into a decision-making process which committed it to decisions taken and eliminated any chain of democratic responsibility to union members. This was a crucial part of the governance of organized capitalism in the Fordist/industrial era.

With organized labour there was a reality to be incorporated, both in terms of representative leaderships and a union movement. What we have in the local post-democratic politics of urban regeneration is the incorporation of two wholly nebulous entities – the 'community', which has no organizational form whatsoever; and the 'leadership' of the 'community', which has achieved leadership through, in general, no known process of selection. Of course, there are community organizations and processes of election associated with them. Shaw and Davidson (2002) assert that there has been more enthusiasm and engagement with the election of community representatives to New Deal for Communities managing boards, although their enthusiasm for the process has to be set against McCulloch's (2004) account of the experience of those self-same representatives when elected. It is also true that in the special case of election of tenants' representatives in relation to the management of social housing, there does seem to be both a real electorate and some genuine accountable representation.

However, the prototype here is the form for Strategic Local Partnerships which, remember, are intended to cover whole local authority areas and not just those which are socially excluded. This raises rather interesting issues. Strategic Local Partnerships exist to play a 'joined-up thinking' coordinating role in relation to all public sector policy development in a particular locality, whether by elected local authority, health services, or any of the numerous quangos which operate public services. Their engagement with community representation generally relates to whatever forms of community organization either really exist or (and more commonly) have in some way been concocted in poor and deprived areas as part of the process of reassertion of community as a mechanism of social control. In other words, if there really was some sort of proper representation of the interests of the excluded then we would be in the odd position of the dispossessed working class having more say in participatory processes than the middle masses. In reality, Strategic Local Partnerships seem wholly devoid of any real democratic accountability at all, which reflects the business-led model on which they are based.

Of course, participation has its own industry of trusts, foundations, experts and academics engaged in 'capacity building' and 'community development' with the objective of enhancing the social capital of an unsocialized society. The UK Home Office identifies this as a process of 'civic renewal' engaged with the formation and utilization of 'social capital'. Some definitions are in order:

> The Government is concerned to promote civil renewal, that is: '. . . *a way to empower people in their communities to provide the answers to our contemporary social problems.*' Civil renewal depends on people having the skills, confidence and opportunities to contribute actively in their communities, to engage with civic institutions and democratic processes, to be able to influence the policies and services that affect their lives, and to make the most of their communities' human, financial and physical assets. Individuals play an important role in this, both in neighbourly action, and in generating ideas and stimulating new activities. However the development of sustainable activity in the end depends on people acting together – in groups, organisations and networks.
>
> (Home Office 2003)

> The UK Government has formally adopted the OECD definition of social capital as: '*networks together with shared norms, values and understandings that facilitate co-operation within or among groups.*' It has also been defined as '*shared understandings, levels of trust, associational memberships and informal networks of human relationships that facilitate social exchange, social order and underpin social institutions*'. . . . In particular, it involves building 'bonds' and 'bridges' between people as a foundation for social support and community relationships. Effective community involvement, especially horizontal involvement and networking, are key elements in the building of social capital.
>
> (Home Office 2003)

And here again we have a deficit model – inadequate people and disintegrating communities now have to be engaged with by a range of 'community developers' working in a therapeutic mode in order to enhance their collective capacity to facilitate the neo-liberal project. The sheer impertinence of the use of the word 'empowerment' in this drivel is breathtaking. But for the moment let us note that this is a vocabulary of a process in which there are no conflicts, no disputes of interest, merely a collective and unproblematic interest in the maintenance of a communally generated and mutually acceptable social order. What we have here is an apparatus of incorporation, not a commitment to social change and the elimination of exclusion.

Conclusion

At the level of the local, we can see rather clearly the character of power relations as they are expressed in relation to competing interests. Without a doubt one real interest is the existing local state bureaucracy, although we should note that, in an extraordinary abandonment of principles which have informed local governance in the UK since the Victorians, high-level careers can now pass backwards and forwards between public service employment and the private sector corporations who are promoting privatization of service delivery and developer-led and profiting urban regeneration. Another very obvious set of interests are the businesses engaged in those activities. The business engagement is not simply a matter of the pursuit of interests. We also have a radical change in the style of governance and the forms which are developed for the resolution of social issues and the local management of crises. Without doubt the local matters, and it is at the level of the local that we can see the bulk of New Labour's efforts at social inclusion in action. The notable but enormously important exception to this is the set of fiscal measures directed at ensuring that poor work is rational for citizens. In general, the conclusion of the review of the activities developed under the aegis of the Social Exclusion Unit lead one to the view that the unit has been well named. The policies developed by it or elsewhere in the Blair government promote poor work, are in general an assault on democratic process, and in practice promote social exclusion rather than do anything to remedy it. Is there an alternative? You bet there is, and we will now turn to it with some relief.

9

Against exclusion:
the radical alternative

The last chapter of the second edition of this book has the same purpose as the conclusion to the first edition. First, it will present a summary account of the nature of social exclusion based on the ideas and data reviewed up to this point. However, we now have nearly seven years' experience of 'inclusionary policies' launched as part of New Labour's third way. This means that we have to understand social exclusion not only in terms of the character of flexible postindustrial capitalism but also in relation to policy regimes and political practices in the kind of post-democratic societies for which Blair's Britain can serve as a prototype. Second, it will examine what we might do about social exclusion, assuming that we want to do anything. We will begin with a consideration of the nature of the politics of social inclusion, with a review of just what political identities might contribute to the restoration of a social world of advanced capitalism which is at least as inclusive as Fordism was, and might even go beyond this both in terms of the internal degree of inclusion and of the extension of that inclusion on a global scale. The term political identity is used here really as a kind of label for political collectives defined by both common objectives and common principles as the joint bases for action. It includes consciousness, but goes beyond it. It is not just about material interest, but about the ideas collectivities of people have about what the future should be and why that future should be.

We will then turn to the practical prospects for a real inclusionary politics which challenges the reality of exclusion and of the economic system and political practices which give rise to it. Here we cannot attempt a discussion of organization without reference to the nature of 'inclusionary policy' at the level of the local. In other words, we have to take the sorts of practices which operate in specific places – whether in relation to education, urban regeneration, New Deal for Communities, cultural policy or whatever, and confront them with a radical practice. Participation has to be pushed to the limits. The contradictions of engaging people as collective social actors in the new post-democratic politics at the local level have to be developed to their full extent. The local is not the only domain of counter-attack against exclusion, but it is a particularly important one.

We must not underestimate the scale of this task. To use the language of complexity theory, we are attempting to redirect local and global social systems away from a trajectory of increasing exclusion towards a trajectory of equality and real inclusion. We have come a long way towards flexible postindustrial excluding neo-liberal capitalism already. There has been a neo-liberal ratcheting in all spheres of social and economic life. Cultural ratcheting is particularly significant. However, that does not mean change, including transformational change, is impossible. Postindustrial capitalism has not settled down into a relatively stable condition in which that system is robust. Rather, postindustrial capitalism is inherently unstable, both in terms of the global system and at every socio-geographical level. The character of the social order can be reconstructed, but this will never be an easy task.

The excluded many, the 'at risk' most, and the excluding few

There are two crucial elements for any understanding the nature and implication of social exclusion under postindustrial capitalism. The first is a grasp of the actual dynamics of social life today. These dynamics are very different from those of Fordism or from the dynamics of advanced capitalist societies at any time between the 1860s and the 1970s. Throughout that period most people in advanced capitalist societies had better lives than their own parents. This is immediately obvious for the very large numbers who were immigrants into the industrial world from peasant peripheries, but it was true generation upon generation for those born into industrial society as well. Not only was there a continuing rise in real living standards, there was a very considerable degree of upward social mobility associated with expansion in the proportion of more desirable occupational roles. Social mobility seemed to be a real possibility, with much of that mobility derived from the acquisition of better educational qualifications.

During the golden years of Keynesianism, the combination of full employment and strong trade unions with a considerable growth in household earnings, derived in large part from increased economic participation by married women, meant that most households could reasonably access a material standard of living which was that of the general social norm. For example, most council housing estates in the UK were occupied by working-class people with steady jobs and a standard of living comparable with that of those living in owner-occupied areas. Movement from council housing to owner occupation was often the product of quite small incremental gains in income. Upward social mobility was general. When Banim (1986) surveyed the residents of a desirable middle-income owner-occupied estate at Chapel Park in Newcastle, she found that the overwhelming majority were the children of manual worker households and had been brought up in council housing or privately rented accommodation. They had achieved upward mobility in space often through a simple combination of a skilled male worker's earnings and those of a clerical female employee. This mobility was absolutely dependent on the availability of well-paid male manual employment. The point is that the real personal dynamics of Fordist industrial capitalism were dynamics of degree. There were very poor people living in appalling conditions in the industrial cities, but for most people the middle range of experience was the norm and most people saw a prospect of upward mobility for themselves or their children. Crucially, throughout this period the incomes of those in the bottom half of the income distribution improved relative to those in the top 10 per cent of that distribution.

The dynamics of personal mobility are very different now, particularly in inter-generational terms. We now find a situation in which upward educational mobility in terms of acquisition of educational qualifications can be associated with downward social mobility in terms of income. There are very many graduates now who earn less in the USA and the UK than their skilled manual worker fathers used to earn, in the USA in real terms and in the UK in relative terms. The skilled manual jobs are now not available, of course, and this is even more true for the semi-skilled jobs where high earnings were dependent on union power. Note that there are a lot of young women graduates in the new clerical employment who earn no more relatively and often less than their factory worker mothers or grandmothers earned under Fordism. They are certainly less powerful as part of a collectivity. The panoptical surveying of call centre workers contrasts vividly with the union-based capacity of female printing or clothing workers 30 years ago. Above all, the relative security of employment, not necessarily but often with the same employer, has gone. It was never so much a matter under Fordism of a 'job for life' as a job always available somewhere.

When we look at the dynamics of income distribution overall in the UK, the nation-state for which the best data is available and where the politics of the third way of which more anon are most developed, we find something really rather remarkable. During the 1990s and including the first term of the New Labour government, the real gains in recorded income went to the top 1 per cent of income recipients, the group most able to use professional expertise to avoid tax. The superclass, composed of business executives, senior public sector managers (these two categories are now interchangeable), a not so petty revived bourgeoisie, and the owners of significant income generating property, are the beneficiaries of the new social order.

The other crucial generative aspect of social exclusion is exclusion from political power in post-democracy. Here the best summary of the position is given by Crouch:

> while elections certainly exist and can change governments, public electoral debate is a tightly controlled spectacle, managed by rival teams

of professionals expert in the techniques of persuasion, and considering a small range of issues selected by those teams. The mass of citizens plays a passive, quiescent, even apathetic part, responding only to the signals given to them. Behind this spectacle of the electoral game politics is really shaped in private by inter-action between elected governments and elites which overwhelmingly represent business interests.

(2000: 2)

We will return to Crouch's important and pertinent account of post-democracy, but here let us take very careful notice of what he is saying. Just as in income distribution the top 1 per cent – the resources superclass – are quite distinctive from the rest of us, so is this true for political power. Most of us have none to speak of.

So what then is 'social exclusion' in postindustrial capitalism? The answer usually given to that question involves examination of the lives of people in the bottom third of the income distribution. It cannot be constructed around income alone, precisely because both the form of the income distribution taken as a snapshot and consideration of the dynamics of household incomes show that there is no easy boundary to be drawn in income terms. Townsend's (1979) efforts to construct an index of social participation and establish a qualitative change in this in relation to the passing of an income threshold are only meaningful in snapshot terms. They would apply if conditions through time were relatively permanent, but if there is a high level of income dynamism they cannot be generalized. If we turn to descriptions of condition as opposed to income, we are little further forward. Social exclusion is often equated with permanent unemployment, but the reality is that permanent unemployment is a relatively uncommon condition in contrast with the phenomenon of *chômage d'exclusion*, the cycling from unemployment to poorly paid work, whether within the regular economy or the irregular economy, and back, with an equal cycling between full dependency on state benefits and dependency on Speenhamland supplements to low incomes. For the young, there is an additional device on this merry-go-round – experience of 'training'. The issue here is not low income taken alone, but the combination of low income and insecurity of employment. Insecurity of employment is inherent in a flexible labour market.

It is much easier to identify 'excluded (and excluding) spaces', the consequence of the transition of cities to a postindustrial status, a transition which of course is as much the product of policy as of inherent shifts in capitalist production and reproduction. Here taxonomic procedures do generate a sharp and clear divide which corresponds exactly with popular conceptions. However, we have to remember that people move in space as well as through time. Those who live in the peripheral estates of the red belt of Paris, or the outer estates of Glasgow or Sunderland in the UK, are clearly living in excluded spaces, but the degree of movement into and out of these places is considerable. This is important when we come to consider the bases for community action.

When it comes to power, we can say bluntly that the overwhelming majority of the people in postindustrial and post-democratic flexible capitalism are excluded from any real engagement with it. The degradation of politics to a state where it is a matter of the competing marketing policies of parties which at all levels of governance are essentially indistinguishable in their relation with corporate power and supine attitude to that power means that we have no say in the determination of future social trajectories. This is particularly evident at the local level in relation to urban regeneration because the processes and consequences of our powerlessness and their power are evident at a level we can all perceive. Crouch (2000) has written with appropriate scorn of the vacuity of a politics in which politicians become objects of blame for failure rather than representing endorsed commitments to a different sort of future. This is the politics of consumerism – what Needham (2003) has called 'New Labour's marketplace democracy':

> . . . recent governments in the UK have been consumerizing citizenship. Rather than exporting the political dimension of citizenship into consumer behaviour, they have sought to import consumer values into the government-citizen relationship. The effect has been to turn democracy into a marketplace, downgrading those elements of citizenship that presume a more collectivist and political linkage between individual and state.
>
> (2003: 7)

In general, public policy in Europe, Canada and Australia sees social exclusion in the weak sense as defined by John Veit-Wilson (1998). In the US under Bush the term is not even part of the policy discourse. In the weak sense of the term, the excluded are understood as marked by personal deficits. Their exclusion can be remedied by the correction of those personal deficits. The argument of this book is that exclusion is not a property of individuals or even of social spaces. Rather, it is a necessary and inherent characteristic of an unequal postindustrial capitalism founded around a flexible labour market and with a systematic constraining of the organizational powers of workers as collective actors – the excluded are excluded by that system – the strong sense of the expression. In terms of income, residence and instability of employment/poor work, the excluded are a minority at any point in time, but the condition of exclusion threatens many more. The excluded are a reserve army of labour for the non-excluded middle mass. In relation to power, 99 per cent of us have no effective say. When we take power into account, the excluded are the great majority.

If we use the language of chaos/complexity to describe the contemporary social order of postindustrial capitalism and the actual trajectories of individuals and households within it, then we can see that contemporary social policies accept a world in which there are quite distinctive ensembles of trajectories. There are multiple attractors and these are taken as given.

Basically, there are three attractor states. First, there is that of being excluded, which is most easily badged in a univariate nominalist way by residence in excluded space, but which comprises a set of life course trajectories revolving around movement among poor work and benefit dependency. Then there is the domain of 'insecurity'. Here people have work and a general standard of living which approximates to that normal under Fordism, but with personal situation being massively less secure than it was in that period. It is very important to note that there is considerable personal and intergenerational mobility between these two condition sets. That is demonstrated absolutely by the information we have about income and employment dynamics and the limited information we have about residential dynamics. Social exclusion policies as they exist at present are all about moving people from the excluded to the merely contingent domains. They seek to do this through either or both of training/education and the supplementation of low wages.

The third attractor set is that of the affluent, the owners of capital and the higher service classes. This category is not closed. It can be entered, particularly through very high levels of educational attainment. These can of course be purchased. Perhaps many of the academic readers of this book will be paying for the private secondary education of their own children, or at the very least arranging their area of residence so that their children have access to those state secondary schools with outstandingly good results in competitive examinations. However, it is perfectly evident that the possession of some combination of cultural and financial resources is the basis of membership of the superclass. In income terms, this comprises the top 1 per cent of income recipients who are the beneficiaries of cuts in the higher rates of taxation and who have accumulated massive real wealth. We should also note that this superclass generally regards itself, in atheistic terms, as a Calvinist elect. Its members have 'achieved' through inherent worth and regard themselves as fully entitled to their consequent differentiating privileges.

Let us be absolutely clear here. So long as a social system exists that can be described in the terms just employed, then we will have social exclusion. What, if anything, can we do about it?

Can we do nothing? Is politics powerless?

Let me quote the summary of conclusions of the MOST Roskilde symposium 'From social exclusion to social cohesion: a policy agenda' held in advance of the United Nations Copenhagen World Summit on Social Development:

> Sixto Roxas . . . feels that since the nineteenth century Western civilisation has made the market and its self-regulating capacity the basis for democracy, the liberal state itself being the creation of this market. The key to this system, which was at one time called into question with

the development of the Keynesian welfare state, resides in the assertion that the laws which govern the market are of the same order as the universal laws of physics. It is therefore to be understood that a major characteristic of dominant economic thinking is that it considers itself to be scientifically based and universally valid. This gives it, in the words of Ignacy Sachs 'an ahistoric and atopic character'. One must attempt to understand, says Roxas, why the market has progressively occupied the totality of the economic terrain and how economic theory has been able to transform itself into a dominant ideology. Such is the case today. Thanks to a powerful network structured by international financial institutions, and those issuing from Bretton Woods in particular, the dominant economic order is in the process of establishing a global hegemony of such omnipotence that one may truly speak of our epoch as the civilisation of the market, or of enterprise. . . . The result of such an evolution is that, in Petrella's words, competitiveness 'is no longer a means; it has become the prime objective not just of enterprises but also of the state and society as a whole.' . . . Petrella agrees with Roxas in asserting that private enterprise is in the process of shaping the values of our times by fixing the rules of the game, not only for itself but also for the state and the whole of society. The constraint of the dominant economism is now such that states are enjoined to run themselves like private firms, whereas the latter take on an increasing number of prerogatives that were once in the exclusive domain of the state.

(Bessis 1995: 17–18)

This is absolutely accurate. If we examine the arguments of that miserable document, the report of Labour's Commission on Social Justice (Borrie 1994), we find that it distinguishes between a political line which it endorses and describes in terms of a political category of 'investors', and the old political objective of equality which it dismissively associates with 'levellers'. Well that is an honourable and acceptable label! I will bear the name leveller any time. What matters, however, is what Borrie's mob meant by 'investors'. Simply put, these are those who have bought the ideological line that there is no alternative to the endorsement of the logic of market capitalism and that the only way in which to achieve social justice is to fit people for the purposes which market capitalism wants of them. Let us understand this absolutely. Whatever the formal rhetoric of politicians and policy implementers, for many in flexible postindustrial market capitalism, what is required of them is engagement in low-paid work alternating with unemployment and benefit dependency. For most, the risk of that condition remains present. We have an active reserve army of labour and a middle mass whose contingent lives are determined to a considerable degree by the existence of that reserve army.

If social exclusion is inherent in a market-oriented flexible postindustrial capitalism, then it is impossible to eliminate it by any set of social policies directed at the excluded alone. It is perfectly true that redistribution through tax credits will benefit the working poor and that this has the enormous advantage for order of making poor work more economically rational for the working poor. However, this will be done entirely at the expense of the working non-poor, not at the expense of the beneficiaries of flexible postindustrial capitalism among the most affluent. Nelson has described the political context of policies of this sort:

> . . . the resources associated with postindustrial capitalism contribute to a more hegemonic political structure favoring business interests and wealthier individuals. . . . This hegemonic structure erodes class conflict under postindustrial capitalism. Unions decline in importance, working-class politics recedes, and a conservative consensus becomes ever more embracing and pervasive. Hence the paradox of politics and class conflict under postindustrial capitalism: As inequality increases, the potential for militant conflict diminishes among those most affected by economic adversity and circumstance.
>
> (Nelson 1995: 104)

These accounts are very similar to Jessop's 'hollowed out state' as outlined in Chapter 2, but there is a crucial distinction. Roxas and Petrella recognize that the issue is to a very considerable degree one of ideological contestation, an important element in which is the assertion by the proponents of flexible postindustrial capitalism, that their future is the only future possible. Therborn (see Chapter 2) has noted the weakness of European Christian and social democratic politics in the face of this onslaught, and we have to recognize that Anglo-American Keynesian politics, if not necessarily economic theory, has essentially ceded both the intellectual and the administrative ground to it. Solidarity is on the retreat and full employment has been ceded absolutely. This is how it is. How might it be made differently? A very large part of the answer to that question has to be sought in the domain of culture, and in particular in the processes through which cultural norms are developed and asserted.

The cultural front: what we need to change – empowerment in postindustrial and post-democratic capitalism

Empowerment is a word to be used with care and reservations. Page has reminded us that all too often it is at best a conscience-saver for professionals:

> . . . social work techniques of this kind may prove to be more beneficial to facilitators and educators who wish to cling on to the vestiges of a personally rewarding form of 'radical' practice rather than to those disadvantaged members of the community for whom the promise of a better tomorrow appears to be as far away as ever.
>
> (Page 1992: 92)

At worst, as in the Home Office document quoted in Chapter 8, it is used in what one wishes was a cynical but in fact is probably a sincerely and dangerously ignorant fashion as part of a process of real disempowerment through incorporation. Nonetheless, with those caveats made, here we are going to think about how empowerment for social change might be achieved, remembering always that whilst the intellectual contest in terms of political ideas and substantive critique is important, it is useless without actual practical engagement, without the redevelopment of a popular democratic politics of solidarity. How is that to be achieved?

In the first edition of this book, I attempted to answer that question by assembling a list of social forces that might endorse a programme of solidarity and equality as a basis for social integration. That strategy will be revisited, briefly, here, but this time around I want to focus more on the issue of 'identity' and how it might serve as the basis of a new cultural politics of social change, which at the same time draws on traditions – to use Raymond Williams's expression 'unincorporated residual culture' – of solidarity which informed the working-class project for most of the twentieth century.

There is one thing to be said here and said very firmly. Transformative social change has to be a project founded in a class analysis and around class identities. Fraser (1997, 2000) has done a service in explicating the absolute and total linkage of issues of economic and cultural injustice – the processes of maldistribution and misrecognition. Her dismissal of forms of identity politics which ignore material injustice and confine attention only to: 'mis recognition as a freestanding cultural harm' (2000: 110) is absolutely correct. However, she then endorses a position which emerged at the end of the twentieth century in cultural politics and which amounts to 'letting class back in'. In other words, the claims of class are recognized as allowable and even equal to the claims of ethnicity, gender and sexual identity. Class becomes an identity among others. Fraser goes beyond this in her account, because she insists on material divisions as crucial to experience, but she does not then make them the basis of common and universal action. Class loses its position as the foundation for a universal claim. This approach will not lead to an effective anti-exclusionary politics in the twenty-first century. Exclusion is a class matter first and foremost. Gender and ethnicity and sexual identity, and even more the matter of citizenship status, matter a great deal, but the fundamental issue is the class organization of flexible capitalism and how class identities can be constructed in opposition to that organization. Saying this is not to endorse the inane drivel of, for example, Collins (2004) in terms of claims for an indigenous white working class in the UK or anywhere else. It is to remember, among other things, that class is something you join when it is class for itself, unlike other identities which are externally imposed.

Personal history and experience signifies here. My grandmother and her brother, first-generation Irish immigrants brought to English Tyneside as children, were part of the group of politically active working-class people –

miners' wives, as she was, and miners, like him, for the most part – who took the decision in 1921 to dissolve the branches of the Irish Labour Party in the northeast into the Labour Party. Of course, the Irish Labour Party was a class-based party, but it also expressed an ethnic identity and they gave that up in political terms in support of the class project pure but perhaps not so simple. In the late 1970s I lived and worked in Belfast in a milieu which had much in common with that in which I was brought up and have continued to live, but which differed in crucial ways. I have family connections with the North of Ireland and shared many formative experiences with Belfast friends and comrades, including of considerable significance for credibility having been educated by the Christian Brothers. However, for them, Protestant and Catholic, despite a strong adherence to class values and goals, identity was constituted around ethnicity. Protestants asserted superiority. Catholics originally demanded civil rights and equal status, and subsequently asserted a superior 'all Ireland' national identity. What is absolutely apparent is that the working-class people of the North of Ireland, and the working class of the Celtic tiger of the post-Catholic South as well, have been utterly dispossessed by a developing postindustrial capitalism which has not figured on the political radar screen of the majority of political activists. Ethnic identity matters not a whit to that system and it accommodates all who will assimilate to it. The neo-liberal project is truly liberal. The alternative class project was defeated in the northeast of England in the 1980s, but at least it was fighting the right enemy.

This is not to say that the forms of class politics which operated in the past will work now. Crouch (2000) is quite right to identify both the miners' strike of 1984 and the resistance of Liverpool Council to Thatcher's cuts as absolutely failed projects of an intransigent proletarianism using old models of struggle which could not work in the circumstances in which they were applied. It is pertinent to note that he is equally dismissive of the rainbow politics based on multiple identities attempted by the radical Livingstone before he became a technocratic servant of development and finance capital in his current role as Mayor of London. Crouch is also correct in his account of the nature of class structure when the North American and European manual working class has been restructured by a combination of technological change and the displacement of manual work to China and other 'developing' countries. That said, I think Crouch neglects the significance of origins. White-collar proletarians, let alone pink-collar proletarians, who are both economically and culturally dispossessed working class, may well have different value systems and a different political potential from the traditional 'lower middle class' of industrial society.

That word 'may' is indicative of how I currently see the potential for change. In the first edition of this book, I attempted to prescribe the nature of coalitions for change based on traditional institutional forms and new social movements. Thinking about the potential of parties, churches, organized labour and the green movement remains relevant. However, what we really need is a different sort of process if we are to develop a programme of real empowerment which might enable those excluded and liable to exclusion in acting in a transformative way – and that category necessarily includes most of us, especially when issues of power and culture are considered. The ideas of Freire (1973, 1977, 1982) are enormously useful here, particularly if read with the assistance of Heaney's (1995) introduction and glossary. The significance of Freire's ideas about social pedagogy are immense because, in contrast to the Leninist account of the role of the party cadre who knows through the principles of 'scientific Marxism' what is right and has the task of raising the mere 'trade unionist' consciousness of the proletariat, for Freire pedagogy is always a process of mutual change and transformation. The idea is perhaps best expressed in Freire's conception of 'participatory research':

> Participatory research is an approach to social change – a process used by and for people who are exploited and oppressed. The approach challenges the way knowledge is produced with conventional social science methods and disseminated by dominant educational institutions. Through alternate methods, it puts the production of knowledge back into the hand of the people where it can infuse their struggles for social equality, and for the elimination of dependency and its symptoms: poverty, illiteracy, malnutrition etc.
>
> (Heaney 1995: 11)

The role of those with expertise in this can only be collegiate participation in empowerment: 'a consequence of liberatory learning. Power is not given, but created within the emerging praxis in which co-learners are engaged' (Heaney 1995: 10). The method must be dialogical: 'The dialogical approach to learning is characterised by co-operation and acceptance of interchangeability and mutuality in the roles of teacher and learner. In this method, all teach and all learn' (1995: 10).

There are very real problems for the development of action in the West which might be qualitatively different from those of Brazil, the real model for a politics which might confront globalism. Auyero's (1997) account of marginalization in Latin America is one of very considerable separation, of an almost uncrossable gulf. Whatever the disadvantages of that, and in Brazil its extent is clearly not such as to make it absolutely uncrossable because otherwise the Workers' Party could not have unified the poor and the industrial working class, relatively permanent spatial exclusion generates a spatial stability of community. Given the nature of postindustrial politics and the capture of important parties of the left and centre by the superclass, this will not be easy. However, European Christian, social democratic, post-Leninist Communist and green parties, the Brazilian Workers' Party, and member-directed trade unionists everywhere have a common cause with those who are dispossessed now.

The city region is probably the most important site at which the battle against neo-liberalism can be fought. The significance of the politics of the local should not be underestimated. The history of the labour movements of advanced capitalism, particularly in their social democratic as opposed to Leninist form, is to a considerable degree one of battles about the level and form of social reproduction in particular places, battles very often fought by women. The reconfiguration of urban space is an essential part of the neo-liberal project. This contest is expressed in many ways – through gentrification, cultural assaults on traditional identities and values, privatization of iconic welfare systems (especially the UK National Health Service), exploitation across the range of employment, and the subordination of radical artistic practice to banal commodification. These things mark out the ground for the fight. Or rather they mark out the ground for the fight, as I and others with whom I work on Tyneside and in the northeast of England understand the fight. The whole point of the Freirian project as outlined above is that it then becomes necessary to enter into a general dialogue with others. Some of the things we have done through the non-sectarian Tyneside Socialist Forum, which brings together socialists of various hues including even some members of the Labour Party, greens and unattached radicals, has taken this dialogical form – notably an event organized in criticism of the Newcastle–Gateshead bid for European City of Culture status 'Reclaiming Culture'.

In many respects the 'social forum' movement, when it transcend its unfortunate tendency to drift into large-scale radical tourism coupled with sectarian backbiting, offers a model for this sort of action, although so far the focus of World or European or national social fora without an equivalent development of local fora has not got things off to the best of starts. However, the idea is good. The Web description of the Irish Social Forum provides us with a general definition of the idea, even if the actual construction of the other world is not so easily identified in practice.

> The Irish Social Forum is a process to assist in, and present, the articulation of the movement of movements of individuals, formal organisations and informal groups from any part of Irish civil society who are negatively affected by and are opposed to the global project known as neo-liberalism. Its purpose is to express the needs felt within Irish society as a powerful statement of the 'other world' that is not only possible but is already 'under construction' in many areas.

The tactical forms of assault on neo-liberalism include all the old weapons of the armoury – participation in electoral politics, publicity, criticism (even academic criticism), and open protest. However, they must also include a critical and active engagement with the actual processes of the new urban governance, and in particular with processes of participation. The ideal of participatory democracy remains important for us, but the objective for the moment is probably disruption and discord. The future is contested and there are mass, indeed virtually universal, interests set against narrow and particular elite interests with most powerful politicians belonging body and soul to the elite. It isn't so much a case of 'be realistic – demand the impossible', as of be realistic – demand what you want and expect to be able to get it. If there is one horrible and very real cultural truth about contemporary, neo-liberal, postindustrial, post-democratic capitalism, it is that most people have a very good idea of what it is like and what it is doing and think there is damn all they can do about it. At the level of the city, the fight can be fought. Moreover, a focus on local issues like school access, health-care organization and urban regeneration processes is a way of engaging the middle masses, without whose participation the politics of inclusion will not work at all. This has to be a universal project.

In my view there is a great deal of mileage in using the idea of the 'sustainable city' as the basis for a local politics against exclusion. The Christian churches and the greens must come together with local labour movement organizations (in the UK, the TUC-funded 'Centres Against Unemployment'), and community organizations to work out a real political strategy. This cannot be confined to attempting to influence policy makers. It must be prepared to put real pressure on them. The democratic process is in terrible trouble in postindustrial capitalism. A truly subsidiaristic local politics founded in civil society is absolutely necessary in order to revive it. My own view is that the regional level is also very important here. In the medium to long term, within one human generation, it is highly likely that the national level of states such as the UK and France will not matter very much. It is certainly desirable that this should happen. In a Europe of localities, regions and a European federal state, a real politics against exclusion should be possible. Note I have no romantic notions about neighbourhoods as part of this system. Frankly, the very high levels of residential mobility out of areas of dispossession mean that any politics based on the neighbourhood level is far more likely to take the form of middle-class NIMBYism than anything else. The local is a level which covers the span of postindustrial experiences. It is a basis for universalistic programmes, at least so far as the internal politics of metropolitan postindustrial capitalism are concerned.

And all this is so much easier said than done. There are obstacles at every level. These include, in no particular order:

- The incorporation of community groups and representatives into official 'participation'.
- The continued nuisance value of the off scourings of Leninism, now most commonly found in Trotskyist form.
- The collaboration of trade unions in the neo-liberal project, exemplified by the way public sector unions in the UK have dropped their opposition to New Labour's privatization agenda in return for rather meagre and probably unenforceable concessions in relation to the rights of new recruits.
- The bemused incapacity of social and Christian democrats in political parties to uphold the principles which inform those political positions.
- The influence of a media dominated by neo-liberal elites and owners.
- The encouragement of racism against non-citizens which is endorsed by Christian and social democratic parties – a dirty disgrace indeed.

Well – what else is there to do but try?

So to conclude: social exclusion derives from inequality. It is a product of the postindustrial social order dominated by globalizing capital and the superclass associated with that globalizing capital. Attractive as the notion might be of watering the fields with the blood of the superclass, practically the way to deal with them is through two other forms of bloodletting – through the proper taxation of high incomes and accumulated wealth with the revenues used to sustain a process of global development on a sustainable basis, coupled with a restoration of basic organizational rights to workers so that they can both resist job instability and reduce the levels of corporate profits and senior executive remuneration to the benefit of wage earners. I think that the development of local coalitions against exclusion, popular fronts based on all social forces which are prepared to set solidarity as the key social goal, is a means towards the development of a political culture in which such a programme has some chance of being put into effect.

And a personal point: an acquaintance to whom I put a preliminary version of these views very properly asked me what I would expect to pay in extra tax myself. On a salary of £45,000 per year I would expect to pay about an extra £1,500 a year – much of that through local taxation – although I would expect to see a lot of benefit for that in terms of an enhanced social wage through ecological, social care and world development programmes. In real terms I would be better off. I wouldn't expect UK households with an income of less than £25,000 a year to pay a penny extra. I would expect those with incomes of over £50,000 a year to see most of the excess over that figure taken back from them through real redistributive taxation. In real terms they would be worse off. An essential component of solidarity is fairness. Unfettered markets will never yield fairness. Democratic politics can impose it.

Bibliography

Aldridge, S. (2001) *Social Mobility: A Discussion Paper*. London: Performance and Innovation Unit, Cabinet Office.

Alexiadou, N. (2002) Social inclusion and social exclusion in England: tensions in education policy, *Journal of Education Policy*, 17(1): 71–86.

Allen, J. (1998) Europe of the neighbourhoods: class, citizenship and welfare regimes, in A. Madanipour et al. (eds) *Social Exclusion in European Cities*. London: Jessica Kingsley, pp. 25–52.

Amin, A. (ed.) (1994) *Post-Fordism*. Oxford: Blackwell.

Anderson, J., Duncan, S. and Hudson, R. (1983) *Redundant Spaces in Cities and Regions*. London: Academic Press.

Apospori, E. and Miller, J. (eds) (2003) *The Dynamic of Social Exclusion in Europe*. Cheltenham: Edward Elgar.

Arendt, H. (1958) *The Origins of Totalitarianism*. London: Allen & Unwin.

Atkinson, A.B. (1999) The distribution of income in the OECD countries, *Oxford Review of Economic Policy*, 15(4): 56–75.

Atkinson, A.B. (2004) Income tax and top incomes over the twentieth century, *Hacienda Pública Española/Revista de Economía Pública*, 168: 123–41.

Auyero, J. (1997) Wacquant in the Argentine slums, *International Journal of Urban and Regional Research*, 27(2): 508–11.

Ball, S.J., Bowe, R. and Gewirtz, S. (1995) Circuits of schooling, *The Sociological Review*, 43: 52–78.

Baker, M. (1997) *The Restructuring of the Canadian Welfare State: Ideology and Policy*, SPCR Discussion Paper 77, University of New South Wales.

Balloch, S. and Taylor, M. (2001) *Partnership Working*. Bristol: Policy Press.

Banim, M. (1986) Occupying houses: the social relations of tenure, unpublished PhD thesis, University of Durham.

Bankston, C. and Caldas, S.J. (1986) *Majority African American Schools and Social Injustice: Social Forces*, 75(2): 535–555.

Barnes, M., Heady, C., Middleton, S., Millar, J., Papadopoulos, F. and Tsakloglou, P. (2003) *Poverty and Social Exclusion in Europe*. Cheltenham: Edward Elgar.

Barry, B. (2002) Social exclusion, social isolation and the distribution of income, in

J. Hills et al. (eds) *Understanding Social Exclusion*. Oxford: Oxford University Press, pp. 13–29.

Bartley, B. (1998) Exclusion, invisibility and the neighbourhood in West Dublin, in A. Madanipour et al. (eds) *Social Exclusion in European Cities*. London: Jessica Kingsley, pp. 131–56.

Bartley, M. (2003) *Health Inequality*. Cambridge: Polity.

Bauman, Z. (1987) From here to modernity, *New Statesman*, 25 September.

Bauman, Z. (1997) No way back to bliss: how to cope with the restless chaos of modernity, *Times Literary Supplement*, 24 January: 4–5.

Bauman, Z. (1998) *Work, Consumerism and the New Poor*. Buckingham: Open University Press.

Bell, D. (1974) *The Coming of Post-Industrial Society*. London: Heinemann.

Bessis, S. (2004) From social exclusion to social cohesion: a policy agenda, MOST Policy Paper, No. 2, http://www.unesco.org/most/besseng.htm

Beveridge, W.H. (1944) *Full Employment in a Free Society*. London: Allen & Unwin.

Bhalla, A.S. and Lapeyre, F. (1999) *Poverty and Exclusion in a Global World*. Basingstoke: Macmillan.

Blair, A. (2000) *The Third Way: New Politics for a New Century*. London: Fabian Society.

Borrie, G. (Chair) (1994) *Social Justice*. London: Vintage.

Bowker, G.C. and Star, S.L. (1999) *Sorting Things Out*. Cambridge, Mass.: MIT Press.

Braun, D. (1997) *The Rich Get Richer*. Chicago: Nelson-Hall.

Braverman, H. (1974) *Labor and Monopoly Capital*. New York: Monthly Review Press.

Brenner, N. and Theodore, N. (2002) From the 'new localism' to the spaces of neo-liberalism, *Antipode*, 34(3): 341–7.

Brown, P. (1995) Cultural capital and social exclusion, *Work, Employment and Society*, 9(1): 29–51.

Burchardt, T., Le Grand, J. and Piachaud, D. (2002) Degrees of exclusion: developing a dynamic multidimensional measure, in J. Hills et al. (eds) *Understanding Social Exclusion*. Oxford: Oxford University Press, pp. 30–43.

Burrows, R. (1999) Residential Mobility and Residualisation in Social Housing in England, *Journal of Social Policy*, 28(1): 27–52.

Bynner, J. (2002) *Young People's Changing Routes to Independence*. York: Joseph Rowntree Foundation.

Byrne, D.S. (1989a) *Beyond the Inner City*. Milton Keynes: Open University Press.

Byrne, D.S. (1989b) Sociotenurial polarization: issues of production and consumption in a locality, *International Journal of Urban and Regional Research*, 13(3): 369–89.

Byrne, D.S. (1995) Deindustrialization and dispossession, *Sociology*, 29: 95–116.

Byrne, D.S. (1997a) Chaotic places or complex places: cities in a postindustrial era, in S. Westwood and J. Williams (eds) *Imagining Cities: Scripts, Signs and Memories*. London: Routledge, pp. 50–72.

Byrne, D.S. (1997b) Social exclusion and capitalism, *Critical Social Policy*, 17(1): 27–51.

Byrne, D.S. (1998) *Complexity Theory and the Social Sciences*. London: Routledge.

Byrne, D.S. (1999) Tyne and Wear UDC – turning the uses inside out – active deindustrialisation and its consequences, in R. Imrie and H. Thomas (eds) *British Urban Policy and the Urban Development Corporations*. London: Paul Chapman.

Byrne, D.S. (2000) Newcastle's going for growth, *Northern Economic Review*, 30: 3–16.

Byrne, D.S. (2003) *Interpreting Quantitative Data*. London: Sage.

Byrne, D.S. and Parson, D. (1983) The state and the reserve army, in J. Anderson et al. (eds) *Redundant Spaces in Cities and Regions*. London: Academic Press.

Byrne, D.S. and Rogers, T. (1996) Divided spaces: divided school, *Sociological Research Online*, 1 http://Kennedy.soc.surrey.ac.uk/socresonline/1/2/contents.html

Byrne, D.S. and Wodz, K. (1997) La désindustrialization dans les villes industrielles en déclin, in A. Martens and M. Vervaeke (eds) *La polarisation sociale des villes européennes*. Paris: Anthropos, pp. 55–70.

Callaghan, G. (1998) Deindustrialization, class and gender – young adults in Sunderland, unpublished PhD thesis, University of Durham.

Cameron, S. (2003) Gentrification, housing redifferentiation, and urban regeneration, *Urban Studies*, 40(12): 2367–82.

Cameron, S. and Field, A. (2000) Community, ethnicity and neighbourhood, *Housing Studies*, 15(6): 827–43.

Catholic Bishops' Conference of England and Wales (1996) *The Common Good*. London: Catholic Bishops' Conference.

CCBI (1997) *Unemployment and the Future of Work*. London: CCBI.

Cleaver, H. (1977) Malaria, the politics of public health and the international crisis, *Review of Radical Political Economy*, 9: 81–103.

Cleaver, H. (1979) *Reading Capital Politically*. Brighton: Harvester Wheatsheaf.

Coleman, D. and Salt, J. (eds) (1996) *Ethnicity in the 1991 Census: Volume One: Demographic Characteristics*. London: HMSO.

Collins, M. (2004) *The Likes of Us*. Oxford: Granta.

Cooper, C. (2002) *Understanding School Exclusion*. Hull: Education Now Publishing Cooperative.

Crosland, A. (1956) *The Future of Socialism*. London: Cape.

Crouch, C. (2000) *Coping with Post-Democracy*. London: Fabian Society.

Crouch, C. and Marquand, D. (1989) *The New Centralism: Britain Out of Step in Europe*. Oxford: Blackwell.

Crowe, G. and Allan, G. (1994) *Community Life*. Hemel Hempstead: Harvester Wheatsheaf.

Dahrendorf, R. (1987) The erosion of citizenship and its consequences for us all, *New Statesman*, 12 June: 12–15.

Dahrendorf, R. (Chair) (1995) *Report on Wealth Creation and Social Cohesion in a Free Society*. London: The Commission on Wealth Creation and Social Cohesion.

Damer, S. (1989) *From Moorepark to 'Wine Alley': The Rise and Fall of a Glasgow Housing Scheme*. Edinburgh: Edinburgh University Press.

Deaton, A. (2003) Letter from America: tax cuts, income distribution and fairness in the United States, *Royal Economic Society Newsletter*, October.

Dennis, N. (1997) *The Invention of Permanent Poverty*. London: IEA.

Dennis, N. and Erdos, G. (1992) *Families without Fatherhood*. London: IEA.

Domanski, H. (1994) Nowe mechanizmy stratyfikacyjne?, *Studia Socjologicsne*, 132(1): 53–76.

Domanski, H. (2002) Is the East European 'underclass' feminized?, *Communist and Post-Communist Studies*, 35: 383–94.

Donnison, D. (1998) *Policies for a Just Society*. London: Macmillan.

Driver, S. and Martell, L. (1997) New Labour's communitarianisms, *Critical Social Policy*, 17(3): 27–46.

Duffy, K. (1997) Review of the international dimensions of the thematic priority on social integration and exclusion: a report to the UK Economic and Social Research Council. Leicester: De Montfort University.

Duncan, G.J., Smeeding, T.M. and Rodgers, W. (1992) The incredible shrinking middle class, *American Demographics*, 14 May: 34–8.

Duncan, G.J., Smeeding, T.M. and Rodgers, W. (1993) W(h)ither the middle class? A dynamic view, in D.B. Papadimitriou and E.N. Wolff (eds) *Poverty and Prosperity in the USA in the Late Twentieth Century*. London: Macmillan, pp. 240–71.

Eder, K. (1993) *The New Politics of Class*. London: Sage.

Ellison, N. (1997) Towards a new social politics: citizenship and reflexivity in late modernity, *Sociology*, 31(4): 697–717.

Engels, F. (1968) *The Condition of the Working Class in England in 1844*. London: Allen & Unwin.

Erikson, R. and Goldthorpe, J.H. (1993) *The Constant Flux*. Oxford: Clarendon Press.

Esping-Andersen, G. (1990) *The Three Worlds of Welfare Capitalism*. Cambridge: Polity.

Esser, J. and Hirsch, J. (1994) The crisis of Fordism and the dimensions of a 'post-Fordist' regional and urban structure, in A. Amin (ed.) *Post-Fordism*. Oxford: Blackwell, pp. 71–98.

Etzioni, A. (1995) *The Spirit of Community*. London: Fontana.

European Commission (1994) *Growth, Competitiveness and Employment*. Luxemburg: Office for Official Publications of the European Communities.

European Commission DGV (1994) *European Social Policy: A Way Forward for the Union*. Luxemburg: Office for Official Publications of the European Communities.

European Union (1999) Definitions of poverty and their link to health, AIDS and population objectives, http://europa.eu.int/comm/development/body/theme/social/1099meeting/backp106.htm

Everitt, B.S. (1993) *Cluster Analysis*. London: Edward Arnold.

Eversley, D. (1990) Inequality at the spatial level – tasks for planners, *The Planner*, 30 March (76): 12.

Fainstein, S. and Harloe, M. (1992) Introduction: London and New York in the contemporary world, in S. Fainstein et al. (eds) *Divided Cities*. Oxford: Blackwell, pp. 1–28.

Fainstein, S., Gordon, I. and Harloe, M. (eds) (1992) *Divided Cities*. Oxford: Blackwell.

Fairclough, N. (2000) *New Labour: New Language*. London: Routledge.

Ferguson, R. (2004) Discourses of exclusion: reconceptualising participation amongst young people, *Journal of Social Policy*, 33(2): 289–320.

Fitch, R. (1993) *The Assassination of New York*. London: Verso.

Ford, R. and Miller, J. (1998a) Lone parenthood in the UK: policy dilemmas and solutions, in R. Ford and J. Miller (eds) *Private Lives and Public Responses*. London: Policy Studies Institute, pp. 1–21.

Ford, R. and Miller, J. (1998b) *Private Lives and Public Responses*. London: Policy Studies Institute.

Förster, M. and Pearson, M. (2002) *Income Distribution and Poverty in the OECD Area – Trends and Driving Forces*. Paris: OECD.

Fraser, N. (1997) *Justice Interruptus*. London: Routledge.

Fraser, N. (2000) Rethinking recognition, *New Left Review* (second series) 3: 107–20.

Freire, P. (1973) *Education: The Practice of Freedom*. London: Writers' and Readers' Publishing Cooperative.

Freire, P. (1977) *Cultural Action for Freedom*. Harmondsworth: Penguin.

Freire, P. (1982) *The Pedagogy of the Oppressed*. Harmondsworth: Penguin.

Geddes, M. (1997) *Partnership against Poverty and Exclusion*. Bristol: Policy Press.

Geddes, M. (2000) Tackling social exclusion in the European Union?, *International Journal of Urban and Regional Research*, 24(4): 782–800.

Giddens, A. (1998) *The Third Way: The Renewal of Social Democracy*. Cambridge: Polity.

Giddens, A. (2000) *The Third Way and Its Critics*. Cambridge: Polity.

Glendinning, C. and Millar, J. (1992) *Women and Poverty in Britain in the 1990s*. London: Harvester Wheatsheaf.

Goodman, A. and Oldfield, Z. (2004) *Permanent Differences? Income and Expenditure Inequality in the 1990s and 2000s*. London: Institute for Fiscal Studies.

Goodman, A., Johnson, P. and Webb, S. (1997) *Inequality in the UK*. Oxford: Oxford University Press.

Gordon, D. (1999) *Inequalities in Health: The Evidence*. Bristol: Policy Press.

Gorzelak, G. (1996) *The Regional Dimension of Transformation in Poland*. London: Jessica Kingsley.

Gosling, A., Johnson, P., McCrae, J. and Paull, G. (1997) *The Dynamics of Low Pay and Unemployment in Early 1990s Britain*. London: Institute for Fiscal Studies.

Gough, J. (2002) Neo-liberalism and socialisation in the contemporary city, *Antipode*, 34(3): 405–26.

Green, D. (1996) *Community Without Politics*. London: IEA.

Green, D. (1998) *Benefit Dependency*. London: IEA.

Grolowska-Leder, J. and Warzyswoda-Kruszjuska, W. (1997) Women in the welfare state of Poland, conference paper, European Sociological Association, Colchester.

Grover, C. (2003) New Labour, welfare reform and the reserve army of labour, *Capital and Class*, 79: 17–24.

Guattari, F. and Negri, T. (1990) *Communists Like Us*. New York: Semiotext.

Hamnett, C. (1996) Social polarization, economic restructuring, and welfare state regimes, *Urban Studies*, 33(8): 1407–30.

Hamnett, C. (1997) A stroke of the Chancellor's pen: the social and regional impact of the Conservative's 1988 higher tax rate cuts, *Environment and Planning A*, 29(1): 129–47.

Hamnett, C. (2003) *Unequal City: London in the Global Arena*. London: Routledge.

Harris, N. (1987) *The End of the Third World*. London: Penguin.

Harrison, P. (1982) *Inside the Inner City*. Harmondsworth: Penguin.

Harvey, D.L. (1993) *Potter Addition*. New York: Aldine de Gruyter.

Harvey, D.L. and Reed, M.H. (1994) The evolution of dissipative social systems, *Journal of Social and Evolutionary Systems*, 17(4): 371–411.

Harvey, D.L. and Reed, M.H. (1996) The culture of poverty: an ideological analysis, *Sociological Perspectives*, 39(4): 465–95.

Hayek, F. (1944) *The Road to Serfdom*. London: Routledge & Kegan Paul.

Hazlitt, W. (1982) *Selected Writings*. Harmondsworth: Penguin.

Heady, C. (1997) Labour market transitions and social exclusion, *Journal of European Social Policy*, 7(2): 119–28.

Heald, D. (1983) *Public Expenditure*. Oxford: Martin Robertson.

Heaney, T. (1995) *Issues in Freirean Pedagogy*. http://nlu.nl.edu/ace/Resources/FreireIssues.html

Heilbroner, R. (1993) *Twenty First Century Capitalism*. London: UCL Press.

Heisler, B.S. (1991) A comparative perspective on the underclass, *Theory and Society*, 20(4): 455–83.

Hill, M., Hill, D. and Walker, R. (1998) Intergenerational dynamics in the USA: poverty processes in young adulthood, in L. Leisering and R. Walker (eds) *The Dynamics of Modern Society*. Bristol: Policy Press, pp. 85–107.

Hills, D. (ed.) (1996) *The New Inequalities*. Cambridge: Cambridge University Press.

Hills, J. (1995) *Joseph Rowntree Foundation Inquiry into Income and Wealth*, Vol. 2. York: Joseph Rowntree Foundation.

Hills, J., Le Grand, J. and Piachaud, D. (eds) (2002) *Understanding Social Exclusion*. Oxford: Oxford University Press.

HM Treasury (1997) The modernisation of Britain's tax and benefit system: employment opportunity in a changing labour market, http://www.hm-treasury.gov.uk/pub/html/docs/fpp/mtb/main.html

Home Office (2003) *Building Civil Renewal*. London: Civil Renewal Unit Home Office.

Hudson, W.H. (1910, 1981) *A Shepherd's Life*. London: Futura.

Imrie, R. and Thomas, H. (eds) (1999) *British Urban Policy and the Urban Development Corporations*. London: Paul Chapman.

Inglis, B. (1972) *Poverty and the Industrial Revolution*. London: Panther.

Inglot, T. (1995) The politics of social policy reform in postcommunist Poland, *Communist and Postcommunist Studies*, 28(3): 361–73.

James, C.L.R. (1950, 1986) *State Capitalism and World Revolution*. Chicago: Charles H. Kerr Publishing Co.

Jessop, B. (1994) Post-Fordism and the State, in A. Amin (ed.) *Post-Fordism*. Oxford: Blackwell, pp. 251–79.

Johnston, L., MacDonald, R., Mason, P., Ridley, L. and Webster, C. (2000) *Snakes and Ladders: Young People, Transitions and Social Exclusion*. Bristol: Policy Press.

Jones, P. (2003) Urban regeneration's poisoned chalice, *Urban Studies*, 40(3): 581–601.

Jordan, B. (1996) *A Theory of Poverty and Social Exclusion*. Cambridge: Polity.

Karn, V. (ed.) (1997) *Ethnicity in the 1991 Census: Volume 4*. London: HMSO.

Keane, M.P. and Prasad, E.S. (2002) Inequality, transfers and growth: new evidence from the economic transition in Poland, *Review of Economics and Statistics*, 842: 324–41.

Kellard, K. (ed.) (2001) *Lone Parents and Sustainable Employment*. Loughborough: Centre for Research in Social Policy, University of Loughborough.

Kempson, E. (1996) *Life on a Low Income*. York: Joseph Rowntree Foundation.

King, A. (1996) Introduction: cities, texts and paradigms, in A. King (ed.) *Re-Presenting the City*. London: Routledge, pp. 1–22.

Kodias, J.E. and Jones III, J.P. (2002) A contextual examination of the feminization of poverty, *Geoforum*, 22(2): 159–71.

Küng, H. (1997) *A Global Ethic for Global Politics and Economics*. London: SCM Press.

Lash, S. and Urry, J. (1994) *Economies of Signs and Space*. London: Sage.

Lavery, G., Pender, J. and Peters, M. (eds) (1997) *Exclusion and Inclusion: Minorities in Europe*. Leeds: ISPRU Publications, Leeds Metropolitan University.

Lawless, P., Martin, R. and Hardy, S. (eds) (1998) *Unemployment and Social Exclusion*. London: Jessica Kingsley.

Lee, R. (1995) Look after the pounds and the people will look after themselves, *Environment and Planning A*, 27: 1577–94.

Leisering, L. and Walker, R. (eds) (1998a) *The Dynamics of Modern Society*. Bristol: Policy Press.

Leisering, L. and Walker, R. (1998b) New realities: the dynamics of modernity, in L. Leisering and R. Walker (eds) *The Dynamics of Modern Society*. Bristol: Policy Press, pp. 3–14.

Lemann, N. (1991) *The Promised Land*. London: Macmillan.

Levitas, R. (1996) The concept of social exclusion and the new Durkheimian hegemony, *Critical Social Policy*, 16(1): 5–20.

Levitas, R. (1998) *The Inclusive Society: Social Exclusion and New Labour*. Basingstoke: Palgrave Macmillan.

Lewis, G. (1836) *Report on the State of the Irish Poor in Great Britain*. London: HMSO.

Lewis, O. (1966) *La Vida*. New York: Random House.

Lipietz, A. (1994) Post-Fordism and democracy, in A. Amin (ed.) *Post-Fordism*. Oxford: Blackwell, pp. 338–58.

Lipietz, A. (1998) Rethinking social housing in the hour-glass society, in A. Madanipour et al. (eds) *Social Exclusion in European Cities*. London: Jessica Kingsley, pp. 177–88.

Lister, R. (1998) *Citizenship: Feminist Perspectives*. London: Macmillan.

MacDonald, R. (ed.) (1997) *Youth, the 'Underclass' and Social Exclusion*. London: Routledge.

MacKay, R.R. (1998) Unemployment as exclusion: unemployment as choice, in P. Lawless, R. Martin, and S. Hardy (eds) *Unemployment and Social Exclusion*. London: Jessica Kingsley, pp. 49–68.

MacLeod, G. (2002) From urban entrepreneurialism to a 'Revanchist City'? On the spatial injustices of Glasgow's renaissance, *Antipode*, 134(3): 602–24.

MacNicol, J. (1987) In pursuit of the underclass, *Journal of Social Policy*, 16(3): 293–318.

MacPherson, C.B. (1962) *The Political Theory of Possessive Individualism*. Oxford: Clarendon Press.

Madanipour, A. (1998) Social exclusion and space, in A. Madanipour et al. (eds) *Social Exclusion in European Cities*. London: Jessica Kingsley, pp. 177–88.

Madanipour, A., Cars, G. and Allen, J. (eds) (1998) *Social Exclusion in European Cities*. London: Jessica Kingsley.

Marcuse, P. (1989) Dual city – a muddled metaphor for the quartered city, *International Journal of Urban and Regional Research*, 13(4): 697–708.

Martin, C. (1996) The debate in France over social exclusion, *Social Policy and Administration*, 30(4): 382–92.

Massey, D. and Denton, N.A. (1993) *American Apartheid*. London: Harvard University Press.

McBride, S. (2001) *Paradigm Shift, Globalization and the Canadian State*. Halifax: Fernwood Publishing.

McCrate, E. and Smith, J. (1998) When work doesn't work, *Gender and Society*, 12(1): 61–80.

McCulloch, A. (2000) Evaluations of a community regeneration project, *Journal of Social Policy*, 29(3): 397–419.

McCulloch, A. (2004) Localism and is neo-liberal applications, *Capital and Class*, 83: 133–66.

McKay, S. (1998) Exploring the dynamics of family change: lone parenthood in Britain, in L. Leisering and R. Walker (eds) *The Dynamics of Modern Society*. Bristol: Policy Press, pp. 108–24.

McKnight, A. (2002) *Young People's Changing Routes to Independence*. York: Joseph Rowntree Foundation.

Mead, L.M. (1997) *From Welfare to Work*. London: IEA.

Meadows, P. (ed.) (1996) *Work Out – or Work In?* York: Joseph Rowntree Foundation.

Merrett, S. (1979) *State Housing in Britain*. London: Heinemann.

Middleton, S., Barnes, M. and Millar, J. (2003) Introduction: the dynamic analysis of poverty and social exclusion, in E. Apospori and J. Miller (eds) *The Dynamic of Social Exclusion in Europe*. Cheltenham: Edward Elgar, pp. 1–15.

Millard, F. (1997) The influence of the Catholic hierarchy in Poland 1989–96, *Journal of European Social Policy*, 7(2): 83–100.

Mills, C.W. (1959) *The Sociological Imagination*. New York: Oxford University Press.

Mlady, M. (2003) Regional unemployment rates in the acceding countries in 2002, *Statistics in Focus*, Brussels: Eurostat.

Morenoff, J.D. and Tienda, M. (1997) Underclass neighbourhoods in temporal and ecological perspective, *Annals of the American Academy of Political and Social Science*, 551: 59–72.

Moynihan, D.P. (1965) *The Negro Family: The Case for National Action*. Washington, DC: Dept of Labor.

Mulderrig, J. (2003) Learning to labour: the discursive construction of social actors in New Labour's education policy, in M. Tönnies (ed.) *Britain Under Blair*. Heidelberg: Univestälag Winter, pp. 123–46.

Murray, C. (1984) *Losing Ground*. New York: Basic Books.

Murray, C. (1990) *The Emerging British Underclass*. London: IEA.

Murray, C. (1994) *The Underclass: The Crisis Deepens*. London: IEA.

Needham, C. (2003) *Citizen-Consumers*. London: Catalyst.

Negri, T. (1988) *Revolution Retrieved*. London: Red Notes.

Nelson, J.I. (1995) *Post-Industrial Capitalism*. London: Sage.

Nove, A. (1983) *The Economics of Feasible Socialism*. London: Allen & Unwin.

O'Connor, J. (1981) The meaning of crisis, *International Journal of Urban and Regional Research*, 5(3): 301–29.

OECD (1997) *Education at a Glance*. Paris: OECD.

OECD (2003) *Education at a Glance*. Paris: OECD.

Office of National Statistics (1997) Mortality decennial tables, *Decennial Supplement*, London: ONS.

Orloff, A. (1996) Gender in the welfare state, *Annual Review of Sociology*, 22: 51–78.

Page, R. (1992) Empowerment, oppression and beyond: a coherent strategy?, *Critical Social Policy*, 35: 89–92.

Papadimitriou, D. (ed.) (1993) *Aspects of Distribution of Wealth and Income*. London: Macmillan.

Papadimitriou, D. and Wolff, E.N. (1993) *Poverty and Prosperity in the USA in the Late Twentieth Century*. London: Macmillan.

Parker, H. (1989) *Instead of the Dole*. London: Routledge.

Parkin, F. (1979) *Marxism: A Bourgeois Critique*. London: Tavistock.

Peach, C. (ed.) (1996) *Ethnicity in the 1991 Census*. London: HMSO.

Pearson, R.W. (1991) Social statistics and an American underclass, *Journal of the American Statistical Association*, 186: 504–12.

Peck, J. and Tickell, A. (1994) Searching for a new institutional fix: the *After*-Fordist crisis and global-local disorder, in A. Amin (ed.) *Post-Fordism*. Oxford: Blackwell, pp. 280–315.

Percy-Smith, J. (ed.) (2000) *Policy Responses to Social Exclusion*. Buckingham: Open University Press.

Perrons, D. and Skyers, S. (2003) Empowerment through participation?, *International Journal of Urban and Regional Research*, 27(2): 265–85.

Peterson, P.E. (1992) The urban underclass and the poverty paradox, *Political Science Quarterly*, 106: 617–37.

Pilgrim Trust (1938) *Men without Work*. Cambridge: Cambridge University Press.

Pinch, S. (1993) Social polarization: a comparison of evidence from Britain and the United States, *Environment and Planning A*, 25: 779–95.

Piven, F.F. and Cloward, R. (1979) *Poor Peoples' Movements: How They Succeed and Why They Fail*. New York: Vintage.

Podkaminer, L. (2003) A note on the evolution of inequality in Poland 1992–9, *Cambridge Journal of Economics*, 27: 755–68.

Polyani, K. (1944) *The Great Transformation*. Boston: Beacon Press.

Powell, M., Exworthy, M. and Berney, L. (2001) Playing the game of partnership, *Social Policy Review*, 13: 39–62.

Prigogine, I. and Stengers, I. (1985) *Order Out of Chaos*. London: Flamingo.

Pryke, R. (1995) *Taking the Measure of Poverty*. London: IEA.

Reed, M. and Harvey, D.L. (1992) The new science and the old: complexity and realism in the social sciences, *Journal for the Theory of Social Research*, 22: 353–80.

Reed, M. and Harvey, D.L. (1996) Social science as the study of complex systems, in L.D. Kiel and E. Elliott (eds) *Chaos Theory in the Social Sciences*. Ann Arbor: University of Michigan Press, pp. 295–324.

Ridley, N. (1987) *Department of the Environment: Observations by the Government on the Third Report of the Employment Committee*, HC 83: 88–89, HMSO.

Rieger, E. and Liebfried, S. (2003) *Limits to Globalization*. Cambridge: Polity.

Roche, M. (1992) *Rethinking Citizenship*. Cambridge: Polity.

Rodgers, J.R. (1993) The relationship between poverty and household type, in D. Papadimitriou (ed.) *Aspects of Distribution of Wealth and Income*. London: Macmillan, pp. 31–51.

Room, G. (ed.) (1995) *Beyond the Threshold*. Bristol: Policy Press.

Rose, N. (1996) The death of the social: refiguring the territory of government, *Economy and Society*, 25(3): 327–56.

Rowlingson, K. and McKay, S. (1998) *The Growth of Lone Parenthood*. London: Policy Studies Institute.

Rubery, J. and Fagan, C. (1995) Gender segregation in societal context, *Work, Employment and Society*, 9(2): 213–40.

Sayer, A. (1995) Liberalism, marxism and urban and regional studies, *International Journal of Urban and Regional Research*, 19(1): 79–95.

Schrammel, K. (1998) Comparing the labor market success of young adults from two generations, *Monthly Labor Review*, February: 3–9.

Sen, A.K. (1992) Minimal liberty, *Economica*, 59(234): 139–60.

Sen, A.K. (2000) Social justice and distribution of income, in A.B. Atkinson and F. Bourguignon (eds) *Handbook of Income Distribution*, Vol. 1. North-Holland: Amsterdam, pp. 59–86.

Shaw, K. and Davidson, G. (2002) Community elections for regeneration partnerships, *Local Government Studies*, 28: 1–15.

Shaw, M. (1999) *The Widening Gap: Health Inequalities and Policy in Britain*. Bristol: Policy Press.

Shepherd, A. (2003) *Inequality under the Labour Government*. London: Institute for Fiscal Studies.

Silver, H. (1993) National conceptions and the new urban poverty, *International Journal of Urban and Regional Research*, 17(3): 336–54.

Silver, H. (1994) Social exclusion and social solidarity – three paradigms, *International Labour Review*, 133: 531–78.

Smith, N. (2002) New globalism, new urbanism, gentrification as global urban strategy, *Antipode*, 34(3): 427–50.

Smith, S. (ed.) (1991) *Economic Policy and the Division of Income within the Family*. London: Institute for Fiscal Studies.

Social Exclusion Unit (1998) *Truancy and School Exclusion*. London: Cabinet Office.

Social Exclusion Unit (2000) *National Strategy for Neighbourhood Renewal: A Framework for Consultation*. London: ODPM.

Starrels, M.E., Bould, S. and Nicholas, L.J. (1994) The feminization of poverty in the United States, *Journal of Family Issues*, 15(4): 590–607.

Steinert, H. (2003) Introduction: the cultures of welfare and exclusion, in

H. Steinart and A. Pilgrim (eds) *Welfare Policy from Below*. Aldershot: Ashgate, pp. 1–12.

Strengmann-Kuhn, W. (2002) Working poor in Europe: a partial basis income for workers?, http://ssrn.com/abstract=386540

Swyngedouw, E., Moulaert, F. and Rodriguez, A. (2002) Neo-liberal urbanization in Europe: large-scale urban development projects and the new urban policy, *Antipode*, 343: 542–77.

Taylor, M. (2000) Communities in the lead, *Urban Studies*, 37(5/6): 1019–35.

Teague, P. and Wilson, D. (1995) *Social Exclusion: Social Inclusion*. Belfast: Democratic Dialogue.

Therborn, G. (1985) *Why Some People are More Unemployed than Others*. London: Verso.

Therborn, G. (1995) *European Modernity and Beyond*. London: Sage.

Thomas, S.L. (1994) From the culture of poverty to the culture of single Motherhood, *Women and Politics*, 14(2): 65–97.

Thompson, S. and Hoggett, P. (1996) Universalism, selectivism and particularism, *Critical Social Policy*, 16(1): 21–43.

Titmuss, R.M. (1958) The social division of welfare, in R.M. Titmuss *Essays on the Welfare State*. London: Allen & Unwin, pp. 34–55.

Tönnies, M. (ed.) (2003) *Britain Under Blair*. Heidelberg: Univestälag Winter.

Townsend, P. (1979) *Poverty in the United Kingdom*. Harmondsworth: London.

Turner, B.S. (ed) (1993) *Citizenship and Social Theory*. London: Sage.

UNDP (1996) *Katowice Human Development Report 1996*. Katowice: UNDP.

Valentine, C. (1967) *Culture and Poverty*. Chicago: University of Chicago Press.

Veit-Wilson, J. (1998) *Setting Adequacy Standards*. Bristol: Policy Press.

Wacquant, L.D. (1993) Urban outcasts: stigma and division in the black American ghetto and the French urban periphery, *International Journal of Urban and Regional Research*, 17(3): 366–83.

Wacquant, L.D. (1995) Red belt, black belt: racial division, class inequality and the state in the French urban periphery and the American ghetto, in E. Mingione (ed.) *New Aspects of Marginality in Europe*. Chichester: Wiley, pp. 234–74.

Wacquant, L.D. (1999) Urban marginality in the coming millennium, *Urban Studies*, 36(10): 1639–47.

Walker, R. (1995) The dynamics of poverty and social exclusion, in G. Room (ed.) *Beyond the Threshold*. Bristol: Policy Press, pp. 102–28.

Walker, R. (1997) Poverty and social exclusion in Europe, in A. Walker and C. Walker (eds) *Britain Divided*. London: CPAG, pp. 48–68.

Walker, R. with Ashworth, K. (1994) *Poverty Dynamics: Issues and Examples*. Aldershot: Avebury.

Walker, R. and Leisering, L. (1998) New tools: towards a dynamic science of modern society, in L. Leisering and R. Walker (eds) *The Dynamics of Modern Society*. Bristol: Policy Press, pp. 17–33.

Walker, A. and Walker, C. (eds) (1997) *Britain Divided*. London: CPAG.

Walker, R. and Kellard, K. (2001) *Staying in Work*. DfEE.

Webb, S. (1995) *Poverty Dynamics in Great Britain*. London: Institute for Fiscal Studies.

Weclawowicz, G. (1996) *Contemporary Poland*. London: UCL Press.

Westergaard, J.H. (1978) Social policy and class inequality: some notes on welfare state limits, in R. Miliband and J. Saville (eds) *The Socialist Register 1978*. London: Merlin Press.

Westergaard, J.H. (1995) *Who Gets What?* Cambridge: Polity Press.

Whitfield, D. (2001) *Public Services or Corporate Welfare*. London: Pluto.

Whitty, G. (2001) Education, social class and social exclusion, *Journal of Education Policy*, 16(4): 287–95.

Williams, R. (1962) *The Long Revolution*. London: Chatto & Windus.

Williams, R. (1980) *Problems in Materialism and Culture*. London: Verso.

Williams, R. (1983) *Towards 2000*. London: Chatto & Windus.

Williamson, W. (2003) The language of mutuality: culture and social policy in contemporary Britain, in M. Tönnies (ed.) *Britain Under Blair*. Heidelberg: Univestälag Winter.

Willis, P. (1977) *Learning to Labour*. Farnborough: Saxon House.

Wilson, W.J. (1987) *The Truly Disadvantaged*. Chicago: University of Chicago Press.

Wilson, W.J. (1990) The ghetto underclass: social science perspectives, *Annals of the American Academy of Social and Political Science*, 501: 182–93.

Wilson, W.J. (1992) Another look at 'The Truly Disadvantaged', *Political Science Quarterly*, 106: 639–56.

Wilson, W.J. and Wacquant, L.D. (1989) The cost of racial and class exclusion in the Inner City, *Annals of the American Academy of Social and Political Science*, 501: 5–25.

Wodz, K. (1994a) The process of marginalization of the traditional workers' communites in Upper Silesia, in K. Wodz (ed.) *Transformation of Old Industrial Regions as a Sociological Problem*. Katowice: Silesian University Press, pp. 258–63.

Wodz, K. (ed.) (1994b) *Transformation of Old Industrial Regions as a Sociological Problem*. Katowice: Silesian University Press.

Wright, R.E. (1992) A feminization of poverty in Great Britain, *Review of Income and Wealth*, 1: 17–25.

Wright, R.E. (1993) A clarification, *Review of Income and Wealth*, 1: 11–12.

Yépez del Castillo, I. (1994) A comparative approach to social exclusion: lessons from France and Belgium, *International Labour Review*, 133: 5–6, 613–33.

Zukin, S. (1995) *The Culture of Cities*. Oxford: Blackwell.

Index

Related books from Open University Press
Purchase from www.openup.co.uk or order through your local bookseller

FAMILIES, VIOLENCE AND SOCIAL CHANGE

Linda McKie

An exciting new addition to the series, this book tackles assumptions surrounding the family as a changing institution and supposed haven from the public sphere of life. It considers families and social change in terms of concepts of power, inequality, gender, generations, sexuality and ethnicity.

Some commentators suggest the family is threatened by increasing economic and social uncertainties and an enhanced focus upon the individual. This book provides a résumé of these debates, as well as a critical review of the theories of family and social change:

- Charts social and economic changes and their impact on the family
- Considers the prevalence and nature of abuse within families
- Explores the relationship between social theory, families and changing issues in familial relationships
- Develops a theory of social change and families through a critical and pragmatic stance

Key reading for undergraduate students of sociology reading courses such as family, gender, health, criminology and social change.

Contents

*Series editor's foreword – Acknowledgements – Introduction – **Part one:** Families, violence and society – Your family, my family, their family – Identifying and explaining violence in families – Families: fusion and fission – **Part two:** Gender, age and violence – Embodiment, gender and violence – The ambiguities of elder abuse: Older women and domestic violence – **Part three:** Towards a critical theory – Unpalatable truths: Recognizing and challenging myths – A critical social theory of families, violence and social change – Conclusions – References – Index*

c.192pp   0 335 21158 5 (Paperback)   0 335 21159 3 (Hardback)